THE LIBERATORS

Jewish Wom
burning
concentration
– germany

THE LIBERATORS

AMERICA'S WITNESSES TO THE HOLOCAUST

MICHAEL HIRSH

BANTAM BOOKS NEW YORK

Copyright © 2010 by Michael Hirsh
Map copyright © 2010 by Mapping Specialists, Ltd.

Published in the United States by Bantam Books,
an imprint of The Random House Publishing Group,
a division of Random House, Inc., New York.

BANTAM BOOKS and the rooster colophon are
registered trademarks of Random House, Inc.

LIBRARY OF CONGRESS CATALOGING-IN-PUBLICATION DATA
Hirsh, Michael.
The liberators : America's witnesses to the Holocaust / Michael Hirsh.
p. cm.
Includes bibliographical references and index.
ISBN 978-0-553-80756-1
1. World War, 1939–1945—Concentration camps—Liberation.   2. World War, 1939–1945—
Concentration camps—Germany.   3. World War, 1939–1945—Concentration camps—Austria.
4. Concentration camps—Germany—History—20th century.   5. Concentration camps—
Austria—History—20th century.   6. World War, 1939–1945—Atrocities.   7. Soldiers—United
States—Interviews.   8. World War, 1939–1945—Personal narratives, American.   9. Holocaust,
Jewish (1939–1945)—Personal narratives.   I. Title.
D805.G3H523 2010
940.53'185—dc22   2009042954

Printed in the United States of America

www.bantamdell.com

9 8 7 6 5 4 3 2 1

FIRST EDITION

Frontispiece drawing by 84th Infantry Division
combat artist Walter H. Chapman. It depicts the
burning of barracks at the Salzwedel concentration
camp, as described in Chapter 7.

Book design by Casey Hampton

FOR THREE PEOPLE
WHO CHANGED MY LIFE

My aunt and uncle
Rochelle and Sam Sola

And my friend
Marvin Zimmerman

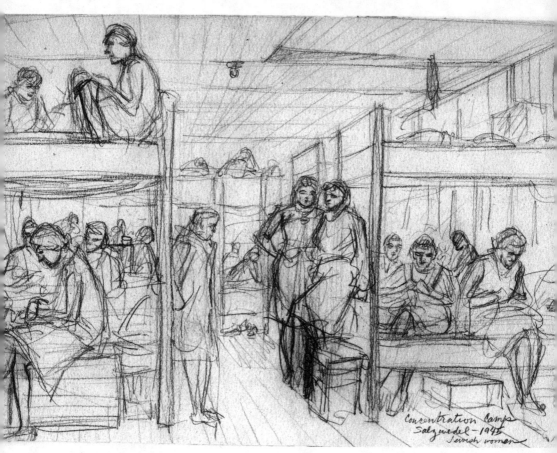

Jewish women prisoners in one of the barracks at the Salzwedel concentration camp sketched by 84th Infantry Division artist historian Sergeant Walter Chapman shortly after the division liberated the camp.

ON LIBERATION

What did we, camp prisoners, perceive of the moment? The SS suddenly left. We are locked inside the barracks. An airplane circles menacingly, close to the roof; hundreds of women crouch on barren floors and contemplate Imminent Death, who is no stranger—and a few do hope and so they speak. Shots are heard sporadically—the jailkeeper's plane vanishes and then silence, long silence. Suddenly out of nowhere, it seemed, or out of another world, some mystical beings appear in shiny armor at the gate. All the prisoners able to move, cry and laugh, embrace each other and shout—"Americans! Americans!" The gates, the doors open, "Americans! We are free!" The words are shouted in innumerable languages. It forms one unified choir: *LIFE!*

... in the name of all of us who were freed, please accept the thanks for our last 37 years of life!

GOD BLESS AMERICA!

> Mrs. Alice Kranzthor Fulop, age 81
> Milwaukee, Wisconsin
> April 22, 1982

———

A letter discovered by the author in the archives of the U.S. Army Center of Military History written to thank the 84th Infantry Division Railsplitters for the liberation of Salzwedel concentration camp, where she survived with her daughter, Nicole Martha Kranzthor.

CONTENTS

HOW DO YOU
PREPARE TO SEE THAT?

I n the final months of World War II, as American soldiers pushed the German army east toward the advancing Russians, the GIs began to discover—and to liberate—dozens upon dozens of camps large and small filled with the multitudes imprisoned by the Nazis. Some had been shipped to the camps to serve as slaves, to dig tunnels into mountains, there to build war machines for the Reich. Others had been shipped from camp to camp for one purpose only: to keep them from falling into the hands of the advancing Allied forces.

The prisoners who are the focus of this book had been liberated by the Americans, British, and Canadians. (The Russians liberated the notorious camps in Poland.) They had been consigned to death; the manner was, for all practical purposes, irrelevant.

They were marched to death, worked to death, starved to death, dehydrated to death, frozen to death, sickened to death, gassed to death, and sometimes shot to death—although this was not a preferred method, but only because bullets were not cost-effective. It also wasn't enough that the victims of the Nazis died; they were always humiliated and usually dehumanized and tormented before death came.

The deaths occurred not just in a handful of concentration camps whose names are familiar to almost everyone, but in literally thousands of camps and subcamps sprinkled all over the map of Germany, Austria, Czechoslovakia, and France. Wherever slaves could help the Third Reich accomplish its aims, there were camps. Some may have been nothing more than a barn where women workers making hand grenades in a forest armory were locked up at night; others were part of sophisticated underground manufacturing facilities where the first rockets and jet fighters were built and thousands of workers were used up.

Each of the major camps in Germany and Austria—like Dachau, Buchenwald, and Mauthausen, to name three of the oldest and largest—had jurisdiction over a wide geographical area, and each may have had a hundred or more subcamps. Workers were often transferred from one to the other as needed and then transported back to the main camp alive, to be killed, or dead, to be burned.

It's this system that American soldiers discovered, much to their shock, horror, and surprise, as they chased the German army toward its mythical Alpine redoubt. The GIs had received no warning as to what they might find, but that may not have mattered, for as one of them said to me, "What if we had? How do you prepare to see *that*?"

Most of the more than 150 Americans interviewed for this book were soldiers. Six were U.S. Army nurses. One was a 4F (physically unfit to be drafted) volunteer civilian ambulance driver who worked at Bergen-Belsen with the British and Canadian forces. Three were U.S. Army prisoners of war—two of them Jewish soldiers—who experienced the Holocaust firsthand alongside slave laborers imported from Eastern Europe. Five were concentration camp inmates who developed special relationships with particular GIs and are now American citizens. And one—also an American citizen now—served in the Polish army attached to the Russian army. With them he discovered some of the worst of the camps in Poland but only after all the inmates had been either murdered or evacuated to the west. He finally liberated prisoners in Sachsenhausen and eventually participated in the battle for Berlin.

At the time they were interviewed, the veterans ranged in age from eighty-three to ninety-six. All are among the relative handful of America's witnesses to the Holocaust who are still alive, still willing and able to recount their experiences, still cognizant of the need to tell their stories.

While researching this book, I discovered that it's not unusual for veterans not to know, even now, the names of the camps they discovered. Some U.S. medical personnel spent weeks at the camps, but it was more typical for combat troops to spend mere minutes to a few hours inside the gates before moving on in their relentless pursuit of the German army. Although they may not know the names, and though they may have spent but a short time inside their gates, they've never forgotten what the camps looked like, how they smelled, how the inmates looked, and how it all made them feel. And that is what this book is about. This is their opportunity, perhaps for a final time, to tell the world what they saw.

Writing about the trial of Adolf Eichmann in Jerusalem in 1963, Hannah Arendt used the phrase "the banality of evil" to explain that the Holocaust had been executed by ordinary people willing to be convinced that their actions were normal. In interviewing American soldiers who confronted that evil face-to-face, I became aware of a banality of the language they use to describe what they saw. And through my own personal reaction I've come to recognize the danger in that for those of us who are anxious to learn from them. The most vivid example: soldier after soldier from camp to camp to camp described "bodies stacked like cordwood," to the point that it's very easy for the shock and horror of such a statement to evaporate into meaninglessness. When an individual soldier was confronted by "bodies stacked like cordwood," he was seeing them that way, in all their brutal horror, through eighteen- or nineteen-, or twenty-year-old eyes, for the first time. Those kids were confronted with premeditated murders and attempted murders on a scale heretofore unimaginable.

A word, now, about the concept of *the liberators*. Aware that the Americans were coming, the SS guards—often with a final orgy of indiscriminate torture and killing—fled. It was left for the GIs to enter the camps, assess the humanitarian needs of the surviving inmates, bring up rear-echelon forces to minister to them, and arrange for the burial of the dead.

While I have observed the pride that members of specific Army units feel at having been officially designated the liberators of a certain camp, the truth is that their greatest achievement was not in cracking open the gates. Their achievement was in doing everything necessary to liberate an entire continent, and it took between three and a half and four million members of the U.S. armed forces (plus those of British, Canadian, French, and other Allied nations) in the European Theater of Operations (ETO) to do that job.

It's unfortunate that because of what I believe to be a well-intentioned but poorly drawn agreement between the United States Holocaust Memorial Museum in Washington, D.C., and the U.S. Army Center of Military History, Americans who died in the surf at Omaha Beach or in the Battle of the Bulge, for example, are not given any credit for liberating concentration camp victims, while an entire 15,000-man division that may have had just a handful of its members drive past a camp en route to battle elsewhere is declared to have liberated that camp and honored with the display of its flag at the museum.*

The soldiers on the scene were certainly, and importantly, American *witnesses* to the Holocaust—a condition that, as you'll learn, often had lifelong negative consequences. Nonetheless, the flag of *every* division that landed on European soil, *every* Army Air Corps unit that flew over European soil, *every* Navy, Coast Guard, and Merchant Marine command that sailed in support of the war in Europe, should be displayed in a place of honor, and all the men and women who served anywhere in the European Theater of Operations should be honored

---

* The agreement effectively holds that if just a truckload of troops out of a 15,000-man division reached a specific concentration camp at any time within the first forty-eight hours after the first American unit had reached that camp, the entire division would be declared to be a liberating unit of that camp and the flag of that division would be provided by the Army and placed on permanent display at the USHMM.

as *liberators* at the magnificent and moving Holocaust Memorial Museum in our nation's capital.

I want to thank every one of the men and women who were willing to dredge their minds and their souls to bear witness to the Holocaust in this book. The process often brought forth painful memories that had never been shared even with wives or children and, quite often, tears from both interviewee and interviewer. There were several instances of a wife learning for the first time of her husband's experiences at the camps by overhearing the interview for this book.

A word of caution: this is a book about crimes against humanity and about the reaction to those crimes by men at war. To soften the images and not tell the complete truth would violate the trust they placed in me when they agreed to speak. It would have been a disservice to them and to history. They know, and want you to know, that war is ugly despite rules and conventions negotiated far from the battlefield to make it less so.

A few words about what this book is not. Though the focus is almost solely on the actions of American fighting units, it is not a traditional military history of the final days of World War II in Europe. There are many of those, nearly all of which share one trait in common: the discovery by the Allied forces of the death camps, the slave-labor camps, and the Nazis' end-of-days attempts to murder tens of thousands of prisoners are barely a footnote, because they were almost never significant to the achievement of military victory. Bearing witness is not a soldier's primary job. Even the U.S. Army's official chronology of World War II, while detailing the day-by-day flow of Allied divisions across Germany—a country only slightly larger than the state of New Mexico—assigns no importance to the horrors discovered by the soldiers.

That said, what *The Liberators* does is trace the course of the final months of the war in Europe, by tracking the American units as they freed the inmates of camp after camp on an almost daily basis from early April 1945 through May 8—VE Day. For this book, bearing witness is the primary mission of the soldiers, whose stories have continued long after the war, when the true cost of war is often revealed.

North Sea

MANCHESTER

GREAT
BRITAIN

NETHERLANDS

LONDON

EINDHOVEN

SOUTHAMPTON   PORTSMOUTH   ISERLOHN
                                  DÜSSELDC
                    ANTWERP
English Channel   BRUSSELS   Rhine
                    BELGIUM   REMAG
                    VERVIERS

CHERBOURG   WIESBADEI
UTAH BEACH   Ardennes
SAINTE-MÈRE-   LE HAVRE   BASTOGNE FRANKF
ÉGLISE   ROUEN
OMAHA   SWORD   DILLINGEN
BEACH   BEACH   REIMS
           JUNO   PARIS   LUXEMBOURG
GOLD   BEACH
BEACH   METZ
                   PHILIPPSBOURG   H
                   GAMBSHEIM
                   STRASBOURG

                                 COLMA

FRANCE

                              SWITZERLA

ATLANTIC
OCEAN

0   75   150 Miles

0   75   150 Kilometers

N
W   E
S

WESTERN EUROPEAN LOCATIONS
CITED BY VETERANS INTERVIEWED
FOR *THE LIBERATORS*

MARSEILLES

Mediterranean Sea

THE LIBERATORS

CHAPTER 1

THE BEGINNING OF THE END

JANUARY 1945

ALSACE, OCCUPIED FRANCE

Some guys have all the luck. Some guys have none. Since they survived the war, you might say that Army veterans Norman Fellman and Morton Brooks belong in the former category. But don't make up your mind just yet—because both these former GIs are among the very few American witnesses to the Holocaust who experienced it from the inside, on the wrong side of the barbed wire. Sent to liberate Europe, Fellman and Brooks would instead personally experience the Holocaust. They would be caught up in the Nazis' compulsion to eliminate all Jews from the face of the earth.

Norman Fellman was drafted into the Army in the spring of 1942, right out of high school in Norfolk, Virginia. He was a well-built kid, six feet tall and weighing 178 pounds. He was trained as a medic and then transferred into the Army Air Corps but was washed out when

Norman Fellman before shipping out to
Europe, where he'd barely survive the Nazi
slave-labor camp at Berga an der Elster.

the training program was shut down because the instructors were
needed to fight the war. The Army was forming the 70th Infantry Division at Camp Adair, Oregon, and since he arrived there on an odd day
of the month, he became a scout in B Company, 1st Battalion, 275th
Infantry Regiment. Had he arrived a day earlier or a day later, he would
have been assigned to the artillery and his entire life would likely have
been very, very different.

In early December 1944, the 275th Regiment sailed aboard the
troopship *West Point,* landing in Marseilles, France, ten days later after
stops in North Africa. Originally commissioned in 1939 as the luxury
liner *America,* the flagship of the United States Lines, the ship was fast
and made the crossing without benefit of convoy. The landing on European soil on December 16 coincided with the German offensive that the
Wehrmacht called Operation Watch on the Rhine. The U.S. Army officially named it the Battle of the Ardennes, but it came to be known as the

Battle of the Bulge. The German intent was to split the British and American line in half, capturing the vital port at Antwerp, Belgium, in the process. It was essential to the Allies that the Germans not succeed, and in an effort to prevent that from happening, they threw every available unit into the fray, whether or not they were deemed combat-ready.

At almost the same time that Fellman's outfit was landing in Europe, Morton Brooks's unit, part of the advance elements of the 42nd Infantry Division (designated Task Force Linden for its assistant division commander, Brigadier General Henning Linden), landed in southern France, rushed there after less than two weeks of training in England. The task force included three infantry regiments and a headquarters detachment, but no supporting artillery units.

Brooks had grown up in Brooklyn and enlisted in the Army Specialized Training Program (ASTP) just shy of his eighteenth birthday. He was sent to Syracuse University, but when the program was shut down because the Army needed line troops, he was assigned to the 42nd—the Rainbow Division—as a rifleman.

Instead of having weeks to acclimate and train with its supporting artillery units, Norm Fellman's 275th Regiment was given just four days, and then loaded onto 40 and 8 railroad boxcars, so named because they could carry forty infantrymen or eight horses, and sent five hundred miles north, arriving in Brumath, France, just north of Strasbourg, on Christmas Eve. The men were now part of Task Force Herren, which would soon be attached to the Seventh Army's 45th Infantry Division. They were about to confront well-equipped German army units that would be executing a surprise attack in the snow-covered ridges of the Low Vosges Mountains. The Germans called it Operation Nordwind. It was designed to cause the Allied armies to shift forces away from the Bulge, where German troop movements had stalled. Nordwind would be the last gasp of the Third Reich, but that would prove to be of little comfort to Norm Fellman.

By January 4, his Company B was tasked to hold Falkenberg Hill, twelve kilometers outside Philippsbourg, a village in the heart of the Alsace region of northeastern France that was valued for the nearby rail lines and road network. Snowstorms began during their first night on the hill. Temperatures plummeted. The winter had already been declared the harshest in decades.

The Germans let loose with constant artillery barrages, supplemented by Nebelwerfer rockets, which the GIs called Screaming Meemies. Communications were cut off with A and C Companies on adjacent hills, and Fellman's company commander was wounded. B Company held the hill for five nights and six days. "By the end of the third or fourth day," Fellman recalls, "we were running short of supplies. Food was pretty much gone. Whatever we had in the way of candy bars or rations went to the wounded, which were beginning to pile up. We had water from melted snow, but that was it."

At the end of the sixth day, the Germans surrounded his unit with flamethrowing tanks, and the surviving officers decided to surrender. They'd sent three or four patrols out; they later learned that only one man had gotten through to the American lines. Fellman says, "We could starve to death or we could freeze to death, or we could surrender, and that was the choice they made."

There were no more than forty survivors out of a company of roughly 160 men. As a private first class, Fellman says he had a very limited view of what went on. "I remember that we assembled, there was a cease-fire, and that we attempted to destroy whatever weapons we had. We were then marched down to an area at the base of the hill, and from there we were marched toward a railhead twelve kilometers behind the lines."

It was during that march that he realized the Germans were probably on their last legs. "They had nothing mechanized. They had horses pulling trucks and wagons. They had no gasoline to use for anything except frontline activity."

But that fact was of little comfort. "You are their prisoner, and you realize that you have no more control over anything. You're subject to their whim as to whether you live or breathe. I had my first lesson—we were passing a concrete abutment on the side of the road, and there was an icicle hanging from it. I stepped out of line to grab an icicle, and I got my first rifle butt. So, you learned quick that you had no choice at all. It takes a little while for everything to begin to build up. But your first feelings are the anger and the fact that you just have no idea what's ahead, so there's some fear involved. And later on, it becomes just a struggle for existence."

They were taken to a holding area for prisoners of war, then packed into boxcars—sixty to ninety men to a car. The doors were locked and didn't open again for four or five days. The train sat on sidings during the day and moved mostly at night. Allied aircraft strafed them, and there were casualties in most of the cars. They stopped in Frankfurt for a day and a half and then moved to the town of Bad Orb, the location of Stalag IX-B, the German's largest POW camp for low-ranking enlisted men. His memory is more of being cold than of being afraid. "Maybe I was too young or too stupid to know just how bad the predicament was." He also underestimated the capacity the Nazis had for evil, but in his defense, in January 1945, American GIs in general knew little, if anything at all, about the thousands of concentration and slave-labor camps scattered all across Germany.

They were processed into the camp by other American POWs functioning as clerks who never asked what religious preference was stamped on their dog tags—P for Protestant, C for Catholic, or H for Hebrew. "Everyone was put in as a Protestant, and I said, 'How come?' And he said, 'They don't like Jews. They don't like Catholics, either.' So as far as the German records were concerned, everybody was a Protestant."

Combat didn't go any better for Morton Brooks. His company was moved from south of Strasbourg to north of the city, where it was overwhelmed by the more powerful German forces. He recalls, "In a way, I was fortunate. I was in a forward foxhole, and we were overrun. And before I knew it, the Germans were behind us, hitting the town of Hatten." There were a number of times during those first days of combat when Brooks was terrified. The way he puts it, "I crawled into my helmet."

The men who survived the initial attack gathered in the command post—a tank trap. Friendly artillery fire was beginning to fall on their position, and their telephone lines were cut. Brooks volunteered to trace the wire back to the breaks to repair it. He made it to a bunker that was part of the French defensive position known as the Maginot Line, but he was unable to make contact with the artillery units that were blasting his unit.

Waiting in the bunker with other Americans, he knew that their situation was dire. They couldn't remain in the bunker because the Germans were all around them, and they couldn't get back to the American lines. They were pondering their options when the ranking sergeant looked out into the early daylight and saw a German tank coming up the road. Brooks recalls him saying, "We gotta surrender." He didn't want to and said so, but the sergeant said, "Look, they'll just put the nozzle into this opening, and they'll blast us to pieces." It was clear that they didn't have much of a choice.

"It's interesting—when you're in training in the States, they tell you you're going to know what's going on, who's on your right, who's on your left. But in a combat situation, it's madness. You really don't know what's going on. He felt we better surrender."

Surrendering was a frightening thing to do. "I knew that the Germans would not be kind to us. I had heard about their attitude towards Jews; I didn't know about concentration camps or anything like that, but I knew about some of the pogroms." That was going through his mind as the Germans marched their new POWs across the road into a trench where they'd set up a machine-gun nest. That's when Brooks realized how lucky he'd been not to have been discovered as he approached the bunker.

Once things quieted down, the Nazis marched the prisoners back to a farmhouse where they'd gathered a number of Americans and were interrogating them. Brooks was shocked to learn how much the enemy knew about his outfit, such as the names of the officers and the date they'd sailed from the United States. After a couple of days, all the prisoners were marched to a railhead and packed into boxcars. He was given a bit of food but remembers going at least three days without eating as the train made its way to Frankfurt, parked on sidings during the day, occasionally being strafed by Allied fighter pilots who had no idea that they were wounding and killing American POWs. Ultimately, they arrived at Bad Orb and were marched into Stalag IX-B, a former children's camp set amid eighty-five acres of pine forest.

The POWs at Bad Orb wore the clothes they'd had on when they were captured. They were ripe—but the good news was that the cold kept down the odor. Their daily ration was a loaf of half-flour, half-sawdust bread, shared by seven to ten men depending upon its size. They had a poor excuse for soup at supper. Brooks remembers it being no better than hot grease with something floating in it on occasion. On the weekends they got what their captors called jelly or jam. The Americans were beginning to know what hunger was like.

On January 27, Norman Fellman marked his twenty-first birthday. It was the day he and his comrades were lined up and threatened with being machine-gunned because some prisoners had broken into the food stores and beaten a guard. According to Fellman, the episode ended when a chaplain convinced the perpetrators to turn themselves in. He never saw the men again.

Early in February, the barracks leaders were told by the guards that at the next roll call, all the men who were Jewish were to step forward. The guy he was closest to knew Fellman was Jewish but advised him strongly not to step forward. He promised to keep the secret, but Fellman still had reasons for being concerned.

"During training, there was some anti-Semitism that we ran into. I didn't want to tempt anybody into turning me in [as being Jewish] for food or whatever. You get hungry enough, God knows what a person will do. And we were beginning to get on the hungry side. The other thing is, I've never been ashamed of what I am—maybe I was cocky or more guts than brains—but I decided to step forward. I told my buddies no, I didn't want to be on anybody's conscience."

At the next roll call, Fellman and somewhere between forty and sixty other men stepped forward. Over the next several days they were transferred to the newly designated Jewish barracks.

Mort Brooks remembers his initial interrogation somewhat differently. The Americans doing the interviewing told Brooks they were required to tell the Germans his religion. Brooks thought about it, then said that he was Jewish. "I wasn't going to hide it. I felt I was an American soldier. I had to be treated like a soldier." At the time, his surname was Brimberg, a Jewish-sounding name. Shortly after the interrogation, he was moved to what was designated the all-Jewish barrack, by then holding approximately eighty men.

Strange as it seems, neither Brooks nor Fellman recalls the Germans ever actually inspecting their dog tags. And while some of their fellow Jewish POWs threw theirs away, they didn't, perhaps because it was tangible proof that the wearer was an American soldier and they clung to the notion that it provided some protection. The Americans were issued German prisoner-of-war dog tags, and at the morning roll calls they had to call out the number stamped on them.

The roll calls for the prisoners in the Jewish barracks seemed to last longer than they did for the general POW population. It was January in the worst winter in decades, and the men had to stand in the freezing cold for hours. They'd been allowed to keep the clothing they were wearing when captured, so many of them still had snow boots and winter jackets. Nevertheless, on their reduced rations, the cold wasn't easy to handle. Brooks still had several packets of cigarettes that had come with military K rations, and he traded them to other prisoners for their bread ration.

On February 8, the guards told them that a contingent of 350 men was to be shipped to another camp, ostensibly to relieve overcrowding (4,700 American infantrymen captured during the Battle of the Bulge had been packed into the camp). The Germans insisted that all the Jews, between seventy-seven and eighty men, be sent on the transport. Survivors claimed that the camp authorities made a point of also including Catholics and "troublemakers." One way or another, the order was to ship 350 men, and 350 were marched by guards with dogs out of the camp, to the train on the tracks that ran along the outskirts of Bad Orb. The guards had fixed bayonets and prodded the men along. Brooks says, "They were a little rougher, shoving us in, packed in so that you couldn't sit down." They gave each man a piece of bread, and there was a little water, which didn't last long.

Brooks recalls the trip lasting five days; Fellman isn't sure but thought it was just three or four. As during their trip to Stalag IX-B from the battlefield, the train was strafed by Allied aircraft. The Germans had no control of the air, and he remembers that American or Allied planes were constantly overhead, "and if they could shoot up a train, they did. There were no markings on the train to tell them what was in it. In every car there was at least one person hit." Helping the wounded was virtually impossible. "You can't move," remembers Fellman, "you can't get across the car. You're packed, you're a sardine.

Whoever was hit in the car with me, I couldn't get over there, I couldn't see. For that I was thankful in a way, too."

In addition to enduring friendly fire, the men had to survive the cold. "If you were lucky, you were in the middle of the car, because that way you were warmer," Fellman says. "If you were near the outside, you had chinks in the wood, and the cold could come through and you'd freeze your ass. Your hands would be frozen, your feet would be frozen, and you couldn't lie down and you couldn't stand. I don't remember a lot of conversation, to tell the truth. I think we were more concentrating on just getting through the day."

The train's route took them east, deep into Germany, passing south of the infamous Buchenwald concentration camp, which had administrative control of the hellhole to which they'd been consigned, the slave-labor camp at Berga an der Elster—Berga on the Elster River. On or about February 13, the train stopped on the tracks just south of the Berga town center, across from a camp identified as Berga One.

The POWs were driven from the boxcars by SS officers supervising elderly Volkssturm guards accompanied by dogs. (Volkssturm was the militia started late in 1944, made up of conscripted males between age sixteen and sixty who were not already part of the home guard.) Facing the tracks were extremely high barbed-wire fences—picture the high fences used at golf driving ranges to keep errant balls from flying out— with towers on each corner and searchlights. As they were marched south toward the separate camp they would occupy, they were spat upon by the townsfolk. But that was a minor annoyance. What really terrified them was the sight through the fence into Berga One.

Norman Fellman will never forget it. "The compounds were packed with the skinniest people you ever saw in your life. Huge, huge eyes. The eyes is what I remember most. And they had pajamalike garb on, blue and white stripes. There were hundreds that we could see, and we never did see the full extent of the camp. And the eeriest thing about it was, there was not a sound. It was just incredible; not a sound out of them. You never saw people like this before."

Norman Fellman didn't know it at the time, but he'd just seen his future.

CHAPTER 2

LIFE AND DEATH IN BERGA

APRIL 1, 1945

Between the time Norm Fellman and Morton Brooks arrived in Berga and the start of spring, the tide of the war had turned. The German army was clearly on the run even as the Americans continued to pour fresh troops off boats and into the conflict. Fellman and Brooks had survived their first six weeks at Berga, but around them men were dying at an increasing pace.

Shortly after arrival they were given showers and a delousing treatment, and their clothing was deloused and returned to them. Unfortunately, when they were assigned to shared bunks in barracks heated only by a wood-burning stove at one end, the straw bedding they received was lice-infested. Fellman says rather sardonically, "So maybe for a period of twelve or fourteen hours we had no lice. [After that] whatever leisure time we had was spent going through the seams of our clothing, trying to catch them and squash them between our fingernails. Oh, yeah, that was an occupation that never stopped."

But lice were a relatively minor problem. The men had been brought to Berga as slave laborers to help drill thirteen tunnels into a nearby mountain. They'd heard that the tunnels, or a huge chamber deep in the mountain where the tunnels would meet, would be used for munitions factories; another rumor had it that they'd be used to make synthetic aircraft fuel desperately needed to replace the lost manufacturing capacity at facilities being bombed to rubble by Allied aircraft. The fact that the war was clearly lost and the construction at Berga would make no difference in the outcome of the conflict was irrelevant. The tunnels had to be bored, and the Americans were going to do the job even if it killed them. Or especially if it killed them. At least forty of them died while working in the Berga tunnels.

According to Brooks, six or eight men worked in each tunnel per shift. There were two or three pneumatic drills at the rock face, each one weighing around a hundred pounds. The drill bit was several feet long, and the man holding the drill had to keep it going straight into the rock. As the prisoners lost muscle mass, just holding the drill became a nearly impossible task. He says, "You'd drill into the wall, and then a German explosives expert comes in and sets the charges, and you go out, they blow the wall, and then you go back in and shovel the rock." There was no waiting for the dust to settle; they were forced back in immediately, breathing the huge cloud of smoke and rock and dust.

Fellman was assigned to Stollen Elf, Tunnel Eleven, where he learned the process quickly. "What they would do is drill a series of holes with pneumatic drills into the face of the rock, and then they would insert in each one of these holes a series of gunpowder sausages. I heard from some other prisoners that they had dynamite, but where we were all they had was black powder. They'd pour gunpowder, a premeasured amount, into a sausage size. You twist the heavy paper together, and you made this individual gunpowder sausage. Depending on whatever the engineer decided would determine how many of these gunpowder sausages went into each hole. And they would blow up, and once they blew, before the dust had begun to settle, we were forced back into the tunnel, and we would load that rock into open-side gondolas, and the gondolas were on narrow-gauge rail tracks, and we would push them to the river's edge, the Elster River ran there, and you would dump them. And then before dawn, every day, they would spray paint the pilings of rock so that it didn't look fresh from the air. We worked mostly at night, and the planes would come over for hours, so that the faces of the tunnels would be draped with a canvas of some sort to block the light."

The POWs wore whatever clothing they'd had with them when they arrived at the camp. "Shredded up, whatever we lost, we lost; that was it. You got a hole in your shoe, you put something in it, a cardboard or whatnot. Whatever. You got no replacement as far as clothing is concerned; you're still wearing whatever you had on. [The overseers] had masks, they had gloves, they had all kinds—we had nothing."

That's not quite accurate. What they often had from the civilian overseer in the tunnel, recalls Morton Brooks, was beatings. "He carried a pickax handle and a rubber hose and didn't hesitate to use it. And we were all beaten on a fairly regular basis because we weren't going to try and help them do it. We slacked off and goofed off as much as we could get away with."

Fellman, who was not working in the same tunnel as Brooks, says that even if it meant a beating, the Americans resisted with acts of sabotage. "We'd be sitting on the side of a pile of dirt making these gunpowder sausages. They'd be watching us. What would happen, though, is somehow—nobody ever knew how it happened—but every eighth or tenth sausage got a handful of dirt. When the explosions went off, it never went off the way it was supposed to, and they would go mad. They would go absolutely bananas. And everybody on the shift, everybody, I don't care who you were, got a beating. Either with a club, a rifle butt, or a rubber hose. And this happened on a regular basis.

"I can only speak for the tunnel I was in, I don't know what went on in any of the others, but we discovered by accident that if you piled all the heavy rocks on the side closest to the river and the lightest rock on the side closest to the bank, that when the gondolas would tip so that the body of the gondola was turned to empty the load, the whole gondola would go down in the water. And that would happen from time to time, whatever could be done to slow the work. One of the prisoners who understood German heard the guards saying, 'That crap began to happen when the Americans got there.' "

Before they went to work on their twelve-hour shift, the men received what their captors called coffee. They drank it or tried to clean themselves with it. After their shift they would get a bread ration, perhaps along with soup of some sort, made with dead cats or rats, some of them were told. It was estimated they were being fed about 400 calories a day—roughly the equivalent of a McDonald's Quarter Pounder. The likelihood of survival under those conditions over a long period of time was nil, and the men knew it. Some took heart in the ever-increasing number of Allied aircraft that flew over the camp on their way to bombing German cities.

"We saw the American Air Force flying overhead," says Brooks, recalling the sight of more than a thousand heavy bombers heading for Dresden. "It was wonderful. The Germans weren't happy, but we were thrilled."

Anthony Acevedo, a close friend of both Brooks and Fellman, who as a medic was allowed to remain in the barracks in order to minister to seriously ill POWs, says that when the bombers went over, he could hear the hinges on the windows shake and feel the building vibrate. He'd look skyward and cross himself, praying that liberation would come soon. And he said the guards—mostly Austrians who were devout Catholics as he was—would also cross themselves. He hastens to add that being devout didn't make them any less brutal than the Germans.

Death was all around them at Berga. "The Germans were sticklers for book work," Fellman says. "Everything had to be recorded. So whenever a prisoner died, they had to wait for the medical officer to come by and make a death certificate out. He would only come periodically, once a week, maybe, and so the guys that died in the interim, they would line [their bodies] up on the outside. Remember, now, this is subfreezing weather, so they were stiff in every sense of the word, and they would line them up right alongside of where we lined up to get our chow. And you have to understand, you're standing there waiting for your food alongside of your buddies who are lying dead on the road, and it didn't bother you. [That gives you] some idea of what kind of a situation you had sunk into—and it didn't take long."

Morton Brooks acknowledges that he didn't even have the strength to cry at the time. "It was so miserable, unreal. It's not like sitting here and thinking about it. You're in that situation, and your behavior's determined by the situation in which you're in."

And the situation? All the niceties of civilized living are absent. Taking a shower, having toilet paper, being able to wash your hands after going to the bathroom or before you eat. Not even having a bathroom, just a perch over a slit trench for months on end, coping with chronic diarrhea and having only straw from your bedding to wipe yourself with. And then wearing the same clothes for months at a time.

Brooks ultimately became a clinical psychologist, and he speaks in the language of that profession. "That's why I say, the situation determines your behavior, and say it's a crazy situation, your behavior is crazy. And so, to understand someone's behavior, you have to understand the totality of the situation. And the human capability of coping with that situation. So you cope. And whatever comes out, comes out.

"You had this piece of bread, and then you try to stretch it. Sometimes if we had the potbelly stove going, you'd take the bread and try and toast it on the outside of the stove. One of our fellow soldiers had stolen someone else's bread, and we went over to essentially attack him for doing that. I remember going to hit him, and it was like a powder puff. The force with which I hit him, and I remember how striking it was for me, the lack of strength I had at that moment. You just don't even realize how the strength disappears. It was a shock to me that I had lost so much strength. But that's how quickly we became weakened."

Brooks never did really pray. "I don't know why," he explains. "Maybe I'd never thought in those kinds of terms, that there was some God up there that would be protecting me or could do anything for me."

Survival under those conditions required both physical and emotional strength. Fellman says, "I always believed, but I was never excessive about it, and I don't remember doing any heavy-duty praying, although I'm sure I must've. So I can't tell you where the strength came from. I'm only glad it was there."

And clearly, it had to be. He says, "I have to reiterate, any time you got the frame of mind that you felt like you weren't going to make it, those guys didn't make it. Every one of them." Fellman says that of the guys who survived, "it never occurred to us that we weren't gonna make it home."

He doesn't know what gave him or the others that outlook, it was just existential, like the barracks humor that buoyed them. "We made jokes about everything, except toward the end, you were so turned in, there was no jokes, no nothing. We used to engage on what we would order when we went to a restaurant, and we would insist that the steak be done a certain way, with a certain number of onions on top. And we'd make damn sure you were listening. 'Are you hearing me? Are you hearing what I'm saying?'

"You never talk about girls. Women became very unimportant. I don't remember anybody talking about women, but we talked about food—how it was gonna be prepared."

The Germans worked most of the Americans in twelve-hour shifts. During their off-hours, they slept—or tried to. Norm Fellman recalls, "We tried, if the lice would let you. If the cold would let you. We slept two to a bunk, tried to keep warm. But it depended. I think we slept no matter what, because we were just so thoroughly exhausted. Between the hunger and the lice and the cold, it was not a guaranteed thing. You did sleep. I'm sure we did; otherwise, we wouldn't have made it."

As the days and weeks wore on, Fellman found it more difficult to be an optimist. "Let me tell you, when we first got into camp, the idea was just to hang on. After you've been on reduced rations for a while, you would concentrate on food an awful lot. Your concern would be to make it through the next month, the next week, the next day, and when things got toward the end, you were trying to make it through the next hour. And then it was the next ten minutes. You just wanted to survive that much longer. By the time we were liberated, I don't believe any of us would have lasted another week. I don't believe I would have lasted another twenty-four hours. I was as close to being gone as you can be and not be."

Fellman doesn't remember having nightmares while in Berga. "I don't know what could happen in a nightmare that could even equal what would happen to us during the day. Your existence was a nightmare. Nobody could believe that something like this could happen, not to Americans, anyway."

CHAPTER 3

INCOMPREHENSIBLE

APRIL 3, 1945
NEAR GOTHA, GERMANY
130 miles northeast of Frankfurt

Lieutenant Colonel Albin F. Irzyk didn't find God on the road to Bastogne during the Battle of the Bulge; he was already a believer. But he was certain God found him on December 23, 1944. There was no other way for him to explain why a high-powered armor-piercing round fired by a German tank at point-blank range hit his huge Sherman tank, knocked everyone inside for a loop, but didn't explode. The impact actually split open the turret. As dawn came up, the crew inside could see a long sliver of light. Only after daylight, when Irzyk, the commanding officer of the 8th Tank Battalion, Combat Command B, of the 4th Armored Division, had a chance to crawl outside his tank, did he discover that the round had, with great precision, pinpointed a stubby piece of steel about five inches by four inches by six inches deep and ricocheted off into the Ardennes forest. Irzyk had been a tanker for most of his military career, and he'd never before even noticed that appurtenance on the tracked monster, much less understood why it was there. But it didn't take him long to figure out that had the round not bounced off that solid chunk of steel, it would have driven through the turret and hit him square in the back, leaving little more than crispy pieces of flesh and bone.

Such are the mysteries of combat: the shrapnel that's stopped from penetrating all the way to your heart by the miniature Bible or prayer book carried superstitiously in a breast pocket. The land mine you learn is a dud only after stepping on it and hearing a *click* followed by—nothing. The rifle bullet that slams into your helmet at the perfect angle, so that instead of killing you outright, it runs an orbital path between the steel pot and the helmet liner, resulting in nothing worse than a hellacious headache. Or the incoming shell that bursts in the trees, killing the buddies you share a foxhole with but leaving you alive and unscathed, save for a lifelong case of survivor guilt.

The men of the 4th Armored had experienced all of that and more since they'd landed at Utah Beach on July 11, 1944, and entered combat barely a week later. To attack the Germans at Bastogne in order to help relieve the besieged 101st Airborne Division—the Battered Bloody Bastards of Bastogne—under orders from General George S. Patton they'd raced into Belgium, covering 150 miles in nineteen hours. Even for an armored unit accustomed to outpacing the infantry and artillery, that's nothing short of incredible.

They fought hard, crossing the Rhine on bridges built by U.S. Army engineers, heading into the heartland of Germany on March 24 and 25. They went east of Frankfurt and drove north to the city of Bad Hersfeld, the last population center in what would come to be known as West Germany. Then they headed east into the future German Democratic Republic (aka East Germany), toward the ultimate objective of Dresden. The map Irzyk switched to in the turret of his tank covered the Erfurt sector of the country. The Americans gambled on traveling down the Autobahn as far as practical, because it was quick going. They were hit; they fought back and kept going. They went through Eisenach and on the following day, April 4, around midmorning, the 4th Armored Division took Gotha without firing a shot, but only because the town's burgomaster had been given an ultimatum: surrender the city or see it destroyed by artillery fire. Combat Command B, which included the 37th Tank Battalion, formally accepted the surrender of Gotha.

The commander of one of the 37th tanks was Sergeant Harry Feinberg. A lanky, six-foot-tall Jewish kid from Brooklyn, Feinberg had left home in 1937 at the age of seventeen without finishing high school to tour the country for nearly four years with a vaudeville act called Borrah Minevich and His Harmonica Rascals. He practiced a lot, made recordings, and even appeared in a movie with the child star Jane Withers.

In late 1940, with the glamour of show business fading, Harry returned home to work in the building business with his father. Little more than a year later, he was drafted, sent to Fort Knox, Kentucky, to learn all about tanks and to discover that training was going to require a good imagination: the entire division had only six tanks; they simulated firing at targets made by painting the word TANK on big Army trucks.

Eventually, while on exercises in the Mojave Desert, the unit got real tanks as well as a commanding general the men loved, Major General John Wood. Feinberg says that prior to deployment Wood was being questioned by reporters who asked him why the 4th didn't have a nickname like the other armored divisions, such as "Hell on Wheels" or "Old Ironsides." According to lore, Wood said, "We don't need a nickname. We will be known by our deeds alone. Name is enough: 4th Armored Division." And that's how the division nickname became "Name Enough."

At the end of 1943, the division sailed for England in a fifty-two-ship convoy and then trained in the British countryside for months until finally being sent to France weeks after D-Day. It didn't take long for the reality of war to strike home. They were in the Normandy hedgerows, just beyond Sainte-Mère-Église (recall the famous scene in *The Longest Day* where the paratrooper's chute is caught on the church steeple next to the clock), and had just jumped off the tanks to begin routine cleaning and maintenance. Feinberg recalls that "As soon as we got off the tank, I hear a whistle. That's the loudest whistle I ever heard. A plane came over, and right into the next hedgerow, a bomb fell there, and you see a flash, and you hear screaming, 'Medic! Medic!' And I started shivering.

"You could hear a lot of excitement. 'Over here, guys, over here, c'mon!' And you'd hear another guy say, 'I can't feel my legs, I can't feel my legs.' And this all came down as a big surprise. You can imagine my head just spinning. What can I do here? Where can I run to?"

Feinberg survived the next several months, which included participation in the Battle of the Bulge. He earned a Purple Heart and screwed up his back for life as a result of the constant jumping down from the tank. By the time his unit stopped in Gotha, he was an experienced soldier, using training, innate smarts, and intuition to survive. But as most war veterans will tell you, it's when you think you've got it figured out that you tend to get careless and take unnecessary risks.

"I was now a tank commander, because our guys were getting killed, so they promoted me. Gave me three stripes. Baloney. I didn't want those three stripes or any of them. Anyway, we're on attack, on a paved road. I don't remember what was on my right side, but on this side I see about eight, ten houses, well-kept two-story homes, and we stopped on the road. We gassed up, oiled up, and greased up and did what we had to, and we're just waiting for a command to move out. So I said, 'Hey, guys, I'm going into this house across the road.' There was a wrought iron fence with fleur-de-lis all on this black fence, and I'm going in there to see what's in the house, which is the most stupid thing I ever did. I go to the door, and I turn the handle, and the door opens. I go in, I look, and I'm in a big, big living room, and there's a woman at the other end. She's dressed from here"—he touches his neck—"down to her ankles, and she had a German honeycomb hair comb. And she says, 'Come in, come in.' Being I could speak Yiddish, I was used as a German interpreter, so I understood her. And I looked at her. All I had was my .45 and my grease gun, and I look around, and I see a door here and there, and it didn't dawn on me until I ran out, what am I doing here? There might be enemy in there. My God, they can make mincemeat of me. Anyway, she says to me, 'Come in, this is my living room.' She asked me, *'Keine Schokolade?'* And I said, *'Nein.'*

She says in German, 'I'll make a trade with you. See this lamp here, on the end table? You take this, you give me chocolate, and you can take this home as a souvenir.' So, I said, *'Nein, die Schokolade ist für die Kinder,'* because in every town we went to, little five-, six-, eight-year-old kids were not afraid of us, even in Germany. They used to come around to see us, look at us around our tanks. Very poorly fed, very poorly clothed. And the American soldier's not a tough soldier, he's a sweetheart, he's a marshmallow, they see kids, they jump off the tank and give them chewing gum and if we had cookies, oh, these kids would love us. And we'd pick them up and just play with them. They would laugh. And, of course, this is when we're not firing.

"She said, 'For a souvenir, take it home with you.' So I looked at the lamp, and something shuddered over my body. I got a feeling, because the light was still on and I could see through there, and it was sort of grayish yellow coloring. She said, 'Do you know what this is made of? This is human skin.' That's when I turned—I wheeled around and just waved her down and ran out, and the guys said, 'Hey, what happened?' I said, 'I just did the most stupid thing that I ever did. What the hell did I go in there for?' "

It would not be the last time that American troops were confronted by such hideous creations.

Probably around the time that Harry Feinberg was recovering from his Gotha adventure, Lieutenant Colonel Al Irzyk's 8th Tank Battalion was literally flagged over to the side of a main Gotha road by the commanding officer of Combat Command A, Colonel Hayden Sears, a huge hulk of a man who dwarfed the much more diminutive battalion commander.

Speaking face-to-face on the sidewalk, Sears told Irzyk that intelligence had received indications that the Nazis had built a huge underground communications installation designed for the headquarters of the entire German army in the event Berlin had to be evacuated. The installation was reported to be somewhere near the town of Ohrdruf, which lay roughly ten miles to the south. Sears's instructions were simple: "Go to Ohrdruf and look for this complex."

Today, that's an eighteen-minute drive. In 1945, in Sherman tanks with bad guys shooting at you, it took a little longer. Irzyk's memory of

Brigadier General (Ret.) Albin F. Irzyk looks
over the map he used to move his 4th Armored
Division tank battalion into the area of
Ohrdruf, the first concentration camp
discovered by American forces.

the day is remarkably clear, and his recitation of the story comes to life
when he spreads out his wartime-era map on the dining room table of
his historic Palm Beach, Florida, home. The route his tank battalion
and accompanying armored infantry followed six decades ago is easy to
see. "The minute we left Gotha, we started hitting resistance." Initially, they were attacked by Panzerfausts—the German antitank
bazooka-type weapon that resembles the rocket-propelled grenades
(RPGs) so common today. Those were followed by mortar and small-
arms fire, as well as occasional artillery rounds. Nevertheless, "This is
April, the ground is dry. I had my tanks spread out, and we advanced."

At the time, he was confident. "If there was a complex, one of my
tanks would have found it. You can't hide a complex, [or] so we
thought as we moved. But we got to Ohrdruf, and it was getting dark.

Joe Vanacore used the bulldozer blade on his Sherman tank to push through the gates at Ohrdruf.

I outposted two towns beyond Ohrdruf," he recalls, pointing at the map. "And then we dug in for the night."

Irzyk had been too busy positioning his troops to focus on chatter that had begun late in the day on one of the tank-commander-to-tank-commander radio channels. They were talking about a lot of bodies being found in the woods.

It was either late in the afternoon of that same day or first thing the next morning—the surviving GIs don't agree—when a barbed-wire enclosure was discovered by a platoon of tanks from Company A that had been sent to observe the area to the front of the 8th Battalion. Twenty-one-year-old Joe Vanacore, from Queens, New York, was driving the only tank in the battalion with a bulldozer blade. He calls it the dirtiest job in an armored unit. Whichever of the three companies was in the lead, Joe's tank was in second position. His job was to clear the roads so the unit's trucks could get through. If, for example, aircraft knocked out a Tiger or Supertiger tank and it blocked the road, Joe had to use his thirty-ton Sherman to move it—a tricky task considering that the German tanks weighed sixty to sixty-five tons.

As their tanks approached the barbed-wire enclosure that afternoon, Joe's view was limited. His world was confined to what he could see through the tank driver's periscope. He'd been across Europe and into Germany buttoned up. "Half the towns I went through, I couldn't tell you what they were." His tank commander, Bill Jenkins, lined him up on the ten-foot-high wooden gates and told him to go, and he pushed them in with the bulldozer blade.

The gates marked the entrance to Ohrdruf Nord, a subcamp of Buchenwald, also known as North Stalag III. Ohrdruf was a small camp but significant because it was the first one discovered by American forces that contained the bodies of hundreds of dead prisoners as well as starved, frail concentration camp inmates who had managed to survive until the liberators arrived. Even though the American high command knew about the death camps in Poland that had been liberated by the advancing Russian army, they had done nothing to prepare their troops for the possibility that they'd be confronted by the unspeakable evil of the Nazis' slave-labor death machine.

A few words about the Nazi camp system. Between 1933, when Dachau accepted its first prisoners, and the end of the war, the Nazis established approximately 20,000 camps, including concentration camps, forced-labor camps, prisoner-of-war camps, and ghettos, among other types. Of the main concentration camps whose names people generally know, nearly every one was responsible for more than a hundred subcamps in its geographical area. Prisoners were often shifted from one subcamp to another as the need for slave labor arose. When they were worn out, they were shipped to a main camp, where they were allowed to starve or sicken and die, or to extermination camps such as Auschwitz, which were equipped for efficient mass murder on a scale heretofore unimaginable.

Beginning after the invasion of Poland in 1939, the Nazis established thousands of forced-labor camps—some very small, some holding thousands of prisoners—where inmates were housed while being used by the SS, private firms, or government organizations manufacturing war materiel and other goods for the Reich. Prisoners in these camps were not gassed and conditions were better than in the concentration camps, but some prisoners died nonetheless, from exhaustion, exposure, and starvation.

Prisoner-of-war camps were distinct from the concentration camps. They were harsh but were not part of the SS killing machine. Conditions varied: British and American prisoners fared the best, while 60 percent of Soviet POWs died of maltreatment, exposure, starvation, disease, or outright murder.

The 4th Armored's Joe Vanacore recalls no shooting going on as the Americans entered Ohrdruf because the Germans who had been there had fled. Another 8th Battalion tanker, New Yorker Paul Glaz, who was living on Long Island when he was drafted in 1941, confirms that the SS guards had left the camp undefended and believes he knows why. "When they heard the 4th Armored was coming, they took off. We had a thing between the SS and the 4th Armored: one or the other had to go. When you fought them, you didn't take them prisoner, you killed them. If they got us, they did the same with us."

As Vanacore drove his tank inside the camp, he remembers the view through the periscope. "The first thing I saw was this big pile of bodies, about five, six foot high, like a haystack. I didn't realize they were bodies—my mind didn't tell me they were bodies until I got a little closer."

The men dismounted from the tanks and began to wander, looking around in disbelief at what they saw. Vanacore says, "The smell got me so bad I couldn't eat for a week." It's what stays in his mind, what he thinks of now when he hears people say "the Holocaust was a fake. I really couldn't stand people to say things like that. We were right there; we saw things with our own eyes."

Glaz recalls seeing stacks of bodies. "They laid them up like cords of wood, one on top of the other. They were naked, and they'd laid them up about four foot high, lime in between. It was a terrible-looking thing. I remember it smelled like hell. God only knows how long they laid there."

Several GIs who were at Ohrdruf tell of being offered a guided tour of the camp by a healthy-looking, English-speaking man dressed in prisoner garb. But before the tour could begin, a Polish prisoner ran up and clobbered the man in the head with a piece of lumber, following up that attack by stabbing him to death with a bayonet. The attacker explained that his victim had been one of the German camp guards, who, for some inexplicable reason, had not escaped prior to the arrival of the 4th Armored. The episode was recounted in several interviews conducted for this book and can be found in so many oral history archives and military documents that it has begun to sound apocryphal. What militates against dismissing it as such is that it is a scene described by GIs interviewed for this book at camp after camp: inmates discovering former torturers among them after liberation and brutally killing them as the Americans stood by watching.

Vanacore stayed in the camp for about three or four hours, doing some bulldozing to fill in holes in order to make it more accessible for the Army vehicles that would soon be pouring in to help the survivors and deal with the remains of those who had been killed by the Nazis. At one point he saw a German three-yard dump truck loaded with what he initially thought was sand. "It was ashes from the bodies that they burnt."

On the morning of April 5, Lieutenant Colonel Irzyk had his jeep brought up and drove to the area where elements of the 8th Battalion's D Company had discovered bodies in a wooded area. "I got out of the jeep and walked through the woods, and the first thing I saw was this clearing. And I just couldn't believe what I saw. I could see an elliptical circle of bodies, with the feet in and the heads out. I was absolutely stunned. I'd never seen anything like this before—never expected to see anything like it." He recalls gasping audibly; his feet seemed leaden as he forced them to move closer. And he gasped again. "Each man had a little red spot here"—he gestured to his forehead—"shot in the head or in the throat, one shot. And these were thin, emaciated, ragged people in this elliptical circle." The ground around the bodies was blood-soaked.

To the battle-hardened Irzyk, the scene was incomprehensible. He kept asking himself, "What is this?" And that morphed into "How did this happen? But that's step one. And as you get to this building, this

These forty-two emaciated, nude corpses, some showing evidence of having been shot or beaten, were found by the American soldiers in a storage shed at Ohrdruf. This was likely the first instance in the war where GIs saw and described bodies of concentration camp inmates as "stacked like cordwood." The soldiers were ordered to leave the lime-sprinkled bodies where they lay, so that commanders all the way up to Eisenhower would be able to see them when they came to inspect Ohrdruf.

horrible smell, you open the door, and there—again—another unbelievable shock. You've got these bodies, probably thirty of them—they're like skeletons without clothing, but all sorts of marks and bruises, covered with lime, like cordwood, from the floor to the ceiling. Just stacked there. So you open the door and you look at—this is unbelievable! You've never seen anything like it. You can't comprehend it. And that was step two."

Lieutenant Colonel Irzyk, deeply affected by what he was seeing at Ohrdruf, was keenly aware that his men were watching for his reaction to the horror, and he managed to keep himself from vomiting. "Then, as we roam around, the third step was the disposal pits. And by that time, the pattern emerges. You know now what this is. This is totally unexpected, you never heard anything about it, and then suddenly you're confronted with it. This is unbelievable. It makes an impact that is unforgettable."

While the horror of a pit filled with the decomposing bodies of slave laborers is incomprehensible, Irzyk saw something worse as he continued to explore Ohrdruf. "The cadavers were stacked on a grill of logs and rails, and firemen with their spruce and pine kept the fires hot and blazing." Later, he learned that captured SS guards had told interrogators that between December and April, perhaps two or three thousand corpses had been burned in the woods near the camp. The evidence was all around. "The ash was shin high, and the skulls were all over the place. We saw fragments of skin that had not burned."

As a career soldier, Irzyk had not only seen combat in all its ugliness—he'd been trained to expect it, to control his reactions. But nothing he'd ever seen or expected to see matched up to Ohrdruf. "The first two dead Germans I ever saw were in Normandy, when we were waiting to break out, and I was roving, trying to learn lessons. I came across a German tank—it was a light tank, yeah—it'd been knocked out. This is where the 4th Infantry had gone. I got out of my jeep, and this tank was buttoned up—the hatches were closed. I opened up the hatch, and there were two Germans sitting there, burned to a crisp. It was like black toast. Those were the first two Germans that I ever saw, dead Germans. We've hit German tanks, they burned. I saw my tanks burned, I saw my men burned. I went back to the aid station one day, and a guy's lying on the table, and you talk about guts being—" He paused, as if recalling that scene, then continued, "So we saw some terrible things."

Stanley Friedenberg had been an accountant in Manhattan before being drafted. He volunteered for Officer Candidate School (OCS) and in 1943 graduated as a Signal Corps officer. Ultimately, he was recruited into the Counter Intelligence Corps and at the end of 1944 went to Europe, where his supervisors at CIC Headquarters on Avenue Victor-Hugo in Paris sent him on what the now-retired attorney describes as "the grand march across Europe." Friedenberg and the men traveling in his jeep wore uniforms with no identification save for the U.S. pins on their collars; they showed no rank, and their ID cards referred to them as "Mr." He spoke a bit of French and passable German, which he says was nowhere near good enough for interrogation. His unit was assigned to the 65th Infantry Division for rations and quarters, but they essentially freelanced around Germany, gathering evidence of war crimes.

Late on April 4, they got word via radio that a camp at Ohrdruf had been discovered, and they drove there, arriving on the morning of April 5, probably around the same time that Lieutenant Colonel Irzyk entered the camp.

Speaking on the patio of his winter home in Placida, Florida, Friedenberg recalls seeing the barbed-wire enclosure and what he describes as shabby buildings. "As I walked through the gate, there was a pit the size of this swimming pool, fifteen by thirty, that was filled with naked bodies of men—real ninety-eight-pound skeletons, bones protruding. And I couldn't tell how many because they were piled one on top of the other. I would guess there were several hundred bodies there. Someone had started to pour lime on the bodies at one end to decompose them. I took one picture—that's all I could take because it was such a horrible sight. I was going to take more, but I couldn't. I was just overwhelmed by the sight. I didn't throw up. Smell is horrible; decomposing bodies. It's astonishment, really, astonishment."

Even as a member of CIC, Friedenberg had had no idea about the concentration camps. At that point in the war, news of them had not made it down the chain of command. Some officers in the line units knew the Russians had run into them, and Irzyk says there were "undercurrents about concentration camps, but I don't think the impact—it never came until we got to Ohrdruf. To see it, to see it"—he pauses, searching for the right word—"it's staggering, staggering."

The questions raised for Friedenberg that morning in Ohrdruf still trouble him today. "How can one human being do this to another, no matter how much you hated them? These people were just used and worked and given very little food until they dropped dead in their tracks and were thrown in the pit. How could it be? Is there a god? What causes this? You just can't believe that it could happen to human beings."

The camp that the 4th Armored Division's 8th Tank Battalion

found had been built just five months earlier to house prisoners brought from Buchenwald, thirty-two miles away, to work as forced labor on the underground Nazi communications center or the railway leading to it. Just weeks before the liberation of Ohrdruf, the prisoner population was around 11,700, but mere days before the arrival of the Americans, the SS evacuated most of them on a series of death marches to Buchenwald. Many who were too weak to walk were loaded into trucks, and when the trucks were full, the remainder were shot to death. The bodies at the entrance had all been killed with pistols by the last contingent of SS guards to leave the camp—a farewell gesture, no doubt, in observance of Reichsführer-SS Heinrich Himmler's order not to permit concentration camp prisoners to fall into enemy hands alive.

But there were survivors at Ohrdruf. Some had hidden inside the many barracks that had housed the prisoners; others had taken advantage of the inevitable confusion that ensued as the Nazis attempted to force march thousands of prisoners away and hidden in the nearby woods. When they revealed themselves to the American soldiers, they pleaded for food, and, as would happen thousands of times in the final weeks of the war, the GIs gave everything they had, often with tragic results. The high-calorie military rations were too much for digestive systems that had been systematically starved for months or even years. Prisoners who had survived to be freed died even as they were being fed by their liberators.

Three days after liberation, *Yank* magazine correspondent Sergeant Saul Levitt arrived at Ohrdruf. In his article published on May 18, 1945, he wrote:

> The men in the camp included Belgians, French, Russians, Serbs, and Poles. There is one sixteen-year-old Jewish lad among the survivors. There are also three Russian officers who made it. Two of them are doctors . . . the doctors worked as laborers until a few days before the evacuation of the camp. Then, just before the end, they were put to work on some of the sick in an effort to get them ready for the movement.

Harry Feinberg, who has detailed memories of Ohrdruf, kept the Tri-State (New York, New Jersey, Connecticut) Chapter of the 4th Armored Division Association going for years.

Levitt continued:

The Americans going through this camp are very quiet. They have already seen much death, but they stare at this death, which is uglier and harder to look at than the death of war, with impassive faces and big eyes.

Major John R. Scotti of Brooklyn, N.Y., Combat Command A's medical officer-in-charge, burst out in a loud voice, not speaking to anyone in particular. He just stood in the middle of the camp and shouted out what he felt and no one acted surprised to hear his voice booming out big like that.

"I tell you," he said, and his angry voice was shaking, "all that German medical science is nil. This is how they have progressed in the last four years. They have now found the cure-all for typhus and malnutrition. It's a bullet through the head."

Doc Scotti was the man Harry Feinberg was looking for shortly after arriving in the camp at Ohrdruf. Feinberg says, "I started walking around, and these bodies laying all over, some were clothed, some had just this striped thing. Their heads were all shaven and none of them are breathing. And I look, and I see one guy, his eyes back, and he's laying. I don't know if he was Jewish or what, but he had no face; everything was just"—at this point Feinberg scrunches his face, looking pained. "And I see him just gasping for air, so I looked at him, so suddenly he looks up at me. I don't know how he opened his eyes, and he says, '*Amerikaner?*' I says, '*Ja, Amerikaner.*'"

The man acknowledged the information with a labored sigh. Feinberg recalls looking at the other bodies surrounding him. "Nobody else is breathing, just this one guy. I ran over to the tank, got on the horn, I said, 'Medics, medics, come out here, I'm in so-and-so area. Get Doc Scotti here.' He was our battalion surgeon, an Italian guy, he was the greatest. He was the salt of the earth, had a heart as big as a whale. And he came over in his jeep, and I motioned to him.

"I said, 'Doc, the guy's still breathing. I see him gasping.' So Dr. Scotti, he gets on his horn and says, 'Ambulance, come here, we're in this sector.'" While they were waiting, the doctor examined the prisoner. Harry recalls how gentle he was. "Somehow he just touched here, touched here, and he listened. Didn't take his stethoscope out, he just touched. He says, 'Get the litter carrier'"—it was just two oak poles and OD canvas stretched between them. "Then Doc Scotti said, 'Very, very carefully, pick this guy up.' This guy didn't have any strength, just enough to say '*Amerikaner.*' So evidently he was one of the guys who knew that we liberated him. But that's the only one I saw."

After helping rescue the lone survivor, Feinberg and some other men from his unit began to walk through the camp. "All of us took our handkerchiefs out, and we had to cover ourselves. It was impossible to breathe because the odor was terrible. At one point, I even went over to one of the barracks. I opened the doors, and there's bodies laying over these wood beds, two-decker beds. I had to close the door. Dead, dead. I didn't go inside; I couldn't go inside. They were just, all of them the same, heads shaven."

Feinberg also saw the trench with the bodies. He remembers it as "a big hole about fifty feet by maybe two hundred feet with railroad ties shoved in there. They were going to bulldoze the bodies in there and then set the thing on fire and then cover it up so the Americans can't see what they'd done."

Continuing through the camp, Feinberg came across the commander of the 4th Armored's Combat Command B, Lieutenant Colonel Creighton Abrams, who would go on to become the U.S. commander in Vietnam from 1968 to 1972 and then Army chief of staff from 1972 until his death in 1974. "I see him with tears. I couldn't believe that. He's a very nice guy. He didn't try to show you how tough he was or anything. And gets on his tank and says, 'Okay, guys, let's settle here.' We found out that the troops that were guarding the camps, they took off, so he had a few tanks go down the road. The little [spotter] airplane was up above, he called the plane and said, 'Let us know [if] somebody's trying to escape. Get their position.' And he got a platoon of tanks, five, six tanks, had them go after them. I understood that they put on full steam ahead and got them and just annihilated these guys. I didn't see them.

"But anyway, Abrams gets on his tank and says, 'Don't touch anything. The best bet is to get away from this area because there must be a lot of disease floating around.' He himself had had no idea. The colonel in charge of a whole battalion had no idea what was going on, had no idea there was concentration camps. And that surprised me."

Bernard Diamond, from the Bronx, was only eighteen years old when his unit, the 89th Infantry Division, came into Ohrdruf to relieve the 4th Armored. He was a member of a weapons platoon: mortars and machine guns. And he had fought in the Battle of the Bulge near Bastogne almost immediately after arriving in Europe. "You know, I was eighteen years old. Was I terrified? I think I was just stupid.

"When I got to Ohrdruf, and I'm walking into a courtyard, and I see piles of shirts and piles of suitcases. And what I thought were baskets of pebbles, but when I looked closer, they weren't pebbles. They were teeth with gold in them. And I said, 'What the hell is this?' You know, I didn't know anything about [the camps]. But when I saw some prisoners there, the first thing they wanted was my weapon because the Germans were still running out and escaping."

On April 8, several days after liberation, while the 4th Armored was still waiting to be relieved by the 89th Infantry Division, Combat Command A's Colonel Hayden Sears ordered his men to go into the nearby town of Ohrdruf with trucks and bring back the citizens to the camp. In his *Yank* magazine article, Sergeant Levitt describes Ohrdruf as "a neat, well-to-do suburban town with hedges around some of its brick houses and concrete walks leading to their main entrances. The richest man in Ohrdruf is a painting contractor who made a lot of money in the last few years on war work for the German Army and now owns a castle on the way to the concentration camp."

Harry Feinberg recalls the scene when the townspeople arrived at the camp: "They came up and had handkerchiefs over their mouths. And they dressed in their Sunday best, every one of them. The women had nice hats, and they were taken through the camp."

The enforced tour ended at the site in the woods where ten bodies lay on a grill made of train rails, prepared for cremation. Colonel Sears said to the townspeople, "This is why Americans cannot be your friends." Then he turned to a German medical officer and asked, "Does this meet with your conception of the German master race?" It took a few moments for a response. "I cannot believe that Germans did this."

In *Yank,* Levitt wrote:

The crowd of the best people in Ohrdruf stood around the dead and looked at the bodies sullenly. One of them said at last: "This is the work of only one per cent of the German Army and you should not blame the rest."

Then the colonel spoke briefly and impersonally through an interpreter. "Tell them," he said, "that they have been brought here to see with their own eyes what is reprehensible from any human standard and that we hold the entire German nation responsible by their support and toleration of the Nazi government."

The crowd stared at the dead and not at the colonel. Then the people of Ohrdruf went back to their houses.

The colonel and his soldiers went back to their tanks, and we went out of this place and through Ohrdruf and Gotha, where the names of Beethoven, Mozart and Brahms are set in shining gold letters across the front of the opera house.

CHAPTER 4

SPRINGTIME FOR HITLER

APRIL 5, 1945

BERGA AN DER ELSTER, GERMANY

   80 miles east of Ohrdruf

S ometime during the first week of April, the Berga POWs began
hearing that they were to be moved to another camp. Morton
Brooks says that initially the men weren't sure whether or not it was an
April Fool's joke. (Strange as it may seem in this context, that custom
actually originated in Germany in the 1860s with the playing of elaborate practical jokes and hoaxes, so the notion was not completely im-
probable.)

   The rumor about being moved wasn't a joke or a hoax—except for
the part about going to another camp. This was to be a forced march,
destination unknown. Surely the SS knew that most of the men were
unlikely to survive, but they'd long ago tossed the rules of the Geneva
Conventions; additional deaths of American POWs were of little con-

cern. The apparent reason for the evacuation of the Americans was the rapid approach of Soviet troops advancing along the eastern front, to the northeast of Berga.

On April 5, instead of being marched the mile-plus distance to the tunnels they'd been blasting into the mountain, the regular camp guards greeted the prisoners with "We're marching out, we're going out." Morton Brooks, who had arrived at Berga about a hundred days earlier weighing roughly 145 pounds, had lost almost half his body weight. He recalls that the men were lined up and marched out the gates and past the townspeople, who threw things at them. Those were the same good Germans who a month or less hence would be greeting the occupying Allied forces with smiles and shouting the quickly mastered welcome *"Nicht Nazi."*

Just under three hundred Americans began the impossible march south on a road alongside the Elster River, guarded by twenty-eight soldiers. Fortunately, the weather was springlike, and the Berga survivors were not required to cope with winter conditions that surely would have felled a good number of them within days. They'd each received subminimal rations for the march, a tenth of a loaf of bread and part of a Red Cross parcel; perhaps their captors thought they'd find additional food along the way, perhaps not.

The first day they managed to travel about ten miles. The prisoners straggled along, stopping often to relieve themselves—diarrhea had been a constant in their lives for months—which caused the guards to berate them, urging them to be quick. An occasional German civilian offered them something to eat, but more often than not the civilians just wanted the men to move quickly past their property lest they dirty it.

They were all wearing the remnants of the clothes they'd had on when they'd been captured four months earlier. Brooks's socks had disintegrated, and his combat boots had worn the skin off his toes; he could actually see the bones. Nevertheless, he continued to trudge along.

Norman Fellman wasn't quite so fortunate. After a couple of days, he couldn't walk. "My boots had burst, and I had an infection in one leg. A lot of people in that situation were shot, but in the particular group that I was with, they put us into a cart. Now, try and picture the cart: it was used to carry vegetables to market for farmers. It was about maybe twenty feet long, and it was narrow on the bottom, with V-shaped sides to it. They were at an angle—they bellied out. And you could probably get eight, nine people on there without crowding. They put thirty. Invariably, somebody on the bottom would suffocate. It was Russian roulette—you prayed like hell you were not the first one on the cart, because if you were, there was a good chance you were not gonna be breathing when they took you off."

The cart was loaded by prisoners who could still move; occasionally prisoners were dumped into it by the guards. For most of the time on the road, the cart was pushed and pulled by POWs. For a short period of time he recalls a broken-down horse taken from a local farmer being used.

Given that the Germans had not been averse to shooting or beating prisoners to death, why not now? "I think if it wasn't for the proximity of Allied troops, they would've shot us, because earlier, when people fell out of line, that's what happened, they shot them. But I think the fear was there," says Fellman. "The only thing that saved our asses, I believe, was that we were pretty close to American lines."

Nevertheless, at least thirty-five Americans died on the march from Berga. Four perished the first night as the prisoners were lodged in a school. A day later, another four died in a castle. Then three died on the road; another eleven died while the group was kept in a barn for five days. Thirteen more died as the prisoners were forced to march farther south.

As the men in Morton Brooks's group trudged along the road not quite two weeks into the march, they began passing hundreds of bodies, nearly all showing signs of having been shot at close range in the back of the head. They'd been following the same route that had been taken by the death march of the political prisoners from Berga. These were the same skeletal figures with the big eyes that the POWs had seen when they'd first arrived at the concentration camp; the same people who had worked near them, drilling tunnels into the mountain. Confronted with the insensible brutality of the Nazis even though the war was clearly lost, it was difficult to keep the faith, to believe that survival was not only possible but probable. Brooks, age nineteen and weighing less than 80 pounds, still had enough strength left to carry his buddies physically and psychologically. "You just say, 'You gotta keep going. We're gonna be freed soon. We're gonna make it.' Those who didn't believe it usually died. People gave up, just went."

The sight of the bodies of the Eastern European Jews compelled Brooks to make a decision. He had to escape. He said to his buddy Seymour Fahrer, " 'This is gonna be our end, let's see if we can get outta here.' So we agreed that we'd make the attempt, and the following day we just kept falling behind, falling behind, like we couldn't keep up, and the guard who was at the end didn't bother too much. We just straggled along until it got dark. And then Seymour and I took off and went into the woods."

His feet were still incredibly painful, which is why he says with a laugh now, "We trudged, we didn't run. The next day we saw this farmhouse. There was some vegetables on the porch, and we tried to get it. The farmer came out with a shotgun, and we were taken into the town for the night and put into a dungeon—an underground hole. The following day there was some sisters of some order who attempted to do something with my feet. But then we were taken back to the group."

Surprisingly, the two would-be escapees weren't punished—perhaps because the German guards' focus had shifted from making the lives of the prisoners more miserable to figuring out how to make sure they were captured by American soldiers rather than the Russians. Word had already spread throughout Germany that the Russian soldiers were brutal; for them it was payback for what the German army had done to the Russian people as they had advanced toward Leningrad. Wholesale rape was the order of the day. Pillaging. A take-no-prisoners policy. And the Russians were already west of Danzig (now Gdańsk, Poland), less than three hundred miles from Berlin. There were even rumblings among the German high command of trying to work out an alliance with the Americans against the Russians.

APRIL 10, 1945

ERFURT, GERMANY

With the 80th Infantry Division

Robert Burrows was working as a produce clerk in Royal Oak, Michigan, when he turned eighteen in October 1942. He tried to enlist as an air cadet but acknowledges that he paid for having dropped out of high school when he flunked the test. So he went down the hall and tried to join the Marines. But there was a sign on the door that said, "Not taking any enlistments." So he volunteered for the Army. After basic training, he became a medic and was stationed at the Breakers Hotel in Palm Beach, Florida. It was tough duty, but someone had to do it. He stayed there working as a clerk in the lab, participated in a couple of autopsies, and practiced his putting. Being young and clearly not recognizing a good thing, he tried to volunteer for the paratroopers but was turned down. But in February 1944, the need for warm bodies in Europe became pressing, and he was assigned to the XII Corps headquarters.

In December, during the Battle of the Bulge, infantry units were crying for replacements, and Burrows volunteered, much to the chagrin of his boss, Major General Manton S. Eddy, the XII Corps commander and former commanding officer of the 9th Infantry Division. After a ten-minute talk, the general gave him the opportunity to serve with any infantry outfit in Europe. Sergeant Burrows said it made no difference to him, so Eddy sent him to the 2nd Battalion, 317th Infantry Regiment, of the 80th Infantry Division, where his former aide de camp was the commander. Burrows was assigned to S2, the battalion intelligence section.

For the next three weeks he saw heavy combat and was the only survivor among a group of six when the last artillery round of a morning barrage near the town of Borscheid, Luxembourg, fell on their position.

Shortly thereafter, rumors began to spread. He heard that a camp with a lot of bodies had been found, and the rumor mill was saying they were POWs. "They weren't talking about Holocaust versus Jews or Poles or Ukrainians or Russians or anything. The rumors were spread person to person. We had no radios. Somebody said something, and that's the way it went. We really wiped these things out of our minds, anyway. You couldn't go on and be concerned about what's happened. You had a job to do."

Their job on April 10 was to take Erfurt, a city about fifteen miles from Weimar. It would mark the last battle of the war where his unit would lose people. One of them would be his own commander, Lieutenant McAlpine. The next morning, the eleventh, they started for Weimar, and they began hearing rumors again. The 6th Armored Division was ahead of them, and it had found something. But at that point there were just rumors.

What they'd found was Buchenwald, which had been taken over on April 10 by Communist-led inmates who had been arming themselves for the day the Allied armies would approach the camp. The underground movement had nearly a thousand armed men, who had taken over after the hard-core SS guards fled as the U.S. Army approached Weimar. The underground fought against a small number of young German soldiers, overpowering and imprisoning those they caught in a place called "the dungeon." A couple of the young soldiers tried to impersonate inmates but were caught, and it's claimed that they subsequently hanged themselves.

Buchenwald was built in 1937 in a wooded area about five miles northwest of Weimar, in east-central Germany. The early inmates were predominantly political prisoners; however, after Kristallnacht in 1938, almost 10,000 Jews were sent to the camp. As the years went on, the Nazi regime sent a variety of people there: hardened criminals, Jehovah's Witnesses, Gypsies, military deserters, and so-called asocials. In its final years, Buchenwald also held POWs from various countries, former government officials of Nazi-occupied countries, resistance fighters, and slave laborers brought to Germany from captured lands.

By February 1945, the population of Buchenwald and its nearly one hundred subcamps reached 112,000, most of whom were being worked by various businesses owned and operated for profit by the SS. In addition, medical experimentation on inmates, similar to that conducted at other concentration camps, took place at the main camp. Prisoners deemed no longer fit to work were usually selected for transport to other camps, where they were systematically killed. Though there was no gas chamber at Buchenwald, there was a crematorium building that the Americans discovered not only disposed of prisoners who died in the camp but contained a macabre mechanism for the killing of undesirable inmates.

Early in 1945, as the Russian army moved through Poland, the Germans emptied the death camps at Auschwitz and Gross-Rosen, sending thousands of prisoners on forced marches to Buchenwald and leaving thousands more dead along the roadside. In the first week of April, with American forces closing in, the Germans attempted to send almost 30,000 Buchenwald prisoners on foot and by train to other camps.

On the morning of April 11, a fourteen-year-old Jewish boy, Menachem Lipshitz, from Częstochowa, Poland, the location of a famous Catholic shrine, climbed to the roof of the hospital building at Buchenwald. He was being hidden in the hospital by Poles who were imprisoned in the camp. Speaking from his home in Nashville, the man, now known as Menachem Limor, says rumors of liberation had been spreading through Buchenwald. When they saw that the Germans had abandoned their guard posts, they began to believe that the rumors might be true. "When we heard that the Americans were coming, we went on the roof of the hospital, and then I saw American tanks coming from both sides of the camp. A jeep with American soldiers came into the camp, and that's the first time I saw an American soldier in my life. And that's how we were liberated."

A few days before the Americans arrived, Limor says, the Germans "took up a lot of the people for the march of the death." The day before, he'd known something was afoot because he'd seen one of the Russians in the camp walking through the hospital carrying a rifle. "We were afraid that maybe the Germans will take everyone out from the camp, and in the hospital, there was a group that say, 'We won't go. We will run away.' And they had even clothes, you know, not inmate clothes, the civilian clothes. And I was lucky to be with them, that they said they would take me with them if we have to go. So there was an underground, but I was a young boy, so I wasn't that familiar with it, but I know that there was." In June, Limor left Buchenwald, which had been converted to a displaced persons (DP) camp after liberation, after his brother, who had been liberated in Poland, found him. They went to Hamburg and from there to Israel, where he was one of the first soldiers in the nascent Israeli army. He settled in the United States in 1969 with his wife, Leah, also a Buchenwald survivor, and their three children.

At about three in the afternoon on April 11, the day the fourteen-year-old Menachem Lipshitz was watching American tanks approach the main camp, Staff Sergeant Robert Burrows and his driver, Ben, were in their jeep, scouting ahead of the 2nd Battalion, 317th Infantry Regiment, of the 80th Infantry Division. It was a lightly overcast day, and they were driving through the slight rolling hills. To their right was a grassy meadow, but on a rise to the left they could see a camp, fenced with barbed wire, with a building right next to the gate. "This gate was here," he says, gesturing with his hands, "and these fellows were standing to the left. Two POWs in their striped uniforms. Just standing there, watching me. They didn't move. Just had their hands on the wire like they were resting, just like this. Both of 'em. And I thought it was strange, but I didn't want to be bothered, to be honest with you. I had things on my mind. I was supposed to be out scouting ahead of the battalion, and if I run into anything to let 'em know [by radio]. But I went up to the front of this office building—it had a walk-in door—here. I didn't go in the gate. The gate was closed. It was on the left side of the administration building. It said, 'Arbeit macht frei.'" (The phrase, loosely translated as "Work will make you free" or "Work will liberate you," was displayed on or above the entryway of many of the Nazi concentration camps.)

Burrows continues, "I went up to the door, and it opened. Nobody inside, nothing. And I went to the office, to the back end, looked out the back end. There were single-story barracks buildings. I didn't see anybody. I didn't go out; I didn't investigate. I couldn't have done anything anyway by myself. So I walked back out and told Ben, 'I don't see anything there. Let's go.' And so I did.

"I thought it was strange, you know, but that's the way it was." Not long afterward he put two and two together and figured that the people in striped uniforms who he knew were creating havoc and looting in nearby Weimar had been imprisoned in this small, anonymous camp.

There were a lot of things that PFC Clarence Brockman found to be strange about the Army and the war. He was twenty-two and driving a truck in Pennsylvania when he was drafted. Brockman was assigned to the 80th Infantry Division, the Blue Ridge, right out of basic training. He was a private first class and stayed one until he went back to civilian life in October 1945. He went to war aboard the *Queen Mary,* crossing the Atlantic in less than six days. He fought in the Battle of the Bulge in Luxembourg, freezing his butt off but making it through with nothing worse than a hunk of Krupp steel shrapnel in one finger— a souvenir he can still feel.

Talking with Brockman today, you find a man with a cockeyed sense of humor and a ready smile. He was like that during the war, but with a hard edge. During the Bulge, he remembers, there were bad things "about us and them too. You didn't want to take a prisoner back in that snow 'cause you've got to walk them down to the PW camp and walk back. You took 'em over the hill and shot 'em. And there was quite a few of them was shot. On both sides. More so on their side than our side. Because the order came down, we're to take prisoners now. No more shootin' 'em. Take prisoners. So there you are."

His comments are more than just a suggestion that the rules of the Geneva Conventions were bendable, depending on circumstances. After a German unit machine-gunned more than eighty American POWs at Malmédy, during the Bulge, many GIs say they received orders to take no prisoners. If, as Brockman relates, those orders were rescinded, the soldiers obeyed—to a point. Often that point was the discovery of a death camp, which in his case wouldn't happen for a few more weeks.

Brockman and his buddies knew nothing about the Holocaust as the terrible winter gave way to springtime, but he was about to learn. The lessons began slowly, as his unit, the 317th Infantry Regiment, began to run across small forced-labor camps. "We saw the camps; usually the guys ahead of us would take the camp and just clean 'em up, getting the prisoners that was in there and trying to doctor them up. And you couldn't feed 'em anything, 'cause it'd kill them. Rich food, too much rich food, was bad for 'em."

Somewhere ahead of Brockman and the 80th Infantry Division in the line of march to the east was Sergeant Harry Gerenstein with the 6th Armored Division. The New Yorker, now of Las Vegas, was an old man of twenty-five when he was drafted in 1942. He crossed the English Channel a month after D-Day, landed in France, and suddenly the war was real. "I saw all those ships that they sunk there, and it was a disaster. It was scary. Up until then, it didn't mean a thing to me."

Harry drove a truck in the division's supply outfit. "We had no top, no doors, no windshield, and my partner had a position with .50-caliber machine gun. What they call a ring mount; it was on the truck and it goes all around, and he just stood there. I drove all through France, Luxembourg, rain or shine, we never had a top on the truck." Like most of the other GIs, Harry knew nothing about the slave-labor camps until they discovered one.

"We liberated one place where there was a hundred twenty Hungarian Jewish women that they kept, not in a camp, but they lived in the barnyard. The Germans took off." Harry was able to speak to the women in Yiddish. Mostly young and dressed in regular clothes, they told how they were marched into the woods every morning to a camouflaged hand grenade factory. "The women said every day they put a handful of sand in their pockets, and when they got to the factory, each one filled a hand grenade with sand instead of gunpowder. One of the women didn't have any shoes; she wore house slippers. I had two pair of shoes, I can only wear one, so I gave her a pair of my shoes. She wanted to repay me some way. I said, 'Forget it.' I took a picture of them, and that was it. Then we left."

On April 11, Gerenstein heard from his unit's radio man that the outfit had liberated a prison camp. It was actually the first time he heard the term "concentration camp." "We took the jeep, and that's when I went to the camp. It was off the main roads, and we got into the camp, there were some medics there, and they called for other help. We were told, 'Don't feed them, don't give them any food. The food we're eating will kill them.' I saw the ovens there; there was about two hundred bodies in there that the Germans never had a chance to cover them up. I went into the barracks. I don't know if you'd call them barracks, the living quarters. I went in there, and it stunk like hell. And we stayed there not even five minutes. I couldn't stand the odor, and we took off and went back to our outfit. I only spent about a half hour in the camp. We had to get out. We got into the jeep, and not one word was said between us. We were dumbfounded."

Somewhere before the city of Kassel, following behind the 6th Armored, Clarence Brockman and three of his buddies from the 80th Infantry Division tired of walking, so they stole a three-quarter-ton truck from a headquarters outfit back of the line. "Changed the number and everything; wiped it off, painted it over with white camouflage paint. And then we got to Weimar, we asked the people, 'Where's the booze?' You gotta have booze. But the people in the city did not have booze compared to what farmers had. So we went out to a farm. It was on a back road, the guy told us there's two farms on that road. He says, 'Check them out.'

"We kinda sneaked around. When you're stalemated, that's when you do all that." He explained "stalemated": "It took two regiments to take that Weimar. Well, we had three regiments that did leapfrogging, okay?" The implication is that he was in the regiment that was in reserve, and therefore a search for liquor in an appropriated vehicle was well within the bounds of off-duty activity.

"So the next day, we inquired again, and they told us about the farms. These farmers make schnapps. Powerful schnapps. And so we was drivin' down the road to the second farmhouse, and I'd say it was about, let's see, from Weimar to the camp was about ten kilometers. We got just a little over halfway, and I told the other guys, I says, 'Corporal Billman,' I says, 'Corporal, they got monkeys over here?' He says, 'No.' I said, 'Well, what's them up in the trees ahead of us?' And he says, 'Oh, they're civilians.' Whatever they had on, their outfits were blacker than . . . it was dirty."

Brockman says the trees were a little bigger than scrub oaks. "And they was up there where you could grab ahold of the branch. So they was up in there, and there was about ten or fifteen of 'em in different trees.

"We called 'em down, and of course with our broken German and their broken English, we got along pretty good. There's quite a few of them who talked English. They didn't look like people. They was, at the end—emaciated and everything else. They had all kinds of disease."

Brockman had no idea how the prisoners had found the strength to climb the trees, let alone to stay alive all that time. "To answer that question is to know what man's like. But they went up there, we saw them. And they explained what was ahead of us. They told us the guards had left. The camp was already empty of German guards three days before.

"We took 'em down there to the gates. The gates were open. And [the inmates] started rushing us. I said, 'Whoa. We can't go in that camp whatsoever.' So we beat it back to Weimar, got ahold of Captain Root, which is our CIC [Counter Intelligence Corps] officer. We never went back to the camp."

But Brockman did see former prisoners again, in both striped and black outfits, a day or two later, in Weimar, where his unit was billeted. They were tearing up the city, looting it under the watchful, even protective eyes of American troops. "We were in apartment buildings there in Weimar, fairly decent apartment buildings—they hadn't been touched by the war. And [the former inmates] come down the street and they started shoving people aside, actually making them get off the walk and walk in the road. And some Germans resented that, and they started fightin' them back, and then that's when we stepped in. Usually we'd fire a shot in the air, and that'd settle it. Everybody'd be calm. It seems strange, though. The Germans would not run. You fired that shot in the air. But those poor PWs, when they'd hear a shot, boy, they'd scram. Because they didn't know if they was gonna get shot or not."

Unlike Clarence Brockman, who deployed overseas with the 80th Infantry Division and served his entire tour in the same outfit, twenty-six-year-old Gerald Virgil Myers of St. Joseph, Missouri, went over the loneliest way, as a replacement. Every place he went, he was with strangers. He landed at Omaha Beach in October, four months after D-Day, and had the hell scared out of him. "There was a packet of of-

Gerald Virgil Myers has never forgotten the horrors he discovered at Buchenwald. For combat operations with the 80th Infantry Division, he received the Silver Star, Bronze Star, and Purple Heart.

ficers and young Army men that were being loaded on the boat that I just got off of that looked like they were, well, we called it 'battle fatigue' at that time, because they just never talked. They stared straight ahead, and you could tell that they had been in combat.

"We were in this pup tent city, probably a mile back from Omaha Beach, and we were there for two and a half days. They put us in pup tents and told us that we were to watch the bulletin board, because our name would come up on the board to be moved. And if you don't meet that deadline, you'll be court-martialed. Well, back in those days, that just scared the hell out of you, so you went down about every two hours to see if your name was on there.

"They had two meals a day, and you lined up and went down to chow, and they gave you a piece of Army bread that weighed about a pound, oh, a half an inch to three quarters of an inch thick. And you held it in your hand and they slapped peanut butter on top of that bread. Then you went down the line, and they put a big piece of warm Spam about a quarter inch thick on top of that peanut butter. And you went to the next place, and they gave you coffee in your canteen cup.

And right at the end of the serving line was a captain. He said, 'Gentlemen, enjoy your T-bone steak.' He said it a thousand times, morning, noon, and night."

When Myers's name finally came up, he and about a dozen other replacements were loaded aboard a truck with a sergeant in charge. The first leg of the journey took them to Neufchâtel. Half a day there, and Myers was loaded onto another truck and, after a five-hour ride, arrived at Pont-à-Mousson. Several of the soldiers were off-loaded, and he recalls the sergeant telling the remaining men, "Now, you're close to the front, and if you hear artillery come in, you better duck. You've never seen what shrapnel can do to you."

"All of a sudden," Myers recalls, "my God, the biggest explosion went off you ever heard. Well, if you'd have turned that truck upside down, you couldn't have evacuated it any faster than we did, and we hit the ditch, and it was muddy water, and we didn't even think about it. The sergeant came over about that time, and he says, 'What the hell is the matter with you guys?' He said, 'Don't you know that's outgoing?' It was a battery of 155s, just over the hedgerow."

After another short ride, they got off the truck, went into the woods, and were introduced to First Sergeant Percy Smith, all five feet five of him. He said, "We're glad to see you, because in the last week, we have lost half of our company." Myers volunteered for the 60mm mortar section, not knowing that it had lost five men just that week. He spent the rest of the afternoon learning his new job.

The very next day, they got their first taste of battle, capturing a forced-labor camp where the Nazis had imprisoned two hundred Polish workers behind a ten-foot-high barbed-wire fence. In the process, one of the new men who'd been on the truck with Myers all the way up from the beach was killed by a chunk of shrapnel in the head. He'd never even fired his rifle.

Myers fought with the 317th Infantry Regiment of the 80th Division through the Battle of the Bulge in January 1945, suffering frostbite twice because the men had only summer uniforms. He recalls getting winter boots in the latter part of February. His outfit went in on the south side of the Bulge, near Ettelbruck, and from there went to Heiderscheid, Luxembourg, where the fighting was vicious, without a lull, twenty-four hours a day. The snow was fifteen inches deep, and the temperature often hit fifteen degrees below zero. The American forces suffered 83,000 casualties; 18,000 were killed, the rest were injured or captured. Now a buck sergeant, Myers suffered a shrapnel wound in one arm, but since he could still walk and carry a rifle with his other arm, he stayed on the line.

On February 12, the men of Myers's unit got an emotional boost: they entered Germany, crossing the Saar River near the town of Dillingen. He recalls thinking, "Now we've got them on the run," but that was before they encountered what he calls "those damned hills. More like up in Georgia, north, northeast of Atlanta. They're not really mountains like the Rocky Mountains; they're more like the Ozarks in Missouri." There was still no discussion of concentration camps.

On March 26, while under fire from 20mm antiaircraft guns mounted in quads, they crossed the quarter-mile-wide Rhine River at Mainz in plywood boats with paddles and a small outboard motor that the combat engineer used to bring the boat back to the western bank to pick up more troops. After an interlude where he single-handedly captured fifty-six German soldiers along with the enemy's map of artillery installations in the area, earning a Silver Star for what still, to him, seems to be an amusing episode, they made their way through Wiesbaden to Kassel, down through Erfurt, and into Weimar, where they were assigned to police the city and maintain order. It didn't take long before they spotted "fellows in striped suits walking around, skinny as hell."

His company commander was able to communicate in Polish with the men, and he called Myers's first sergeant over and said, "This guy says there's a camp outside of town here. Go out and see what it is." That's how First Sergeant Percy Smith, Myers, and Don Smith came to be driving a jeep toward Buchenwald. "As we rounded the hill and came up behind these trees, here was a camp that had, we estimated, over thirty barracks up there. And the people were standing, holding on to the fence, and they could see you, but they were looking right straight through you. They just were so malnutritioned that they could hardly stand up, and they were nothing but skin and bones.

"And there was a couple of guys that was taking a bath from a wash

Skeletonlike survivors of the Nazi concentration camp at Buchenwald wash themselves, probably for the first time in months or even years, with pans, soap, and water provided by GIs of the 80th Infantry Division.

pan, just using a cloth. And they had their shirt on, but the rest of it was bare, and you couldn't believe that people that were so skinny could still stand up, but they did."

Myers recalls that First Sergeant Smith found an inmate from Lithuania who could speak some English and asked him about the place. The man said, "This is a labor camp. This camp furnishes labor for all of the industry that is within thirty kilometers of here." The man said he'd been captured when the Germans invaded Lithuania. "They took everybody from sixteen years old on up that was healthy and could work and sent us all to different labor camps."

Myers says the inmate also explained to the GIs that most of the SS guards had fled the day before when they heard that the Americans had taken Erfurt, a city just thirteen miles to the west, adding that the inmates had caught seven or nine of the guards and had them "locked up downstairs." Then the Lithuanian said, "There was a tank that pulled up here yesterday, but they just asked us what it was, and we told them it was a Nazi labor camp, and they just went on. Nobody even stopped." The man described three Americans in a small tank. Myers's best guess is that it would have been a recon car from the 6th Armored Division.

"When we were out there, we saw six guys that were pulling a cart, and it was a two-wheel cart, and the inside of that cart had a zinc lining or some kind of metal. They were going around to the different barracks, picking up dead bodies that they would lay outside. The cart had at least six or eight bodies laying in it. And they were taking them to the crematory. And at that time, they had four crematories there. And they claimed that that had been running seven days a week, twenty-four hours a day, up until the SS left, and then they shut it down."

Asked if during the forty minutes he spent inside the camp he saw any evidence of torture, Myers said, "The only torture that I could honestly say that I saw was just them not being fed. They told us that all that they'd had for the past week was potato peelings; that the SS had eaten the inside and they had taken the potato peelings from that and then went out and pulled green grass and mixed it into a soup. And that soup was all they had."

The three 80th ID men went back to Weimar and reported to their captain. "He called regiment and regiment called division, and they said, 'Round up the prisoners that are pilfering in town and take them out to the camp, and we will have food there within a reasonable time. Keep them there, and we'll send medics and food there.' That evening food arrived."

Though the sights inside Buchenwald were disturbing to Gerald Myers, the assignment to patrol Weimar wasn't much easier on his mind. "We had a six-by-six [truck] that we were traveling in around Weimar, looking for these people. We saw one guy come out of a house, and he had a great big potato. He was eating on that thing like he was eating an ice cream cone. We hollered at him to come towards the truck, and about halfway there, he dropped the potato and keeled over. And we picked him up and took him out to the camp, and Dr. Bob said, 'His system is just so weak that he couldn't stand all of that starch and nutrition from that potato. The poor sucker is liable to die from it, because he ate too much of it.'

"You were in disbelief that people could be treated that way, and when you saw them, you just felt so damned sorry for them that you wanted to help them, but you didn't know how. All you were trying to do was to get them out to the camp so somebody else would take care of them, because you really didn't want to know what happened to them. You didn't want to see them die. You just couldn't believe that the Germans could treat people this way and still think that [the Germans] were human beings."

Myers says he and his buddies tried to go into a mode where they didn't let what they were experiencing at Buchenwald affect them emotionally. "We'd been hardened to the effects of war, seeing people killed and seeing injured laying along the road. This was actually just something else that happened in a war."

But years later, denial didn't work. "I thought about that a lot for a long, long time. I would be going to sleep, and I would think about it. And it affected me probably more after the war than it did at that particular time, because I was used to seeing people killed and wounded." After the first few months back home, he stopped talking about what he'd seen because people didn't want to hear it or thought he was exaggerating. He didn't start talking about it again until 1998, more than half a century later, when a schoolteacher friend invited him to speak about the war.

CHAPTER 5

LITTLE BOYS BECAME MEN

APRIL 11, 1945

NORDHAUSEN, GERMANY

  168 miles southwest of Berlin

  45 miles north-northwest of Buchenwald

  10 miles west of Berga

As mid-April approached, there was no doubt that the war would soon end, with the Nazis crushed between the Russians pouring in from the east and a tsunami of Americans, British, Canadians, and French flooding Germany across a wide front from the west.

April 11 saw American forces discover two of the worst-of-the-worst concentration camps. At Buchenwald a significant number of prisoners were found alive with the potential to survive. At the Nordhausen Dora-Mittelbau complex, forty-five miles to the north-northwest, thousands were found dead and unburied all over the grounds. Unlike at Buchenwald, survivors at Nordhausen were relatively few.

The outfits that found the camps believed they were still on a headlong rush to reach Berlin. They'd learn within a day or two, much to the chagrin of their commanding generals, that General Dwight D. Eisenhower had already made up his mind not to go after the capital city, believing the cost in lives would be too great and a victory bittersweet. Rejecting Winston Churchill's desire, Franklin D. Roosevelt declined to order the Americans to take Berlin. This meant that the Russians would control that part of Germany. In addition, within three months, Ike's troops would have to cede the territory they currently occupied to the Russians.

Within twenty-four hours of the liberation of Nordhausen and Buchenwald, FDR would die.

Just a week before the Americans arrived at Nordhausen, three-quarters of the city was destroyed by bombers of the Royal Air Force. Roughly 8,800 people died in the raid, including hundreds of inmates who were confined by the SS in aircraft hangars that were targeted by the raiders.

Major Haynes Dugan, the public affairs officer of the 3rd Armored "Spearhead" Division, witnessed the arrival of the division at Nordhausen. A year later, in unusually frank language rarely found in military histories, he published *Spearhead in the West,* in which he wrote:

> Although the taking of Nordhausen did not constitute the heaviest fighting of April 11, that city will live forever in the memories of 3rd Armored Division soldiers as a place of horror. The Americans couldn't believe their eyes. It is all very well to read of a Maidenek, but no written word can properly convey the atmosphere of such a charnel house, the unbearable stench of decomposing bodies, the sigh of live human beings, starved to pallid skeletons, lying cheek to jowl with the ten-day dead.
>
> Hundreds of corpses lay sprawled over the acres of the big compound. More hundreds filled the great barracks. They lay in contorted heaps, half stripped, mouths gaping in the dirt and straw: or, they were piled naked, like cordwood, in the corners and under the stairways.

Everywhere among the dead were the living emaciated, ragged shapes whose fever-bright eyes waited passively for the release of death. Over all the area clung the terrible odor of decomposition and, like a dirge of forlorn hope, the combined cries of these unfortunates rose and fell in weak undulations. It was a fabric of moans and whimpers, of delirium and outright madness. Here and there a single shape tottered about, walking slowly, like a man dreaming.

Nordhausen was taken by Task Force Welborn and Task Force Lovelady, under the command of Brigadier General Truman E. Boudinot. Colonel John C. Welborn's assault elements approached from the north as Lieutenant Colonel William B. Lovelady's men came in from the south. As John Toland writes in *The Last 100 Days,* "The commanders had been alerted by Intelligence to expect something a little unusual in the Nordhausen area. They thought at first this meant the town's concentration camp, where about 5,000 decayed bodies were lying in the open and in the barracks. But several miles northwest of Nordhausen, in the foothills of the Harz, they ran into other prisoners in dirty striped pajamas who told them there was 'something fantastic' inside the mountain."

What lay inside were two tunnels that had originally been salt mines, approximately two miles in length and fifty feet in width and height, connected to each other by forty-eight smaller tunnels. For more than two years, some 60,000 prisoners had slaved in them, building the V-1 unmanned radio-controlled aircraft and V-2 medium-range ballistic missile used to attack England, in a program supervised by physicist Wernher von Braun. Just days before the Americans arrived, von Braun had supervised the removal of fourteen tons of documents detailing his research. They were hidden in an underground iron mine and eventually removed by U.S. forces and brought to America, along with a hundred complete V-2 rockets, most of which were ultimately test-fired at White Sands Proving Grounds in New Mexico. Von Braun, who was delivered to the United States as part of the secret Operation Overcast, became known derisively as one of "our Nazis," as opposed to "their Nazis"—the rocket scientists snatched up by the Soviets—and later as "the father of the American space program." (Unlike the U.S. government, the satirist/folk singer Tom Lehrer pulled no punches in the song he wrote and named for the ex-Nazi scientist: " 'Once the rockets are up, who cares where they come down / That's not my department,' says Wernher von Braun.")

———

Lieutenant Ernest James of Berkeley, California, was part of the 238th Combat Engineer Battalion, an outfit that was moved around, attached to, and detached from fighting units as needed. James's tour of duty in Europe began inauspiciously on D-Day, when the small boat he was on with a company of men and thirteen vehicles began to sink. They used their own equipment to keep the thing afloat and managed to explain to the powers that be that either they had to land quickly, ahead of the actual fighting outfits, or they weren't going to make it at all. As a result, they were among the first troops to land on Utah Beach. Their job, as the invasion force fought its way inland, was to build bridges, blast defensive installations, and build and repair roads. Although they were not tasked to fight, they were always close to combat operations.

James was in a position to watch troop-carrying gliders land close by. "It was quite a spectacular sight to see these gliders come down right over your head and watch bullets going through them." He also had the sobering experience of seeing the same thing happen to American paratroopers. Confusion reigned, with the one positive thing being the quick surrender of impressed Ukrainians, who had been captured in their homeland by the Nazis and "then given their so-called freedom if they'd come and fight for Germany."

His battalion lost twenty or thirty men during the Battle of the Bulge, with another couple of hundred wounded; roughly a quarter of the outfit. They stayed with the 104th Infantry Division, the Timberwolves, after the Bulge and built both floating and Bailey bridges while under fire to get them across the Ruhr River.

As they moved into the Harz Mountains, they began to encounter farms being worked by forced laborers kept under guard behind barbed wire, but the Army did not forewarn them about the elaborate concentration camp system they would soon confront. James did run into a very different aspect of Adolf Hitler's grand plan. "Going through the Harz Mountains we came into this beautiful little town, only women there, and a lot of them were pregnant. It was one of the places where they were breeding a master race. When we went into the town, we started getting some small-arms fire and so we quickly set up a line and somebody contacted those that were firing at us. They were boys in their preteens and their early teens. They had rifles, and they were shooting at us. The mothers would keep these kids until they were a certain age, and then they had to put them in the military schools."

The next day, the 104th entered the Nordhausen Dora-Mittelbau complex. James doesn't recall what he saw first, but he remembers what made an impact on him the most. "My platoon had to go down into a railroad yard to see if there were any engineering materials—lumber, steel, anything we can use for roads or bridges. And we got in there, and the German civilians were breaking open the railroad cars and looting what was in them. I remember seeing one that had bags of sugar, and the people were fighting over that.

"Anyhow, there's a train, I don't know how big it was, but it was more than ten cars. Nobody was around, and the sergeant and I went over there and we busted open the doors and out slithered dead bodies. Slithered out, that's the only word that I could use, 'cause they'd been dead for days and in various degrees of decomposition. What the Germans had done was go load up these people as we were moving forward, they'd load these people up and move 'em back towards Germany, trying to find ways of getting rid of 'em."

"All I know is that I did not have emotional reactions except hate. How the hell can people do this?" The railcars holding the dead bodies were within easy sight of the cars being ransacked for sugar by the townspeople. "That's the thing that pissed me off so much, was that there were these people looting. Of course, they didn't have anything to eat, either. But they knew, they knew what was down there. You could smell it. Everybody didn't know what was happening, that's the damn thing." To be clear, James was being ironic with that last comment.

Other American units encountered additional Nazi handiwork at the Nordhausen train yards. Robert Miller wrote a letter to the Minnesota chapter of the 104th Infantry Division Association detailing what he'd seen on April 11. He was a member of an armored patrol that was sent to check and secure the train station and the nearby warehouses. The station had been bombed, and the cleanup was still under way. They heard a train approaching.

> One could tell it was a really loaded steam engine. Someone suggested we move one of our three tanks so as to cover the track. The tank was a new one from the states with a high velocity 90mm rifle.
>
> Suddenly, the train could be seen and we debated whether to use the tank's gun. We realized the shell would go right through the engine and the cars behind it, probably killing anyone in them. Within minutes, the train pulled into the station and stopped. The engineer was looking for the station master and was totally surprised to find the Americans. He became argumentative and ended up getting whacked with a rifle butt. Some of us could speak a little German and asked him what the 42 padlocked box cars contained, but he wouldn't say. Unknown to us was that only three miles away was a concentration camp called Dora.
>
> My friend, David Peltier, a street-wise guy from Chicago who taught me how to stay alive, went to the first box car, knocked off the lock and pushed open the door. The car was jammed with people standing, packed together like sardines, and appeared to be in a catatonic state. All 42 of the cars were filled with Polish Jews.

Miller and his buddies unlocked all the boxcars, telling the people that they were *"Americanish soldatin."* He wrote, "They could hardly believe that they had been saved from certain death and that they were free. Stan Pokrzywa, another Chicago man in heavy weapons, spoke Polish and did a wonderful job in comforting the people. We moved them in to the station and warehouses where a large supply of food had been found—food stolen from box cars by the station master—and gave this food as well as water to these former prisoners. Colonel Lovelady approved of this, and let the war wait."

Private John Marcinek was part of D Company, 414th Infantry Regiment, of the 104th, and recalls riding on a 3rd Armored Division tank the day they discovered Nordhausen. He was twenty-three years old and had been drafted two years earlier while working for his folks' beer distributorship in the Shamokin, Pennsylvania, area. He was a veteran of fighting all the way from Holland, where he had spent most of seventeen days immersed in water because the Germans had flooded the area, to the crossing of the Rhine on the famous Remagen bridge and on into central Germany.

As they approached the Nordhausen area, the tanks his unit was riding on stopped. A call came over the radio asking if anyone could speak a Slovak language. Marcinek says that growing up he had eight years of exposure to fractured Slovak, Polish, and Russian languages, so he responded. Turns out that the major who was commanding the lead vehicle was trying without success to interrogate several slave laborers dressed in striped clothing who had escaped from a nearby camp.

Marcinek had difficulty with the translation, but with a combination of charades and language he determined that the emaciated men had, indeed, escaped when several SS guards had abandoned their posts, presumably because they knew the Americans were approaching. The major directed him to take four GIs and one of the escapees to investigate while the tank convoy continued down the highway.

About a mile down a side road, the lightly armed group approached several buildings with white sheets hanging from the windows. Just a day or so before they'd gone through Paderborn, and the townspeople had used the same device to signal surrender. These buildings were behind a double barbed-wire fence, and there were more emaciated prisoners holding on to the wires and watching them approach. As they moved in closer, he suddenly heard a woman scream out, "They're going to shoot at you," and he hit the dirt. He remembers the shooting being erratic, nothing even coming close to him. When they moved forward, he and his men discovered that the shots were coming from what appeared to be the mouth of a tunnel. Once the gunfire stopped, the GIs moved in and were surrounded by about two hundred emaciated people, begging for food. "Some were saying, 'Thank you, Americans,' but they were more concerned about getting some food. They weren't clapping hands or doing anything like that. It was a rather somber-type thing."

His reaction was similarly restrained, and he's very deliberate as he describes his emotions at the time. "I shouldn't say that we were—you're not hardened, but you get the feeling that you're kind of a changed person. You're dealing with realism, and I don't think there's a lot of emotion, at least there wasn't in my case. It was business."

Marcinek's little squad was directed by the prisoners to the commandant's office, but the man he found there was not a hard-core SS veteran. "This commandant appeared to be about thirty years of age, with reasonable command of English. He apologized for the unauthorized gunfire and surrendered his sidearm, a P38 pistol. In response to the clamoring for food, the commandant relayed our promise to have medics and food [provided] by our military support personnel. The commandant explained that his former guards were members of the elite SS." He had been in a Catholic seminary, where he had been studying to become a priest when he was drafted into the army.

Marcinek had no way of knowing at the time, but the tunnel he'd discovered was part of the complex at Dora where the Germans manufactured the rockets he'd seen flying overhead earlier in the war.

By the time he got to Nordhausen, Sergeant Aurio J. Pierro had already earned a Silver Star and a Purple Heart commanding a Sherman tank platoon in the 3rd Armored Division's Task Force Lovelady and had been recommended for a direct commission. Now retired from the practice of law, Pierro has lived in the same house in Lexington, Massachusetts, for all of his ninety-one years.

Recalling the discovery of what was most likely the camp at Dora, three miles from the field of death they would soon discover at Nordhausen, he says, "I was moving the platoon in an area there, and I came to a fence. I didn't know what it was. There was a gate, and there was a barracks on the other side of the fence. And then we waited, and all of a sudden the prisoners came out of the barracks, opened the gates, and they realized who we were—they started jumping for joy, but my crew stayed in their tank. They didn't know what was happening, what could happen.

"One individual there, he was hoppin' around on one foot, just as happy as the others. In a little time my guys were wandering around on foot there, and they came back and said, 'You gotta look in that building over there.' So it was a brick building. I went in, and there was, like, an operating table with dead prisoners, emaciated bodies there, tied hand and foot, on the floor, on the table. Why tied hand and foot? No clothes on, naked bodies."

Pierro's men weren't able to do any extensive exploring. "We had to stay with the tanks. If you were out of the tank, all you had was your sidearm, and you never knew what was going to happen. A crew outside the tank is defenseless, really."

At age ninety-one, he's able to deflect the remembered horror by recalling the bigger picture. "Well, you know, it's not like with something new, but at the time we'd seen a lot of dead people and a lot of hurt people. We had a mission to move forward, long as we were able. We took casualties, and those that were casualties stayed behind and the rest of the crews moved forward. We had casualties, we got replacements, and we went forward."

Private John Olson from Duluth, Minnesota, was one of the youngest men in the 415th Infantry Regiment. He'd been drafted the previous October and had joined the 104th Division near Aachen after riding in 40 and 8 railcars from Le Havre to Verviers, Belgium, and then by truck into Germany. For more than sixty years he's held on to one indelible memory of Nordhausen. "I don't know why we were riding on a jeep trailer, but we were. It was a dark kind of rainy day. We were in a long column of trucks, tanks, and jeeps—I think we were near the beginning of the line. I was sitting on the trailer facing to the left, and as we went along the street, I looked down this side street and I saw this ten-foot-high wire fence and a big gate. The gate was open, and I saw these two prisoners in their striped suits standing by the gate, and they had these beautiful smiles on their faces because they knew now they were being set free. We never went into the camp ourselves. But I just saw these two there, and I hope I never forget what they looked like. They just beamed, although they were just human skeletons, so thin. I had no idea what kind of camp it was; I'd heard about concentration camps, but I really didn't know much about them. I would've loved to have been able to go over and talk to them, but I couldn't do that."

Olson returned to Minnesota, where he became a Baptist minister, a career choice he made, in part, as a result of his experiences during the war. "I think I realized a little better how fortunate I, and we, are to be in America. As I look back, I count it a privilege to have served in the Army and Europe and to have been a part of that. And to think that I was a part of releasing those guys from that prison, that makes me feel good about it. I don't boast about it. I'm just glad I was a part of it. I count all of it by the grace of God that he took me through it, protected me. It was all a positive experience, even though it didn't seem so at the time."

Corporal Robert Ray, who'd been a photographer for the *Nashville Banner* before he enlisted after Pearl Harbor, was riding with his squad from the 36th Armored Infantry Battalion aboard a 3rd Armored Division tank when they arrived outside the walled prison. "We didn't know anything about this Holocaust, didn't have no idea, but we saw flatcars on the side track there that was loaded with bodies, some of them you could see they'd move a foot or a leg once in a while, have a little life in them. The people lived around there, they claimed they didn't know anything about it, but that was a bunch of nonsense, because they could smell it as far as that's concerned.

"We reached this prisoner-of-war camp, and one of the tanks just busted a big hole in the wall—brick, concrete wall, or something. And all them poor devils come screaming out of there, some of them so dadgummed thin from malnutrition, we gave them all the rations we had. They'd eat cigarettes just like they're candy."

Morris Sunshine was a twenty-year-old from Brooklyn who ended up in a combat engineer battalion because, of all things, he played drums and piano and the unit's band was looking for musicians. He played at Newport News, he played at Camp Gordon, Georgia, he played in Nashville and the Mojave Desert. He wasn't playing on the *Susan B. Anthony* on the way to Omaha Beach at H-Hour when the ship hit a mine. His unit lost all its equipment as the captain balanced the ship by having the troops on board move from side to side, and eventually Sunshine ended up on an English vessel with "no helmet, no guns, no nothing," and they watched the *Anthony* sink. He thought they'd take him back to England, but instead he and a few of his guys were dumped on Utah Beach. It took almost three weeks before his

Morris Sunshine was part of the 294th Combat Engineer Battalion attached to the 104th Infantry Division when Nordhausen was liberated. He says the sight was indescribable and the smell was unimaginable.

unit was put back together again and took off on the great march across Europe, where they eventually built the first bridge across the Rhine.

Back in Brooklyn before the war, he'd heard stories about the Germans from people they called refugees who spoke about prisons that they'd come from. But he knew nothing about concentration camps. On the morning of April 12, they began to smell Nordhausen from ten or fifteen miles away. And then they arrived at the camp, which he recalls as being adjacent to the road, next to the town. "We saw these skeletonlike people, dressed in the striped uniforms, and some of them moved. Some of them didn't move. It was a shocking sight. This was some kind of something that's indescribable, you know. And the smell—it was horrible, such a horrible smell of death that hasn't been put into the ground, it's unimaginable.

"I do remember that some of these people got out, and they wandered into some of the German houses looking for food. I was a buck-ass sergeant, and [the Germans] came out looking for me 'cause I spoke Yiddish, and I was able to converse with these people. And they told me that there were some people in this house, and the woman of the house is screaming and yelling, panicking. I went in, and what the story was, the member of the concentration camp, there was bread on the table and he grabbed it. And she was screaming at him that 'This is for my family!' and she was appealing to me that I should get the bread from the concentration camp guy, which, of course, I didn't have any sympathy for her at all.

"I mean, I was so angry at what you saw, and the depravity. Some of them couldn't walk. [They ate] whatever we gave them, some of them threw up; it was too much for their stomach to take. But this—of course we didn't know at the time. We found that out in a day or so, two days—they were collapsing on us."

Sunshine went into the yard at Nordhausen where hundreds of bodies lay because he was curious. He wanted to know who the people were, what they were doing. "Most of them could not speak; it was kind of an unintelligent gibberish to me. They might not have been speaking German. Could have been speaking Russian or Hungarian or anything like that. But I didn't know that. I just went at them with my Deutsche.

"I did get that they had been captured. The story I got was the German guards knew that we were coming—how they knew that, I don't know, but they knew it. And [the guards] tried to get gasoline, kerosene to burn some of the camp and some of the victims. Somehow, some of these internees, the concentration camp victims, were able to overpower some of these guards, which to me sounds strange, because they had such little strength. But evidently, something like that did happen, and they beat up on a few of them and they never got to fire up the camp."

John Rheney, Jr., was a staff sergeant, a rifle squad leader in the 413th Infantry Regiment of the Timberwolves. After the war, Rheney spent forty years as a pediatrician. He's now retired in Orangeburg, South Carolina, where he does physicals five days a week on recruits coming into Fort Jackson. He was twenty-two when he got orders to go see Nordhausen, which had been liberated by the 414th, and he's never forgotten what he saw there. "It didn't look too bad from the outside, but when you got inside there were just stacks and stacks of corpses. All of them had apparently starved to death. There were a few people up that I remember, and they greeted us like we've never been greeted before. Most of them, I think, were French.

"They were in rags. They, too, were starved, but for some reason they had survived a little bit. They just greeted us like we had saved 'em, which I guess we had." Rheney didn't go into the tunnels at nearby Dora, but he went fairly deep into Nordhausen, where the bodies had been accumulated for disposal. "It shook everybody. I'd read about the Civil War and the slaughter that took place there, and the camps they had such as Andersonville, but even those were not like this was."

Corporal Forrest Robinson was a military policeman with the 104th. That's probably why his commanding officer asked that he accompany him into the barracks buildings at Nordhausen. On a visit to the camp fifty years later with his son to participate in the dedication of a museum at the site, the now-ordained minister had a full-blown flashback. "In a searing flash, horrid memory swept over me, and I could see it all once again—row upon row of devastated human bodies, emaciated, starved, mutilated, gray, and rotting in the hot sun. There were open pits in which bodies were burning. The stench was horrid, doing almost final violence to the senses."

Questioned (in writing because of his extreme hearing loss) about his experiences on April 12, 1945, he writes of being nearly overwhelmed, feeling he would lose it all having just walked with his CO through the open yard. "You would have thought that the previous moments would somehow have prepared me for what I was to experience [inside the barracks], but it was even worse.

"Along the full length of the wall to our left, iron cots had been jammed together, and on the cots were the dead and the dying, side by side. I'm certain some of the dead had been so for weeks, their grotesque and distended bodies emitting the foulest of gases. Occasionally a figure on one of the cots would stir and cry out for help. But

Corporal Forrest Robinson was a military policeman with the 104th Infantry Division at Nordhausen. After going inside buildings and finding survivors lying among dozens and dozens of dead bodies, he suffered what he now describes as "total physical and spiritual exhaustion." Now an ordained minister, Robinson says he has no memory of anything that occurred in the two weeks after Nordhausen.

we were helpless. We weren't medics! The horrid stench of it all is indescribable.

"Under a stairway, there were bodies stacked like cordwood. I simply could take no more and suddenly bolted and ran out the door back onto the concourse, grabbing the side of our commander's jeep to steady myself. But a strange thing was happening. One of our men had managed to sneak overseas a portable radio and it was playing in the back seat, and of all songs, Glenn Miller's 'Sunrise Serenade.' It was hideous.

"Utterly overwhelmed by this crushing mixture of circumstances, I literally lost it. I raised my head to the heavens and cursed God in the vilest of language. I screamed there could not be a God who could allow a thing such as the Holocaust, and dismissed civilization as but a thin skin covering a basic savage. Suddenly, in total physical and spiritual exhaustion, I fell over the side of the jeep and vomited." Reverend Robinson writes that he has no memory of anything that occurred in the subsequent two weeks. "That period is a total blank in my mind."

Chicagoan Arthur Leu was part of a military police company of about 175 men, broken into three units: one guarded headquarters, one dealt with traffic control, and the third, his section, handled POWs. He was in a forward compound; his unit's job was to take prisoners from the advance units and contain them, have them questioned by intelligence officers, sort out the SS from the Wehrmacht and Volkssturm, and then ship them to the rear.

By the time Leu got to Nordhausen, the first units in were already starting to bring survivors out and, at the same time, moving bodies from inside buildings to the open area. Leu says there were hundreds and hundreds of bodies. "You can't believe it. You cannot absolutely believe that the human body can be that thin, that devoid of any substance. You can't believe that people could be treated like that, that a human being could exact that kind of punishment on another human. You're horrified."

Leu watched survivors being carried out on stretchers, "and there were some of them sitting against the walls that had been brought out, that were obviously alive and barely so. Men and women. Most of them naked." In the early hours, he says, there were not enough medics on hand, because no one had expected to be confronted with the horrors they found.

"It was very busy, but it was quiet," he recalls. "These people were hardly even capable of being noisy, their moaning or whatever it was. There was no shouting, there was no screaming, none of that going on. But they must have been grateful that there was an activity there that was being of help to them as opposed to what they were going through before."

Arthur Leu's unit probably spent less than an hour inside Nordhausen before leaving to set up a prisoner compound not far from the camp.

Almost as soon as the 3rd Armored Division medics arrived at Nordhausen, they notified the 104th Infantry Division following behind them that a full-blown medical rescue operation would be needed if any of those still living in the camp were to survive. The weight of that mission fell on the 329th Medical Battalion, with its four companies of personnel plus a headquarters unit. One of the men there was Ragene Farris, who, in 1996, described that day in exquisite detail for the division association's newspaper, *Timberwolf Howl*:

Going immediately to the scene, the Timberwolf medics found a square of bomb-scarred buildings, reminiscent of a large college campus, which until six weeks previously had housed the motor shops of the German SS troopers. Upon entry, litters in hand, the men saw rows of bodies stretched out the length of the large concrete floored room. Grotesquely still, evident that they had hung tenaciously to a last breath of life, these prison-marked men lay in an indescribable symbol of death. The initial shock of the bestiality, the inhumane cruelty of this deed, did not register with the men. Their job was to evacuate the living; to hospitalize and nourish; to bring men and women, and children back to the realm of human decency.

In many cases the living had been too weak to move the dead from their sides. One hunched-drawn French boy was huddled up against a dead comrade, as if to keep warm, having no mental concept that the friend had died, and unable to move his limbs. . . . In their prison garments of striped coats, huddled in rags or old dirty blankets, it was like reaching into another world apart, to bring these shadow-men from their environment onto a litter, and into a clean American ambulance.

Not long after the evacuation of the living had begun, troops were sent to the nearby town to bring back several hundred German civilians to assist with the rescue effort. Many of those same Germans would be pressed into burial details in the days to come. Farris wrote:

These were the people who lived in unconcern as thousands of people had been driven as slaves, then left to die. Each medic learned several German words: "schnell" (hurry) and "tempo" (the same— hurry) and with a mixture of emotion soon had a fast-moving litter line going from building, shell and bomb craters, cellars, etc., wherever the patients were found to be yet alive. For seven hours with truck and ambulance, drivers carried away load after load of these shadow-men, taking them to hospital facilities set up by other Timberwolves Medics (section hospitalization). Litters carrying men of every disease and condition, continued to flow into a central evacuation point.

The final score of evacuated patients was well over 700. Fifteen patients died enroute to the hospital area. Three hundred patients were so eaten away by malnutrition that their bodies will never respond to treatment or gain health again. Lying in the camp area were 2,800 bodies.

PFC Rip Rice's mission was to take him past Nordhausen, where his job was to find a water source and set up a purification unit to supply the American forces moving through the area. Now a PhD living in Maryland and lecturing worldwide on the subject of ozone, Rice was one week shy of his twenty-first birthday when he stopped at Nordhausen with the 104th Infantry's engineer battalion. Until that day, he'd had a rather positive outlook on the war and his fate, often saying that he had the safest job a guy could have in a combat zone. "I was always in back of the front—except in the unusual event of maybe a counterattack—and I was not at the rear echelon. I was in between them, so that I was too far back from the front to get any small-arms or mortar fire, and I was too close up to get any artillery [since] that would go over our heads and get to the rear."

He credits the good fortune of that assignment to the unlikely combination of "God and chemistry." He was pulled from one of the line companies in the engineering battalion when the captain asked, "Who knows the definition of the term pH?" When no one else responded, Rice reluctantly raised his hand and said, "Sir, pH is the potential of the hydrogen ion." At that moment, he says, "college paid off. But I was lucky. Something told me to volunteer. I didn't know why. Against my principles, I volunteered. Thank God I did; that's where he gets into the act and gets some credit for this, because I didn't do it on my own."

Next thing he knew, the captain said, "Rice, fall out. Company dismissed. Rice, you're transferred to headquarters; they need a chemist at the water point." From that time on, his job was to leapfrog with one of the four division water points to keep the units supplied with fresh water, sourcing it from local streams or rivers. From the perspective of sixty-four years later, he looks back on what they did in World War II and says, "My God, how could we have drunk that swill? But that's another story."

On April 12, 1945, Rice recalls being on his unit's ten-ton truck, trailer in tow, heading east from Kassel in a valley roughly ten miles from Nordhausen, when they began smelling a strange odor that reminded him of the Fort Worth stockyards. "They didn't care much about air pollution at the time, and when they did the slaughtering, they'd have things left over that they'd burn. From the animals. And that's what it smelled like: burning animals. Only it wasn't exactly that; there was something more to it. And that odor kept getting stronger and stronger, and we didn't know what the heck it was."

As they approached an intersection with a rural road, an MP stopped them. "Guys, the captain wants you to make a detour here. Turn left and go into town, there's something you gotta see." They drove a couple of miles to the outskirts of Nordhausen, and then "We turned into this yard where all these bodies are—and the stench was just—I mean, we got there and every one of us, we just tossed our cookies, we couldn't stand it."

Rice says there were hundreds of bodies—"they were stacked five and six high, in big mounds. And there were more inside buildings—it could have been two, it could have been three. I was so upset by this horror that I was looking at. We didn't know that this was the day or the day after the camp was liberated. We didn't know anything about making missiles in the mountains there. We thought this was a concentration camp, but we didn't know what to call it. Well, it turns out it wasn't that—it was a slave-labor camp. They just worked these folks to death and didn't feed 'em right, and oh, jeesh, it was just total horror. I got sick as a dog. Everybody else did."

Rice, it turned out, was dealing with more than just the horrific sights and smells. He was dealing with his heritage. "I stood there, see—half of me is Jewish. I had no idea what these bodies were. You couldn't tell anything about their religion. The other half of me is German. And I just sat there, stood there, throwing up my guts and saying 'I never want to see another German as long as I live.' The saving grace was when the commanding officer, whoever he was, had sent a detail into town to get the German civilians to come through this area to see what had happened. And as they came in, every one of them threw up his cookies. That's the only thing that saved the German people as far as I was concerned at that time. They were human beings, too. But it didn't bring these people back to life."

Nowadays, when he hears some kid say, "Hey, it never happened, it was just a figment of everybody's imagination," it pushes the wrong button, and he responds. "I'm just—'Bullshit, buster. I wish I could have rubbed your nose in that smell, you'd never forget it.' And anybody who says it didn't is just doomed to repeat history. I was just an observer that came by after the liberation of Nordhausen. But I can sure tell you what a revolting experience that was. Little boys became men all of a sudden."

On the second day, unit commanders sent men into the town of Nordhausen to round up civilians to help with the burial detail. Private Sigmund Liberman, a twenty-two-year-old Texan who'd been raised as a conservative Jew and had been aware of the Nazis' treatment of the Jews before he enlisted, drew the assignment because he could communicate in Yiddish with the Germans. In the process, the civilians told him they hadn't even known there was a camp nearby. He helped herd them onto the division's trucks after ordering them to bring shovels. Asked if they argued or tried to fight, Liberman said, "No, no, they were worried we were going to kill them. I was wanting to do something, but I never did."

Combat Engineer Morris Sunshine, also Jewish, had to confront the good citizens of Nordhausen, who protested. "Some people, they didn't want to do it, and [they asked], 'What is this? We don't know anything about it.' The usual thing. How anybody couldn't know anything about it, the stench was so terrible, it's amazing to me that they were able to live with this smell." He supposes that the citizens "were probably afraid of the [German] leadership—they were still afraid of the leadership at that time, too." But he doesn't excuse them. "The anger—my hate for the German language and the German people is terrible. It's something that I've never forgiven them for."

The assignment of actually burying those bodies fell, in part, to the men of the 238th Combat Engineer Battalion, including Lieutenant Ernest James. He, too, was not impressed by the civilians' "we know nothing" defense. He says they found out later that many of the same civilians from Nordhausen had been working down in the tunnels at nearby Dora. "For Christ's sake, you had to know what was happening," he said. "Down in the tunnels, if an inmate got into trouble, they'd hang 'em on hooks for everybody to see."

James says that an area for mass graves was selected near the town, on the opposite side from the tunnels, and the unit came in with its bulldozers. The trenches were four or five feet deep and as wide as a dozer blade. He doesn't recall how long they were, but they were long enough to accommodate almost 3,000 bodies. The German civilians were made to get into the trenches and clean out the loose dirt, so that the final resting place would be "neatly prepared." James says the commander of the 104th ordered all able-bodied German men to work, no gloves, no masks. "He made them handle these dead bodies with their bare hands. Mean as hell."

But the Americans weren't shedding any tears for the Germans. One artillery battalion commander said his men had to be restrained from physically attacking the civilians. And as for the townspeople, James says, "They'd fabricate things to carry them out—a door, a piece of carpet, or they'd take two poles and put them through the arms of the clothes to make litters. And then four men would carry one body— they wouldn't put two bodies on or anything like that. They laid them out neatly, and God, I've got pictures of one, a little baby, apparently with its mother."

When all of the bodies had been laid in the trench, a memorial service was held with division chaplains leading the prayers.

And within a day or two, the 104th Infantry Division moved on, leaving the recovering survivors in the care of behind-the-lines medical units.

CHAPTER 6

MERE DEATH WAS NOT BAD ENOUGH FOR THE NAZIS

MY FIRST ENCOUNTER

On a Walk from Ettersburg to Buchenwald

One Mile and 200 Years Long

By Warren E. Priest

(Priest was an orthopedic surgical technician with the 120th Evacuation Hospital at Buchenwald. Forty-five years after the liberation, he wrote this poem describing his initial approach to the camp and his first contact with survivors.)

Walking up the pathway, through the forest of beech trees,
Leaves April green; the smooth, gray bark
Soft, clean and oh, so manicured,
How could I know what those trees concealed
At the brow of the hill, amidst the beech trees—the buchenwald,
In that land where Goethe and Schiller wandered in the summer months?

But, suddenly, unexpectedly, who are these strange men, dressed in
Their striped nightclothes
Moving to the side of the pathway as I approach?
I hold my GI issue carbine ready for any possibility
I approach them; they stop, a halting tentative progress
Emaciated, fleshless faces, bearded, unclean;
They stretch out their bony fingers to me like street beggars
Yet they seem to want nothing from me. I am bewildered.
There is no hostility here!
They fall to their knees; their hands now clasped together
as if in prayer, Durer-like.
They reach out skeletal arms tentatively as I approach, as
if I am the Christ, wearing the clothes of immortality
I think, what have I done to, for these four men, a mere 21-year-old soldier
From Massachusetts, in the service of his country?
Hesitantly, wordlessly, I pass them by, embarrassed because I
must be the good soldier; I must not fraternize.
But I cannot ignore their glistening, dark eyes,
Their hands still extended, one so feebly clutching at my calf
but his weak hands lose their grip, more like a caress.
I recalled pictures of saints at the moment of beatification having such
expressions on their faces!
I cannot understand what is happening, for no words have been spoken;
Dutifully, I move on to the fence just beyond
An electrified fence, a double fence, one inside another, with barbed
wire barriers at the top of each, an impenetrable barrier to me, so
I walk along the periphery,
I arrive at the opening to the fence, a towering gateway,
At the top of the gate is an iron inscription: "Jedem das Seine"
I know the meaning:
You get what you deserve.
And I enter the compound through the gate;
How could I know that my journey has just begun?

*Warren E. Priest served with the 120th
Evacuation Hospital at Buchenwald and
never forgot what he saw there. After the war,
he became a teacher in Newton,
Massachusetts, and started a camp for inner-
city children as well as the Center for
Affective Learning in New Hampshire.*

APRIL 12, 1945

BUCHENWALD CONCENTRATION CAMP

Near Weimar, Germany

M ax Schmidt got to Weimar with G Company of the 317th Infantry Regiment, 80th Infantry Division, on April 12, a day
after the city was taken. Max was an eighteen-year-old from Brooklyn
who had shipped out of Boston just six weeks earlier. By the time he
hit Weimar, it had been declared an open city. "In other words, there
was no real fighting to liberate Weimar. The Germans surrendered.
When you got close to it, you know there was something wrong because you could smell it in the air. In my opinion, that was the key,
that's why the Germans came to us, they came to our commanders and
wanted to surrender, because they knew what we'd find, and that
would be Buchenwald."

Louis Blatz was another eighteen-year-old in the 80th, but he got
lucky and arrived in Europe from the Detroit area just in time to serve
as a rifleman at the tail end of the Battle of the Bulge. He was maybe
five feet six and weighed 135 pounds, and he believed that he was in-
vincible. "I never thought about dying. I've always had a feeling, all my
life, even when I was a kid, you're gonna die, there's nothing you can
do about it. Why worry about it and get sick?"

Blatz, like Schmidt, smelled Buchenwald long before he saw it.
"We were walking along the road, our company, and all of a sudden
somebody said, 'Ooh! What's that odor?' And I said, 'It smells like
Mount Clemens.' In the old days Mount Clemens, Michigan, was
noted for mineral baths that smelled like rotten eggs, sulfur gas, an unpleasant odor. And farther along, we see the gates were wide open, we
went in, and we see all these people standing there. And some of them
had already been disrobed. Somebody had gotten there before us, and
they were taking all their clothes away from them, spraying them
down, washing them.

"Seeing it, you think, how could anybody be so inhumane as to
treat people, fellow human beings, in that manner? All that ran
through my mind was these people had no conscience; they didn't care

one way or another. They treated them as animals. It was just horrible. Because it was hard to breathe. The odor, the smell, the air. The crematoriums, some of them still had bodies burning in 'em, so you could still smell it. And it was a relief on our part to get away from it, but you couldn't forget, you couldn't forget. After that, you just say to yourself, nobody better tell me that this didn't happen."

Eugene O'Neil was yet another eighteen-year-old who made it to Europe in time for the end of the Bulge. But the Marylander wasn't as optimistic about his chances of surviving combat as Blatz was. He was sent from Le Havre by 40 and 8 railcar across France to a replacement depot in Belgium. "It was strange, and it was so cold, we even set the thing on fire trying to light a fire in the middle of the car to keep warm." It was early January. He was trucked from the depot to C Company of the 1st Battalion, 319th Infantry Regiment. "When we got in, nobody said, 'Hello, good-bye, go to hell,' nothin' else. Because the feeling, I think, was these guys are coming in to die. So nobody wanted to make any friends." His first battle was at the Our River and then on the Siegfried Line, where he was pinned down for five or six days. "We couldn't get out of the foxhole, and constant shelling, mortar fire, Screaming Meemies, rocket fire—it was enough to blow your mind. Some guys did lose their minds there."

O'Neil's unit stayed on the outskirts of Weimar. He doesn't remember how he got to Buchenwald, but he recalls what he saw. "A lot of men who were nothing but skin and bones. The smell was real bad. I didn't go into the camp." He says there was so much horror—one thing after another, not just the camp but in war. Somehow, he just dealt with it all. "You gotta realize the difference between an infantryman and some of the other guys that came in afterwards and did the police work, did the cleanup. They were strictly the support troops like the MPs that come in along behind you. But when the infantry hits something, they get them out as quick as they can, particularly in a situation like that. I can picture those human beings there with nothing but flesh and bones, which was one of the most horrible sights that you could see. I didn't know and didn't understand the full horror of the camp until after the war was over." Which may have been what helped him deal with it at the time.

Ventura De La Torre was just twenty years old when Cannon Company of the 317th Infantry Regiment, 80th Infantry Division, came to Buchenwald. He'd been drafted out of the citrus groves of Orange County, California, and gone to Europe with the division on the *Queen Mary*. He was a truck driver, towing a 105mm howitzer and hauling the shells for the gun. And he'd never heard of the mass killings or concentration camps until April 12, 1945.

"I couldn't believe it. It was a terrible sight, feeling sorry for these people that couldn't help themselves, nobody to help them. When we arrived, the people just walking toward us, like asking us, 'Get us out of here.' That was their feeling.

"Some just had a piece of blanket covering them. And their knees were nothing but skin and bone. Their ribs . . . a terrible sight to see them. When we went in, some of those guards, they had changed into inmates' [uniforms]—but some of the people recognized them. I heard that [the prisoners] killed some of them. And then they had the ovens there. Oh, it was the smell—when I think about it, I can almost smell that."

De La Torre was in the camp only three or four hours. His description of the dead—"stacked up like wood"—would be echoed by almost every American who set foot inside this camp and dozens of others. He remembers opening a door to one of the barracks. "Those people lined up shoulder to shoulder, and they were just staring at us. They were so weak; a lot of them couldn't even get out. And there were dead with them in there, but I guess [the prisoners] just take them out and pile them up outside the barracks."

Sixteen days after the 80th arrived at Buchenwald, the War Department Bureau of Public Relations issued a report on Buchenwald, first releasing it to war correspondents in Paris. The late Lieutenant Colonel Edward Temple Phinney, who had been with HQ VIII Corps in the final months of the war, tucked a copy of that report in his footlocker. There it remained for more than sixty years until his great-nephew and the latter's wife, Carl and Donna Phinney of Houston, Texas, discovered it and provided it to the author. The report puts into precise, often mathematical terms what the GIs were seeing and experiencing in the camp.

TEXT OF OFFICIAL REPORT
OF BUCKENWALD [*sic*] ATROCITIES

The following text of the official report of the
Prisoner of War and Displaced Persons Division,
United States Group Control Council, has been
forwarded from Supreme Headquarters Allied
Expeditionary Forces to the War Department. It's
[*sic*] contents were made available to correspondents
in Paris, April 28, 1945.

The text:

Inspection of German Concentration camp for
political prisoners located at Buckenwald on the
north edge of Weimar was made by Brigadier
General Eric F. Wood and Lieutenant Colonel
Charles K. Ott on the morning of April 16, 1945.

. . . 2. History of the camp: It was founded when
the Nazi party first came into power in 1933, and has
been in continuous operation ever since although its
largest populations date from the beginning of the
present war. U.S. armor overran the general area in
which the camp is located on April 12. Its SS Guard
had decamped by the evening of April 11. Some U.S.
Administration personnel and supplies reached the
camp on "Friday the 13th" of April—a red-letter day
for the surviving inmates.

3. Surviving population: Numerically, by
nationality, as of April 16, 1945:

    French 2,900
    Polish 3,800
    Hungarians 1,240

```
Jugoslavs  . . . . . . . . . . .570
Russians . . . . . . . . . . .4,380
Dutch  . . . . . . . . . . . . .584
Belgians . . . . . . . . . . . .622
Austrians  . . . . . . . . . . .550
Italians . . . . . . . . . . . .242
Czechs . . . . . . . . . . . .2,105
Germans  . . . . . . . . . . .1,800
Anti-Franco Spanish and Misc. . .1,207
                                 ———
TOTAL . . . . . . . . . . . .20,000
```

(Four thousand of the total were Jews.)

. . . 5. Mission of the Camp: An extermination
factory. Mere death was not bad enough for anti-
Nazis. Means of extermination: Starvation;
complicated by hard work, abuse, beatings and
tortures, incredibly crowded sleeping conditions
(see below), and sickness (for instance, typhus
rampant in the camp; and many inmates tubercular).
By these means many tens of thousands of the best
leadership personnel of Europe (including German
democrats and anti-Nazis) have been exterminated.
For instance, 6 of the 8 French generals originally
committed to the camp, and the son of one of them,
had died there.

The recent death rate was about 200 a day. 5,700
had died or been killed in February; 5,900 in March;
and about 2,000 in the first 10 days of April.

The main elements of the installation included
the "Little Camp", the "Regular Barracks", "The
Hospital," the medical experimentation building, the
body disposal plant, and an ammunition factory
immediately adjacent to this camp and separated from
it only by a wire fence.

Melvin Rappaport first heard the words "concentration camp" in a Hollywood movie just before the war. He saw his first one—Buchenwald—on April 13, 1945, and recalls that "the stench was beyond your wildest dreams." The Queens, New York, native stays in touch by e-mail with dozens of World War II veterans.

In the week preceding the arrival of the Americans, the Nazis moved 23,000 prisoners out of Buchenwald, lest they fall into enemy hands. Two trains with 4,600 prisoners were sent to Theresienstadt, Czechoslovakia, 160 miles to the east. Another train, with 4,800 prisoners destined for Dachau, was liberated en route. Still another, with 4,500 prisoners bound for Dachau, made it only to Gera, forty-five miles east of Buchenwald, where it was liberated. A train with 1,500 prisoners was sent 170 miles east, to Leitmeritz, Czechoslovakia. And two trains were dispatched to the concentration camp at Flossenbürg, 120 miles to the south. One train, with 3,105 inmates, arrived there. The other, with 4,500 prisoners, was detoured through Czechoslovakia, taking its human cargo on a hellish three-week journey that ultimately ended at Dachau.

Captain Melvin Rappaport was part of a headquarters unit with the 6th Armored Division. He'd been going to the City College of New York when he opted to join the Army six months before Pearl Harbor. He volunteered for Officer Candidate School (OCS) and was commissioned a second lieutenant assigned as a platoon leader in the newly organized 6th Armored Division. He went overseas with the unit and became a liaison for air support, wandering the countryside in a half-track talking to the fighter planes overhead via UHF radio. He was at Bastogne, where he remembers losing about a third of the division in the bitter fighting. "Somehow we survived it. Youth, that was the thing," he recalls in his Queens, New York, home. "When you're twenty, twenty-one years old, you can take anything. We got through the Siegfried Line, etc., and then it was April."

Mel knew a bit more than his buddies about Germans and Jews: he'd learned it from the movies. "There was a movie with James Stewart and Margaret Sullavan called *The Mortal Storm,* a 1940 film in which they played a couple in Germany. Her father was a professor and they were Jewish, so they threw them in a concentration camp. That was the first time I ever heard the words 'concentration camp.'"

He *saw* his first concentration camp on April 13. "The stench was beyond your wildest dreams. It was unbelievable. And I still remember this crazy thing. On top of one of these carts—actually it had rubber wheels, it wasn't a wagon—there was this naked body on the top, big fat guy about 220 pounds like me, with a crew cut and his tongue sticking out. So I remember I spoke to one of the inmates, a Polish youngster, twenty years old. He was in there because his father and his two brothers were members of the underground, so they threw them into the camp. He spoke English rather well, and I said, 'Who's that?' He said, 'Oh, that's Herman the guard.' Before he could get out, the prisoners grabbed him and stripped him and killed him and threw him on the top there. So there was this big fat German guy, all nude, laying on the top. All the bodies were like skeletons, all black and discolored, and he was laying up there, nice pink skin, you know.

"I can't explain what I was feeling. First of all, the war was still on, and I shouldn't have been here. Literally, we were supposed to be in headquarters in case something happened, and I was hoping to God the chief of staff of the corps headquarters wouldn't be looking for me. I realized my time was limited, so I wandered around, and maybe two hundred yards to the rear was a little concentration camp within a concentration camp. A big huge barbed-wire entanglement, double barbed wire, and big chains on the front, and behind it was these young boys, as I found out later on, there were 850 of them, ages of about six to sixteen. I found out one was Elie Wiesel, and the other, six years old, later became chief rabbi of Jerusalem. His name was Rabbi Israel Lau. They were starving and hungry and cold and miserable. It was like a pack of wild beasts, just running around this enclave in there. They looked at me, and I was looking at them. I didn't know what to say. It was unbelievable. All youngsters. They had snot coming out of their nose—they all had colds. Oh, God, what a mess."

Many of the children had been relocated to the barbed-wire enclosure from the *kleine Lager,* the little camp. It was actually the first place Mel was dropped off. All he could say about it was that "it was even worse than the main camp, if that's possible." The Army's press release says more:

```
6. The "Little Camp." Prisoners here slept on
triple-decked shelves, each shelf about 12' x 12',
16 prisoners to a shelf, the clearance height
between each shelve being a little over 2'. Cubage
figured out to about 35 cubic feet per man, as
against the minimum for health of 600 cubic feet
prescribed by U.S. Army Regulations. All arriving
new prisoners were initiated by spending at least
six weeks here before being "graduated to the
'regular barracks'." During this initiation,
prisoners were expected to lose about 40 percent in
weight. Jews, however, seldom if ever graduated to
the regular barracks. Camp disciplinary measures
included transferring recalcitrant prisoners back to
```

the "Little Camp". As persons became too feeble to
work, there [sic] were also sent back to this camp,
or to the "Hospital". Rations were less than at
regular camps, and death rate was very high here;
recently 2 per cent to 4 per cent, per day.

While the *kleine Lager* was the worst that Buchenwald had to offer
adult inmates, release to the main camp and the "regular barracks" did
not offer a life that, objectively, was appreciably better. Mel Rappaport
still remembers his first look at those regular barracks.

"We kicked the doors open to some of the barracks, and again the
stench was just unbelievable. It just hit you in the face. The latrines
were out in the street, the toilets, all the toilets right in the street
there, and the inmates, they had huge boards where they slept on,
where maybe you could hold maybe normally thirty people, they had
maybe three hundred in there, packed in there."

Rappaport's vivid description is supported by the Army's press report:

7. The "Regular Barracks." The dormitory rooms were
approximately 42' x 23', about 10' high; or a
content of less than 9,500 cubic feet. In such a
room, there were installed triple-deck 38 stacks of
3 cots each; or a total of 114 cots, each cot 32" by
72" outside measurement. Most of these cots were
double (i.e. 2 parallel cots occupying a space of
60" by 72"), aisles were too narrow (less than 24")
to permit movement except with body edgewise, 114
cots into 9,500 makes less than 85 cubic feet per
person. But since the war 250 persons have been made
to sleep in each such room (5 persons on each 60" by
72" double cot, and 2 persons on each 30" by 72"
single cot); or less than 40 cubic feet per person.
There was less than one blanket per prisoner.
Blankets were thin and shoddy, and undersize. There
was no heat in these dormitories.

The troops who came through Buchenwald on the first couple of days were in combat units. Their job was to keep the pressure on the enemy, and as a result, they often spent no more than a few hours inside the concentration camp. It would be another two days before the first Army medical unit would arrive and attempt to save the 20,000 inmates who remained in Buchenwald.

CHAPTER 7

IKE KNEW THIS
WOULD BE DENIED

APRIL 12, 1945

AHLEM, GERMANY

    180 miles west-southwest of Berlin

    140 miles north-northwest of Buchenwald

With the end of the war in sight, the objective for U.S. Ninth Army units was to reach the Elbe River and link up with the advancing Russians. Ultimately, the Elbe would be part of the border between what became known as East and West Germany. By mid-April, advance units of both the 84th Infantry Division and the 102nd Infantry Division had caught up with the spearheading 2nd Armored Division—Hell on Wheels, which was halted at the Elbe.

In the course of its rush eastward, the 84th liberated the slave-labor camp at Ahlem, a subcamp of Neuengamme, near Hannover. The inmates were primarily Jewish men and boys from the liquidated Lódź ghetto in Poland. Corporal Vernon Tott, a 335th Infantry Regiment radio operator from Iowa, took photographs there and at Salzwedel, a camp they would liberate a day later, and, when he came home, stashed the photos in a shoe box that remained in his basement for more than fifty years. Tott, who died of cancer in 2005, also left a highly detailed written description of his day at Ahlem, which he said was "hell on earth."

He wrote:

My memory of what we saw when we first entered the camp was the pile of dead bodies. The men alive were in ragged clothing and they were just skin and bones. They came towards us with smiles on their faces. They knew their horrible nightmare was finally coming to an end. We motioned them back as we didn't want them to get too close to us. We feared they were full of disease and lice. Then we went into one of the barracks. What we saw in there is something that a person could never forget. There were prisoners laying in bunks too weak to get up. There were dead bodies in some of the bunks. In one particular bunk, there was a boy, about fifteen years old, who was lying in his own vomit, urine, and stool. I could see he was near death. When he looked at me, I could see he was crying for help. Over the years, every time I would think about Ahlem, I could still see the look on this boy's face.

Next, I went into another barracks and it was just as bad as the first one. There was a prisoner there that could speak English. He told me he was a doctor from Belgium, and said that this was the infirmary. He explained that he was the camp doctor. The prisoners here, I could see, were near death. He had no medicines or bandages to help treat the prisoners. Then he took me to look out the back window. There were trashcans full of dead bodies. What a horrible, inhuman way to die! Our troop had just come through six months of bloody battle but what we were seeing here made us sick to our stomachs and some even cried.

What I saw in this camp was so shocking that I wanted pictures to send home to show my family. I took eighteen photos of everyone that was alive in the camp. In the Army, we had no radios or newspapers so I didn't know Hitler was treating the Jewish people in this manner.*

Wayne "Roy" Ogle, then of Knoxville, Tennessee, now a retired horticulture professor at Clemson, was a college student when he enlisted in the reserve. He was called up and went to Europe as part of an antitank platoon in the 333rd Infantry Regiment, 84th Infantry Division. Ogle spent six weeks fighting in the Battle of the Bulge, but he says it felt more like six years. His time on the line ended when a chunk of shrapnel lodged in his chest, just millimeters from his heart. It was probably the freezing cold that saved his life. "I had on a real heavy overcoat, plus a field jacket, plus everything else I could get on. The shrapnel went through that double lining of the lapel on the overcoat, and went through my field jacket, and all the other clothing, and it lodged in my chest. [The clothing] slowed it enough to where it didn't kill me. I was lucky." He managed to get out of the hospital in about two weeks, just short of the time limit after which he'd be sent to a replacement depot rather than back to his old unit. He was with the buddies he'd trained and fought with when his unit discovered Ahlem.

"I was never as shocked in all of my life when I saw those guys. They were skeletons." The first units to liberate the camp had the job of corralling the newly freed inmates and getting them back behind the barbed wire for their own safety. The gates had been closed by the time Ogle arrived.

"The thing I remember best is they had really become jubilant about the fact that they were free. They had run all over camp, and they had spilled flour on the ground. They were rebelling, basically, is what it was, they were just having a fine time of it.

"I also remember that there were some British and some American prisoners there. Not many, maybe a half dozen, and they got those guys out, pronto."

* A film has been made about Vernon Tott connecting with the survivors of Ahlem. It's entitled *Angel of Ahlem* and was produced by the Documentary Institute of the University of Florida. It's available on DVD.

Ken Ayers was with the 84th Infantry
Division at the liberation of Salzwedel.
Ayers, who is still active in veterans'
affairs, celebrated his ninetieth birthday
in 2009 at home in Tallahassee, Florida.

Like others who liberated camps, Ogle has dreamt about the experience. "About those scarecrows that came out, it was terrible. It's worse
than seeing a corpse, I'll tell you that, and I've seen plenty of those."

Two days later, other units of the 84th Infantry Division led an attack to liberate another subcamp of Neuengamme, Salzwedel. First
Lieutenant Kenneth Ayers, from Tallahassee, Florida, was a twenty-
five-year-old platoon leader in A Company of the 333rd Regiment.

Ayers had been part of a National Guard unit at West Palm Beach
that was federalized late in 1940. His unit eventually ended up at Fort
Benning, Georgia, serving as what he calls "demonstration troops."
After a year at Benning, he was the only man left in the outfit with a
high school education, so he was sent to OCS. He became a ninety-
day wonder, graduated from Officer Candidate School with an infantry
commission, and was sent to Camp Wheeler, Georgia, to train troops.
"I was a southern boy, and they sent me to a colored regiment." Those

were the days of the segregated Army, and he knew the assignment was no accident. "I stayed there one year and was reassigned to the 84th Infantry Division at Camp Claiborne, Louisiana."

The 84th arrived in Europe in October 1944, and Ayers is a bit understated in describing what it was like for a twenty-five-year-old to be leading men in combat for the first time. "Don't overlook the word 'scared,'" he says, "because I was." The men in his platoon were from all over the United States and from all walks of life. Not surprisingly, he has a fairly forthright assessment of their fighting ability. "Let me say this: the ones that caused the most trouble in civilian life sometimes turned out to be the best soldiers. In other words—I won't use this word literally—but a gangster on the streets of New York was a helluva soldier in the field."

Despite the fact that he was his company's executive officer as well as a platoon leader responsible for dozens of enlisted men, Ayers was given no advance warning that they might encounter concentration camps. His introduction to the subject was intense: "I literally saw the guards on the gate there in Salzwedel shot and killed. I personally didn't fire a shot—I was behind."

Salzwedel had begun operations with a thousand female slave laborers less than a year earlier, in mid-1944. This subcamp of Neuengamme existed to provide workers for a privately owned company whose primary mission was the production of explosives and bullets. The factory operated around the clock, with the women working under brutal SS supervision in twelve-hour shifts with one fifteen-minute meal break.

By the beginning of April 1945, Salzwedel was being used as a collecting point for transports of female prisoners from camps being evacuated to avoid the oncoming Russians. In its final days, there were more than 3,000 crowded into the camp, including a large contingent of Dutch women evacuated from Ravensbrück. The guards outside the barbed wire were generally Wehrmacht soldiers unfit to serve in combat units. On the inside, security was provided by approximately ten male SS members supervising an equal number of female guards, some of whom attempted to blow up the camp and its inmates as the American soldiers approached.

Lea Fuchs-Chayen was a teenager standing near the gates of Salzwedel when an American tank rolled up. In 1997, from her home in Tel Aviv, she wrote a public letter describing her liberation and thanking the GIs:

A U.S. soldier jumped off the tank, opened the gates and announced, "You are free." To us, he and the others from the U.S. Army were angels from heaven. I was standing fairly near the gate and tried to say "thank you" in English, German or even Hungarian, but no sound would pass my lips.

I ran back to my room in my hut, where several girls were lying on the floor, burning with fever, some even vomiting blood. I wanted to tell them that we were free, but no sound came out. It seems that

The burning barracks at Salzwedel described by survivor Lea Fuchs-Chayen was sketched by 84th Infantry Division combat artist Walter Chapman.

the excitement of that morning was too much for my dilapidated condition.

For the past 48 hours, we had heard gunfire and that morning, we could hear the noise of tanks. When our liberators arrived, the Germans lifted their hands above their heads in capitulation. A few U.S. soldiers rounded them up. One SS officer started to run away and was shot dead.

The Army organized food for us and told us we would be taken to decent quarters. After we left the infested camp, it was burnt down. A doctor came and took note of the patients who needed hospitalization. About three days later, trucks took us to a German air force training school. The buildings were pleasant and roomy and our liberators had expelled all the cadets, after having made them clean the place for us. We were told not to drag anything and should we want to rearrange our rooms, we should ask a U.S. soldier and he would give orders for it to be done. Each of us received a bar of soap, the first in a year. We had hot water for 24 hours a day and so we could shower three or four times a day, as if to wash away all the mental hurt inflicted by the Germans. We had proper beds with sheets and received clean towels every day. After our first shower, we were asked not to put on our old rags, as they were full of lice. We were given clean clothes.

The U.S. Army had organized a special diet for us as we had to get used to eating again. We had the normal facilities of a dining room and we sat on chairs at tables, like human beings again. There were always several Army people present to make sure that all was well, and all this at a time when the United States was still fighting a war.

The most astonishing thing I found, then and today, was how wonderfully kind they were to us. How remarkable it was that under the dirt, disease, rags and lice, these soldiers could see human beings, young girls. Their kindness and their thoughtfulness gave us back our belief in the human race.

A doctor came around to each room to examine us, recommended treatment or said, with a smile, "You will be fine, miss, with good food inside you again."

In the evenings, time and time again, there would be a knock on the door and soldiers would come in and do conjuring tricks or other silly things to get us to laugh or at least smile again. It took some time before we learned to smile again.

Today, 52 years after my liberation, I stand in awe and thank you not only for liberating me, but for being so humane, efficient and kind.

God bless you.

Immediately after the liberation of the camp, Ken Ayers remembers seeing the freed prisoners running amok in the streets of the town of Salzwedel. "They were getting hundred-pound bags of sugar and splitting them open with a knife and coming out with double handfuls of it. They were looting stores. One of them brought me the most beautiful accordion you ever saw in your life—they were just looting and giving stuff away."

Creighton Kerr of Waterford, Michigan, was a machine gunner with D Company of the 333rd Regiment. He was in a jeep driving past the gates of the Salzwedel camp when two GIs came running down the walk inside the gate, calling out to the Americans. It turned out that both men had been captured on the first day of the Battle of the Bulge, both were medic sergeants, and both had been working in the Salzwedel camp hospital. But that's where the similarity ended: one man asked for food and was given a breakfast K ration, which he sat down on the curb and ate. The other man asked for a weapon. Kerr gave him a carbine with a couple of magazines of ammunition, and the guy disappeared back into the camp.

Kerr's other memory of Salzwedel was seeing women pouring out of the wide main gate into the street, singing and dancing. One was stark naked—except for several hats piled on top of her head and a green shoe on one foot, a red shoe on the other.

The 333rd spent less than an hour outside the Salzwedel camp. Then they went on to the Elbe River, where they met the Russians and waited for orders. Within days, Kerr was asked to return to the town of Salzwedel to assist the occupying 334th Regiment as a special services officer. His primary job: to keep the former women prisoners from Salzwedel and men who had, presumably, been in smaller slave-labor barracks in the area entertained. He did it by organizing them by coun-

The women who survived Salzwedel were moved to a nearby German military base, where they were cared for by American soldiers. Several weeks after liberation, three of them made an American flag, which was presented to the 84th Division Railsplitters.

try of origin, and each night of the week, a different group would put on a show. The memory that sticks with him? "We had a famous French male singer—I can't remember his name—who sang the French national anthem for the first time in five years on that first Monday night."

APRIL 12, 1945
OHRDRUF CONCENTRATION CAMP

More than a week after the liberation of Ohrdruf, on the same day that U.S. Army units were liberating Buchenwald, General Dwight D. Eisenhower, supreme commander of the Allied forces in Europe, flew to Ohrdruf because of the unbelievable stories he'd

Private Don Timmer, with two years of high school German, was assigned to serve as Eisenhower's interpreter for the supreme Allied commander's tour of the Ohrdruf concentration camp. Timmer was nineteen years old.

heard. He was met there by Generals Omar Bradley, the Twelfth Army Group commander, and George S. Patton, commanding general of the Third Army, to which the 4th Armored Division, which had discovered the camp, was assigned.

Private Don Timmer, a nineteen-year-old kid from Mansfield, Ohio, had just arrived at Ohrdruf with the 714th Ordnance Company of the 89th Infantry Division. Because he'd had two years of high school German, he'd been interpreting for his unit. On the first nice day of spring, they'd driven from Gotha through the town of Ohrdruf, and he remembers that the German civilians had hung white sheets of surrender in their windows. He also recalls a German plane flying low over their small convoy but not strafing them.

As Eisenhower came into the camp, Timmer was told that the general's interpreter was on a plane that had not yet arrived. Timmer would have to do the job. "I said to him, 'General, I'm not that good at German.' And he said, 'Don't worry, I know German, but I need time to formulate my responses.' "

So Timmer followed Ike, Bradley, and Patton around the camp, tagging along even after the general's interpreter arrived. Though some of the bodies had been removed, the ellipse of dead at the entrance had deliberately been left in place, as had the stack of bodies in the shed. Timmer recalls, "The most pathetic thing happened [when] we came into a barracks of maybe five hundred men. There was one that was unconscious, and a fella shook him and said, 'Eisenhower's here.' The guy sat up, smiled, and then fell over dead."

One of the former prisoners who emigrated to the United States, whose name became Andrew Rosner, had given the generals a tour of the camp. He spoke about the experience in Wichita, Kansas, at a celebration on April 23, 1995, honoring the 89th Infantry Division fifty years after the liberation of Ohrdruf. Rosner was twenty-three when he escaped from one of the SS death marches from the camp. He was found on the outskirts of the town by two American soldiers and hospitalized. Days later, when he awoke, he remembers the nurse running to get waiting American officers and members of the press. He told the Wichita audience, "I was taken back to the concentration camp Ohrdruf by jeep in a convoy headed by Generals Eisenhower and Bradley themselves. Several survivors and myself gave General Eisenhower and his men a personal tour of the horrors, which you had discovered at Ohrdruf. I never forgot how General Eisenhower kept rubbing his hands together as we spoke of the horrors inflicted upon us and the piles of our dead comrades. He insisted on seeing it all, hearing it all. He knew! He wanted to have it recorded and filmed for the future."

Don Timmer recalls that after nearly two hours in the camp, Eisenhower's staff tried to get the general to leave. He remembers one of them saying, "Ike, we've got a war to fight," and Eisenhower responding, "Don't bother me. I've got to *get* this."

That's what impressed Timmer the most—Eisenhower's reluctance to leave. "It was almost prophetic that he knew this would be denied."

Supreme Allied Commander General Dwight Eisenhower (third from left), 12th Army Group Commander General Omar Bradley (fourth from left), and Lieutenant General George S. Patton (right) observe the charred remains of prisoners whose bodies were burned on "the griddle" at Ohrdruf.

Before leaving Ohrdruf, Eisenhower issued an uncharacteristically emotional order. He said, "I want every American unit not actually in the front lines to see this place. We are told that the American soldier does not know what he is fighting for. Now, at least, he will know what he is fighting against." It would become evident over the course of the final month of the war that detours to Ohrdruf would not be needed; tragically, American soldiers would have ample opportunity to see Ohrdruf-like vistas of much greater scale as they moved east, trapping the fleeing German army between U.S. and Soviet forces.

Timmer did one more translating job at Ohrdruf after the Eisenhower visit. The bodies of the burgomaster of Ohrdruf and his wife were discovered in their home a day after they'd been brought with other townspeople to see the camp. They had hanged themselves. Timmer was asked to translate their suicide note. He says it read, "We didn't know! But *we* knew."

After the visit, Eisenhower sent a cable to the chairman of the Joint Chiefs of Staff in Washington, General George C. Marshall. It said, in part:

> The things I saw beggar description. While I was touring the camp I encountered three men who had been inmates and by one ruse or another had made their escape. I interviewed them through an interpreter. The visual evidence and the verbal testimony of starvation, cruelty, and bestiality were so overpowering as to leave me a bit sick. In one room, where they piled up twenty or thirty naked men, killed by starvation, George Patton would not even enter. He said that he would get sick if he did so. [Patton went behind the shed and vomited.] I made the visit deliberately, in order to be in a position to give first-hand evidence of these things if ever, in the future, there develops a tendency to charge these allegations merely to "propaganda."

Ohrdruf had a lasting impact on Patton as well. He recorded precise details about the camp in his diary, describing it as "one of the most appalling sights that I have ever seen." He went on:

> In a shed . . . was a pile of about forty completely naked human bodies in the latest stages of emaciation. These bodies were lightly sprinkled with lime, not for the purposes of destroying them, but for the purpose of removing the stench.
>
> When the shed was full—I presume its capacity to be about 200, the bodies were taken to a pit a mile from the camp where they were buried. The inmates claimed that 3,000 men, who had been either shot in the head or who had died of starvation, had been so buried since the first of January.
>
> When we began to approach with our troops, the Germans thought it expedient to remove the evidence of their crime. Therefore, they had some of the slaves exhume the bodies and place them

on a mammoth griddle composed of sixty-centimeter railway tracks laid on brick foundations. They poured pitch on the bodies and then built a fire of pinewood and coal under them. They were not very successful in their operations because there was a pile of human bones, skulls, charred torsos on or under the griddle which must have accounted for many hundreds.

At 5:47 P.M. Eastern War Time on April 12, radio networks in the United States flashed the bulletin that President Franklin Delano Roosevelt had died earlier that afternoon at his retreat in Warm Springs, Georgia. It was nearly 11 P.M. in Germany when the word reached Eisenhower, Bradley, and Patton, who had returned to their headquarters from Ohrdruf.

In Berlin, the official German news agency, Deutsches Nachricht-enbüro, received the Reuters bulletin: "Roosevelt died today at midday." The historian John Toland wrote in *The Last 100 Days* that when word reached Reichminister Joseph Goebbels, he said, "Now, bring out our best champagne and let's have a telephone talk with the Führer!" Toland continues:

> Some ten people hung over him as he telephoned Hitler. "My Führer," he said feverishly, "I congratulate you! Roosevelt is dead. It is written in the stars that the second half of April will be the turning point for us. This is Friday, April the thirteenth!" It was just past midnight. "Fate has laid low your greatest enemy. God has not abandoned us. Twice he has saved you from savage assassins. Death, which the enemy aimed at you in 1939 and 1944, has now struck down our most dangerous enemy. It is a miracle!

American soldiers would learn of the president's death in *Stars and Stripes* and by word of mouth on the thirteenth. While most of them knew little about their new commander in chief, Harry S Truman, they were reasonably certain that FDR's death would not affect their own lives in the waning days of the war. Toland reports that the three generals were not so sure, "wondering what effect Roosevelt's death would have on the future peace" and agreeing that "It was a tragedy that America had to change leaders at such a critical point in history."

————

The postscript to the Ohrdruf story is told by two men from the 89th Infantry Division. The first is Ray Little, now of Hobbs, New Mexico. He was part of M Company, 355th Infantry Regiment, which had been attached to the 4th Armored Division during this period.

Days after Ohrdruf was discovered, PFC Little and another soldier were given orders to patrol the camp and keep down any disturbances by the inmates. Apparently, U.S. forces were rounding up displaced persons who had escaped from the Nazis and bringing them into Ohrdruf in order to maintain order as well as centralize them so they could be fed and seen by doctors. Little recalls that "Some of them had gotten out and they'd gotten some schnapps, gotten some rifles, and were gonna go out and kill some of the Germans. That's when they sent us in there. To keep 'em calmed down. Just our presence was about all it amounted to, because we didn't actually do anything.

"I remember one intersection, they had built a bonfire, and they were dancing, these Russians. You know how you've seen how they dance squatted down? They were having a ball. They were really enjoying their freedom. I guess they'd been fed, too, but obviously they weren't lookin' for food."

Little and the other soldier had been told to use one of the camp's administration buildings as their billet, and, as young soldiers do, they took it upon themselves to look around. Apparently, they found at least part of what the 4th Armored had been sent to Ohrdruf to find: the secret communications bunker. "Underneath the room we were in there was an underground, and it was full of electronics. I've never known for sure what that was all about, but it looked like it could be a telephone exchange or something. There were several rooms. There was just a mass—walls of wiring and switches and stuff. It was obviously complicated electronics."

The other man from the 89th tells what amounts to a post-postscript to the Ohrdruf liberation. Charles T. Payne was another GI

Charles T. Payne's unit drew double duty at Ohrdruf.

who had been part of the ASTP program, sent to college by the Army until the Army decided it was more important for him to be in the infantry than to get an engineering degree. Payne, of Augusta, Kansas, shipped overseas as a member of K Company of the 355th in the bitterest winter in decades. They landed at Le Havre, going ashore in a landing craft standing in six inches of icy cold water. Then they were taken by truck in the middle of the night and dumped in a snow-covered field with a pile of tents to erect. "That night, we essentially created Camp Lucky Strike. It was one of the most painful episodes of my life. It was the night when grown men cried."

Payne was lucky; he survived frostbite that turned his toes black but, unlike many of his buddies', didn't require amputation. Once their equipment finally caught up with them, he was assigned to a mortar squad, and they were sent to the area where France, Germany, and Luxembourg intersect. Still they didn't face combat—just the aftermath, the bodies, both German and American. One, in particular, had an impact: a GI who'd been shot and then had fallen into the road, his head crushed by a tracked vehicle.

Not long thereafter, PFC Payne was transferred to regimental headquarters company, assigned to accompany a telephone wire-laying crew as their guard. It was a far cry from the infantry, almost enjoyable at times as they wandered the countryside in a jeep.

He got the sense that the tide had turned and war's end was approaching when they crossed the Rhine in a U.S. Navy landing craft, a sobering experience not because they were under fire but because they could see the wounded, burned, and maimed Americans making the trip in the other direction.

In early April their unit approached Erfurt and then Gotha, and they watched the numbers on the road signs indicating kilometers to Berlin getting smaller. Like other GIs, he was disappointed when word came down that they wouldn't be taking Hitler's capital. Instead, he was ordered to Ohrdruf. Close to the camp, he began encountering hundreds of people who had been inmates, out loose, wandering the roads and towns.

When the just-turned-twenty-year-old got into the concentration camp itself, nothing had been touched. The same ellipse of bodies lay at the entrance. The small shed with the stack of bodies covered with lime that had sickened Patton remained untouched, an exhibit ordered by Eisenhower. The body of the SS guard who'd tried to escape by posing as an inmate lay almost at the entry gate, his head beaten in by vengeful former inmates. Speaking from his home in Chicago, Payne recalls not being overwhelmed by the horrors of Ohrdruf. "It was in the middle of the war. I guess I had become able to see all kinds of horrible things and keep going. To me, was this more horrible—except in numbers—than a dead soldier whose head had been run over by a tank? I guess I handled it; I mean, I kept going."

When his outfit moved on to the territory between Ohrdruf and the Elbe River, Payne thought he'd seen the last of Ohrdruf. But when that region was turned over to the Russians at the end of the war, he was ordered back to pull guard duty for what was being converted to a displaced persons camp. It was there that he had his first opportunity to speak—sort of—with one of the victims of what would come to be known as the Holocaust.

He was on guard duty, and a man who he believes was a Polish Jew came to him and wanted to talk. "We did not have a common language; we both knew a little bit of pidgin German, but that was it. So we just stood there and talked. And what he wanted to tell me, if I understood it, was that the Germans had killed a million Jews and nobody knew about it. And he thought it was important to get the word out. He was talking to anybody he could talk to, and I think that was what he was saying."

After returning home in mid-1946 and coping with the kinds of postwar adjustment problems experienced by many veterans, Payne moved to Chicago, where he became a graduate student at the University of Chicago and ultimately did some of the pioneering work in library automation and computerization. He married and had one son and doesn't recall ever telling his family about the time he spent at Ohrdruf. "I've never really liked to talk about it; I like to tell more interesting, funny stories. Everybody's heard my war stories about liberating a baby buggy full of fine German wine. I don't know that anybody's heard about the grim part of it." Not even his great-nephew, the boy who would become President Barack Obama.

CHAPTER 8

BUCHENWALD

THIS AIN'T NO PLACE I WANNA BE

APRIL 14, 1945
FRANKFURT, GERMANY

The men and women of the Army's 120th Evacuation Hospital had spent more than a month chasing Patton—"playing catch-up" is the way one of their truck drivers, Sergeant Milton Silva, put it. "He would move into an area, and we would be moved up to where he was supposed to be, no sooner had we set up our equipment and tents, he'd moved on, we'd knock them down. We just chased him all over until we got to Frankfurt. By that time, everything was sort of quieted down. The Germans were on the way out, and it was sort of an R&R area at the time."

Silva, who grew up in the family-run funeral business in Fall River, Massachusetts, and was drafted while attending the Boston School of Anatomy and Embalming, says the 120th had set up in the center of a racetrack in the middle of Frankfurt and everyone was having a good time, which included racing a liberated motorcycle on the track. The good time ended with word that they were being moved on a priority basis.

"We got word that FDR had died," recalls Silva, now a retired Massachusetts judge whom local prosecutors referred to as "Not Guilty Milty," "and all hell broke loose. We were told to pack up but not to load any vehicles. Up to this time, what we would do is operate in tandem. We would take the people [to the new location] who were supply and maintenance, the guys that put up the tents and so forth. And we would come back for personnel, and while we were doing that, they'd be setting up the equipment, so by the time we got there with the nurses and the doctors, the hospital would be operational."

This move, however, was different. At about six in the morning on April 14, an all-black quartermaster unit showed up with trucks, loaded their vehicles, and with 273 personnel, the 120th Evac moved out. Silva recalls that they drove all day, then into the night under blackout conditions, occasionally hearing small-arms fire. "We didn't know where we were going. We thought that Patton had started a big offensive and he'd met a lot of resistance from the Germans and there were gonna be a lot of casualties. And as we approached our destination, we started to get this odor."

Riding in the truck with Silva was his buddy, truck driver Herbert James, Jr. "Herbie said to me, 'Milt, there's something that smells around here.' I said, 'Herbie, there's somebody dead around here.' Having grown up in the funeral business, the smell of death was not unfamiliar to me, and I thought that we had probably run by some bodies that had been left by the side of the road and had decomposed. But the smell got stronger as we got to wherever we were going. And, lo and behold, with the light of day, we arrived at our destination, which was Buchenwald concentration camp."

Corporal Leonard E. Herzmark of Kansas City, Missouri, had just completed his second year of college when he decided to enlist in the Army at the end of 1942. He was eighteen years old, and since he'd been studying chemical engineering, the Army trained him as a combat medic, which was some cause for concern on his part. "You'd go

The future judge Milton Silva during World War II.

out with a combat company, and you know, you're wearing a red cross on your helmet, which is a good target." He also wasn't armed. "Medics are not supposed to be armed, and that meant you can't shoot a medic, because they haven't got a gun. I think that was probably a rule that was promulgated by the Geneva Convention, but nobody paid any attention to that."

Fortunately, before he went overseas with an infantry unit, he was pulled out and sent to Mississippi, where the 120th Evac was being formed, and he was assigned to be a laboratory technician. That's where he met Milt Silva.

Herzmark says that though the unit wasn't told their specific destination when they left Frankfurt, something was mentioned about a prisoner camp. He remembers getting to the area outside Weimar and bivouacking for the night. But he vividly recalls what happened the next morning. "As we drove up the road, I saw a lot of stuff hanging from trees, and, having come from Mississippi, we had what's called Spanish moss that used to hang from the trees. My eyesight wasn't the best—I wear glasses. But as we got closer, I saw those were soldiers, German soldiers, hanging from the trees." Herzmark surmised that before the SS guards left Buchenwald, they'd blown up the power plants, thrown down their guns, and left. "Since the electrified fence was no longer electrified, the inmates climbed through the fence—this was either two or three actual fences, one inside the other, I should say. And so they took out after the Germans, captured a lot of them, and hung 'em right there. A mass lynching, for which you cannot blame anyone. The Germans had asked for it.

"We dismounted from the truck just outside the camp and went to the gate. And as I walked through the gate, I remember seeing a gallows with three bodies hanging from it. Those were not German soldiers, those were inmates who had been hung. This struck me as 'this ain't no place I wanna be.' "

Milt Silva had a similar reaction. "We got beyond the entrance, and we saw these people walking around, almost naked and looking like living skeletons. It was sort of an eerie sight. People were whimpering. I just couldn't believe what I was seeing. This is not so, you know? Who the hell would treat people like this? And I remember wandering off into an area where a bunch of inmates were surrounding an individual, and they were pelting him and beating the hell out of him. He was one of the guards, and I remember standing there shouting, 'Kill the sonofabitch!' " Silva now calls that one of his moments of shame.

At the time, he was so upset about it that he just walked off. "I didn't want to stay there anymore. I just didn't want anything to do with what was going on up there, and I went down and started to fix tires. Remember fixing eighteen flats and beating the hell out of the tires with a sledge hammer and feeling pretty good about it."

From the Army's Buchenwald press release:

11. Miscellaneous: A. Rations: 600 to 700 calories per day for the regular camp, 500 for the Little Camp, both of an unbalanced ration, as against 3,000 to 3,600 calories required for adult health. Black bread, potatoes twice a week, and beet root twice a

```
week served as weak soup, soy bean (or other
vegetable "sausage"), jam twice a week, margarine
about once a week. Never any greens or fresh
vegetables. Heavy deficiency in animal fats and
vitamins. No meats. Red Cross packages almost
entirely appropriated by SS camp commander, and
distributed to suit himself to SS personnel, to
citizens of Weimar, even to Nordic German camp
prisoners. In two months Commander [René] L'Hopital*
received 1/10, 1/14 and 1/7 of one-person weekly French
Red Cross parcel. Meals were prepared and "served"
by prisoner personnel under SS supervision.
```

Warren Priest was an orthopedic surgical technician with the 120th. He'd grown up in Haverhill, New Hampshire, gotten a full scholarship to Boston University in 1940, and been drafted at the end of 1941, when he was nineteen. After basic training, he was selected to attend Fordham University as part of the Army Specialized Training Program (ASTP), where he majored in German. The plan was for him to be part of a group that, at the end of the war, would be involved with occupation administration. But after nine months, the special program was dissolved and he was sent to the 104th Infantry Division and, from there, to the newly organized 120th Evac at Camp Shelby, Mississippi.

Before the unit left Frankfurt, he remembers the colonel calling everyone together and saying they had an assignment to go into a camp where they could practice their medical training. "My experience as a kid growing up was that camp was a place where you went swimming and went barefoot in a bathing suit. So I had difficulty trying to deter-

---

* Commandant René L'Hopital, former aide-de-camp to Marshal Ferdinand Foch (supreme commander of the Allied armies in World War I) and a personal friend of Theodore Roosevelt, Jr., and Admiral Richard Byrd, accompanied the Americans inspecting Buchenwald. According to the report, "[L'Hopital] weighed 95 pounds against a normal weight of 175 pounds; but was in far better physical condition than the average of his fellow prisoners (due to his having been in this camp only two months)."

mine the nature of the camp. I knew there were people needing medical care, but I had no idea what we had to face."

The odor was his first clue that Buchenwald was not summer camp. On the night of the fourteenth, the unit was bivouacked at Schloss Ettersburg, within two or three miles of the concentration camp. Some men stayed in tents, others slept inside a school. "The whole area was permeated by an odor that I had never experienced before, and I later realized it was the odor of burning bodies and decaying bodies that wafted down from the mountains into the valley below. It was something you couldn't escape.

"It's the first thing you encounter and the last thing you forget. I can tell you from experience that I know that I'm not a victim of post-traumatic stress, theoretically, except at those times when I am present and there's some burning flesh of some kind, it comes back, and it really does a job. For example, I live in a home where I have a wood stove now, and several years ago, I was stoking the fire in the morning with my bathrobe on and didn't realize in doing so a spark came up and lit the back side of my sleeve, went up my arm to the back of my bathrobe, and ignited my hair, and I smelled that burning flesh, burning human. And it kept me awake for months." Priest went into Buchenwald the following morning with the men of the 120th.

Initially, the female nurses of the unit went into the camp with the men. Rosella Willis Lane, who'd been a farm girl in Iowa before becoming a nurse and joining the Army, still recalls the ride from Frankfurt to Weimar, with the trucks stopping frequently and the women ordered to crouch behind the wheels because the convoy was being strafed. Now ninety-four years old, she says that what she saw inside Buchenwald can never be forgotten. "The crematorium with the doors open, ribs and bones. DPs on stretchers and walking around, just skin and bones." She met the fifteen-year-old Elie Wiesel and spent time with him, wondering how he'd ever gotten through *that*. (Long after the war, Wiesel would attend reunions of the 120th.)

Her unit was camped at a castle in Weimar, a couple of miles from the concentration camp. Two or three days after arriving, she says a couple of SS soldiers were killed very near their mess tent, and her commander decided that it was no place for women to be assigned. All the nurses were sent on temporary duty elsewhere, while the men of the 120th remained to work in the camp.

———

Robert Duoos, a Minnesota boy who was drafted in 1942 and spent some time with the 20th Armored Division before being assigned to the 80th Infantry Division's reconnaissance troop, arrived at Buchenwald on April 17, five days behind his unit. His recon jeep had broken down, and he was playing catch-up. He spent a short time in Buchenwald and managed to see some of the horrors described in the Army report. "In the hospital, I saw lampshades that were made from human skin, with tattoos, and they had every part of the human body displayed in alcohol jars. And one of the things that was really unusual was that they had cut an inmate's body in two, from the head to the seat, cut him lengthwise, and he was mounted on a glass inside a tank of alcohol. So you're looking at the cross section of the inside of a human being."

Robert Duoos at home in Cambridge,
Minnesota.

8. The "Hospital". A building were [*sic*] moribund persons were sent to die. No medicines being available, hence no therapy was possible. Typhus and tuberculosis were rampant in the camp. About half the wards in the "Hospital" were about 15' deep with one window at the outside end, by 5$\frac{1}{2}$' wide. From 6 to 9 "patients" occupied such a ward, lying cross-wise on the floor, shoulder to shoulder. Room too narrow for most of them to extend their legs. Death rate in the "Hospital" 5 per cent to 10 per cent a day.

9. Medical experiment building. Block 41 was used for medical experiments and vivisections, with prisoners as "guinea pigs." Medical scientists came from Berlin periodically to reinforce the experimental staff. In particular, new toxins and anti-toxins were tried out on prisoners. Few prisoners who entered this experimental building ever emerged alive.

Shortly after the arrival of the 120th Evac at Buchenwald, Milton Silva and several of his buddies toured the camp. Fairly quickly, they arrived at the crematory building. "Just outside the crematory there were bodies stacked up like cordwood. And I remember peeking in and seeing the incinerator doors open with remains of bodies that had started to be incinerated." But considering what he would discover next, that was a relatively modest horror.

Silva saw a staircase that led to a lower level, beneath the incinerators. "There were hooks on the wall, a meatpacking plant, where they go ahead and hook up the carcasses on the hooks and moved them along. And you could see on the walls where they would be scratching and kicking, trying to prevent themselves from being strangled by the wires that were put around their neck. I was upset that they hadn't buried these bodies. But the word came down to leave everything this way; they wanted to record this to make sure no one would ever forget

Robert Duoos of the 80th Infantry Division's recon unit came around the corner of the crematorium building at Buchenwald and was confronted with a stack of corpses the Nazis hadn't had time to burn.

that it actually happened, and they wanted to bring the brass in to see it. And the commanding general, I remember, had everybody in the town walk through.

"That was weird. People were looking at it like they'd never seen it before, and probably they never had. I think they knew what was going on, but they just didn't want to get involved. And I can recall Margaret Bourke-White, she was there from *Life* magazine, and there's a picture of her taking a picture of these people from the town, walking around, and I remember standing behind her, so that when I see that picture, I can place myself in the area when she was doing this."

The facility described by Milt Silva was given considerable attention in the Army press release two weeks hence:

```
10. The Body Disposal plant: The design of this
installation was a striking example of "German
industrial efficiency." It had a maximum disposal
capacity of about 400 bodies per 10-hour day. All
```

the bodies were reduced to boneash, thus destroying all "evidence". All gold or gold-filled teeth were extracted from bodies before incineration. This plant was entirely enclosed within a high board fence. No one except the small operating force of SS personnel was allowed even to look inside this fence, and no prisoner who passed within it (as a member of a fatigue party or any other reason) ever came out alive. Inside this fence was: (A) a large front yard on the left; (B) a small back yard on the right; (C) the incinerator building centrally located between the two yards. This building was of substantial brick construction with cement floors, one story, with a full-size 12-inch [*sic*—should be 12-foot] high basement beneath. The main floor contained an Administration office at the front end, a locker and washroom for SS personnel at the far end, and the incinerator room in the center. The latter contained, in line, two batteries of three fire-brick incinerators, each incinerator having a capacity of three bodies or a total charge of 18 bodies. Fifteen to twenty minutes were required for the incineration of a charge. The floor of each incinerator consisted of a coarse grate through which the days' accumulation of boneash was extracted at the end of operation. The fire came from a furnace room occupying the rear two-thirds of the basement. The flames being deflected downwards onto the bodies by baffleplates in the roofs of the furnace. The front end of the basement was occupied by the strangulation room.

The method of collecting bodies was as follows: Roll call was held every evening, outdoors outside the dormitory buildings. Internees were required to strip, and bring to roll call, the naked bodies of

all comrades who had died during the previous 24
hours. After roll call a motor truck drove around
the camp, picked up the bodies, and was driven into
the frontyard of the incinerator plant to await the
next day's operation. But this was not the only
source of bodies. Emaciated prisoners who "had been
around long enough" or who committed infractions of
discipline, or who "knew too much," or who refused
to be broken in mind, were arbitrarily condemned to
death. For instance in the "Little Camp" where
prisoners slept 16 on a shelf, an infraction of
discipline (and particularly an attempt to escape)
not infrequently resulted in all 16 being condemned.
Such persons were immediately marched on foot to a
small door into the fence of the backyard, at a
point immediately adjacent to the right hand front
corner of the incinerator building. This door opened
inwards until it hit a doorstop which held it in a
position parallel to the building wall—thus creating
a corridor about four feet wide and three feet deep.
At the far end was an opening about four feet by
four feet flush with the ground, the head of a
concrete shaft about 13 feet deep, the bottom floor
of which was a continuation of the concrete floor of
the room at the front of the basement. The condemned
prisoners, on being hurried and pushed through the
door in the fence, inevitably fell into this shaft
and crashed 13 feet down to the cement cellar floor.
This room on the floor at one end of which they now
found themselves, was the strangling room. As they
hit the floor they were garroted with a short double-
end noose by big SS guards, and hung on hooks along
the side wall about $6\frac{1}{2}$ feet from the floor, the row
of hooks being 45 in number. When a consignment had
been all hung up, any who were still struggling were

stunned with a wooden mallet (the mallet and a noose were being held by Commandant L'Hopital). The bodies were left on the hooks until called for by the incinerator crew. An electric elevator, with an estimated capacity of 18 bodies, ran up to the incinerator room which was directly above the strangling room. The day's quota of approximately 200 bodies was made up of from 120 to 140 prisoners who had died (mostly in the "Hospital," the "Medical Experiment Building" or the "Little Camp"), and of from 60 to 80 supplied by the strangling room.

For a period of about 10 days in March the coal supply for the incinerator ran out. Awaiting the arrival of a new supply, bodies to the number of about 1,800 were allowed to collect in the front yard, stacked up like cord-wood. To the annoyance of the SS this over-crowded yard with undisposed "evidence", and a spell of warm weather created a sanitary problem. Moreover, burial was a good deal more troublesome than incineration, and was out of the customary routine. But something had to be done, so a truck detachment and a fatigue detail of internees was organized. The bodies were loaded in the trucks and hauled out of camp. The fatigue detail dug one huge burial pit, threw the bodies into it filling it except for one end, and covered the bodies. Then the SS shot all the members of the fatigue detail, threw their bodies into the vacant end and covered them up.

Shortly afterwards a new supply of coal having been received, the process of incineration was resumed. This process was so abruptly interrupted by the arrival of U.S. armor in the area that the SS had no time to "tidy up", so that the cycle of operation could be plainly examined and understood. The previous day's quota of upwards of 120 corpses

of prisoners who had died in the camp was parked in
a truck in the front yard. The incinerator furnace
grates had not yet been cleared of unconsumed
hipbone joints and parts of skulls. In addition, the
bodies of about 40 inmates who had died since U.S.
arrival, in spite of prompt medical and ration
attention, were stacked up like cord-wood against
the wall of the yard. American surgeons stated that
the adult corpses weighed only 60 to 80 pounds,
having in practically all cases lost 50 per cent to
60 per cent of their normal weight, and also having
shrunken in height.

The initial job of the 120th Evacuation Hospital was to try to keep surviving inmates alive, which wasn't exactly its specialty. Nearly all of its doctors were surgeons skilled at caring for battlefield casualties, not specialists in internal medicine or infectious diseases. Inmates were dying at the rate of several hundred a day, and Warren Priest remembers that "it was a fairly common experience to see a man walking along feebly and then suddenly collapse and fall, and he was gone. Part of my function was to carry a stethoscope and as bodies were brought into a barracks, lined up on the floor, it was my task to determine if there were heartbeats. If there was a heartbeat, we sent them on to an aid station, and if there was no heartbeat, we had them assigned to a morgue."

How do you get through a situation like that, hour after hour, day after day? "You do what you have to do. When you're faced with a situation where you can save people, you save them. And if you find a sign of life, then that is, in a sense, a measure of hope. And you try always to bring that hope back as fully, as vibrantly as possible."

Which doesn't speak to those moments of absolute, total heartbreak that the Americans assigned to Buchenwald experienced. The children's barrack was one of the most difficult places to work, because conditions for inmates were perhaps the worst of all there. Many children were actually born in Buchenwald to women who were forced to work in the camp brothel. The children were removed from the camp on the first day the Americans arrived, and the personnel of the 120th had very little to do with them. "Very little," says Priest. But not little enough. "I was assigned the task of going through the [children's barracks] to ascertain that there were no more, of which I did. It was one of those moments that I can describe in some detail and force because it was so horrifying to walk where those kids, some four hundred to five hundred, were kept. I can't say 'housed,' because housing suggests a sense of decency and civilization.

"But they were all of them in the chronic state of diarrhea and diseases of all kinds, and the odor was indescribable. They were not using the toilets, and the bedding, the clothing scattered about, you can imagine what the odor must've been. And I kind of held my nose and walked through, checking as quickly as possible. Went down to the end of the barracks and about to turn to come back, and I saw a movement in the far corner. I took—I think it was the pole of a broom—and I poked the clothing aside, and there was a little girl in a fetal position. And I grabbed her by the ankle, pulled her out and wrapped her in my jacket, and I started running toward the aid station, because I sensed that there was life there. I heard a kind of a whimper. And I got about halfway to the aid station, and then I felt the little body collapse. She died in my arms. I think that, as much as anything, represented a kind of a turning point in my whole experience with Buchenwald, that here were young people so affected by the folly of what the elders were doing, and she was the symbolic victim, as young people are so often, of the terrible things that we do as adults. So that, I think, was as powerful a persuasion for me to focus my life on schools and education and young people as I did."

That incident and the smell of the children's barracks has stayed with Priest for more than half a century. In a memoir he wrote:

As I recall my exposure to the children's barracks, I remember the litter everywhere, piled one or two feet high in places, making access to several parts of the barracks impossible. Everything was covered with excrement, urine, vomit—blankets, clothing, shoes, jackets, underclothes—to call the scene indescribable is inadequate. The human urine, diseased flesh mixed with the wafting smells of the burning bodies from the ovens—all this is beyond the human capacity to forget.

Members of the 120th Evac not directly involved in patient care were utilized to transport the very sick out of the camp, across the road, to the SS hospital, where the more than three thousand guards had received high-quality German army medical care. It was rescue by assembly line. Milt Silva recalls that it began the first night they were in the camp, using two-and-a-half-ton trucks to take twelve to fifteen people at a time. They continued the evacuation until in excess of two thousand very sick people had been moved.

During most of that time, Silva did his best not to personally interact with the survivors. "They looked so bad—if you gave them anything, they wanted to respond by hugging you, and I was just afraid to get a disease from them." Years later, the now-retired Judge Silva went to hear author Elie Wiesel speak at the Dartmouth campus of the University of Massachusetts. Silva's eyes mist up as he tells the story. "I went over and talked to him and told him that I was with the 120th Evac Hospital, and he put his arms around me and said, 'Thank you,' and then I said, 'Let me hug you,' and I hugged him. It's redemption, because I wouldn't let those other guys hug me in the old days." And then Judge Silva cried.

First Lieutenant May Macdonald (later Horton), a registered nurse, was in charge of the contingent of nurses assigned to the 120th Evac. She was born in 1916 and recently celebrated her ninety-fourth birthday at her home in Healdsburg, California, in the wine country. She still speaks publicly about her experiences in the Army and at Buchenwald in particular. Toward the end of the war, when censorship of mail was less stringent, she sent a series of lengthy typewritten letters home. On April 28, 1945, she described the prisoners at Buchenwald and her interaction with them:

> With few exceptions, all were ragged, dirty and unkempt. Whenever we passed them in groups or singly, they saluted, smiled and in every

way tried to show how much they appreciated us. We could see that they were dazed and happy, yet so weak that they could not show their enthusiasm. Some of them spoke English and whenever we stopped to talk to one a crowd would gather around us, nodding assent to all the stories of horror he told us and every once in a while interjecting comments in their own language, so anxious were they to have someone know what had happened to them. They showed us the prison number that was tattooed on their arms and other marks where they had been wounded or tortured. I recall in particular a Jewish inmate from Vienna. He had been a lawyer and spoke excellent English. He was about 40 years old and looked 60. You could see that it was only his spirit that had kept him alive during the six years he had spent in concentration camps. He spoke intensely, eagerly, his frail body trembling with the weakness of excitement.

"I shall remember the 11th day of April 1945 as the day of my rebirth," he said. "On that day I became a free man again."

We spoke to many others. Everywhere it was the same story of brutality, long years of imprisonment, and thankfulness at their deliverance. The ex-prisoners seemed to be agreed on two points: 1) Shortly before the Americans arrived about half their number, some 25,000, were carted off by the SS and killed. 2) If the Americans had arrived a few hours later all of them would have been dead.

Her letter on that day concludes with this account:

When we told a French inmate that the civilians at Weimar claimed not to have known of Buchenwald, you could have touched off a match with the fire in his eyes.

"Not know," he croaked fiercely, "when we fell out of the box cars into which they had herded us naked in the winter to travel from France to Weimar, the people of Weimar spat on us and called us dogs." His indignation was so great that he could hardly talk. Today, no German citizens of Weimar can claim "not to know" of Buchenwald. By command of General Patton every civilian in Weimar capable of walking has been led through the camp and forcibly shown the things "they had not seen."

On April 12, before the 120th arrived at Buchenwald, CBS war correspondent Edward R. Murrow reached the camp with one of the early units. He spent the better part of a day there, wrote his report, but, because of problems accessing shortwave radio transmission facilities, was unable to broadcast to the United States until April 15. The recording of that broadcast is available online. Murrow's report is somber; it is straightforward. It uses the language of journalism. It is not especially eloquent. Murrow was holding back, and he said as much. "I pray you to believe what I have said about Buchenwald. I have reported what I saw and heard, but only parts of it. For most of it, I have no words."

The Army press release managed to find words for one component of the Buchenwald horrors Murrow refused to mention:

C. Tattooing: The April 20 Paris edition of the
Stars and Stripes carried on page two a story
regarding the use, by the SS officers of tattooed
human skin for souvenirs. The story is true in every
respect. Commandant L'Hopital stated that the wife
of one of the SS officers started the fad; that any
prisoner who happened to have extensive tattooing of
any sort on his body was brought to her; that if she
found the tattooing satisfactory the prisoner was
killed and skinned; the skin with the tattooing was
then tanned and made into souvenirs such as lamp
shades, wall pictures, bookends, etc; that about 40
examples of this artistry were found in SS officers'
quarters in the camp. This statement was confirmed by
1st Lt Walter F. Emmons, and we ourselves saw six
examples at Camp headquarters including a lampshade.

At the 120th Evac's Buchenwald facility, Warren Priest met a man in relatively good health who had been part of an underground group in Belgium. The man, whose name he never learned, had been a former superintendent of bridges and highways there, and they were able to converse in German. On the day the 120th was to leave the camp, he gave Priest a handmade model sailboat which he had taken from the home of Ilse Koch, the wife of the former commandant of Buchenwald, and urged Priest to send it home. He placed the boat in Priest's hands, then pointed to the sails and said, *"Diese—."* The man searched his mind for the proper word, but it didn't come to his lips. "And then," Priest says, "he took my hand and squeezed the skin at my wrist."

Pointing to the sails again, the Belgian said, *"Menschen, viel Menschen, tot—alles tot, alles kaput!"* People, lots of people, dead; everything dead, everything destroyed!

"Then he turned away as he began to sob," Priest recalls, his voice quivering.

Had it not been for the good that they could see they were doing, the men and women of the 120th might not have been able to cope. It's something that Warren Priest has thought about for years. "Well, it happened that the time was so brief, and we did see good things happening. You understand that we were the liberators. That expression on the faces of those men that I saw walking up the hill [the men he referred to in his poem], we saw again and again and again. That softened in so many ways the inhuman conditions that we saw."

They were also aware that the death rate had dropped from hundreds daily to a handful. He attributed it not to medical miracles but to hope. "They suddenly had hope, they suddenly had some reason for living, and it showed up in their reactions and their relationships.

"And, of course, we had by that time stabilized their eating conditions so they could feed, and we were aware that the best thing we could do was to give them whole blood, especially those more severely impacted, that they couldn't tolerate food in the stomach; they could tolerate whole blood with some nutrients from a healthy person, which we did. We had to get blood from everybody we could. I think all of us gave some blood."

Eleven days after the 120th arrived at Buchenwald, on April 26, the unit received orders to pack up and move to Cham, where they'd be available to care for inmates of some of the concentration camps, including Dachau, which would be liberated in the last two weeks of the war. Even while their medical teams were caring for Buchenwald inmates, their truck drivers, including Milt Silva, had helped move another U.S. Army hospital unit into the Nordhausen area, to care for the survivors of Dora-Mittelbau, which had been liberated by the 3rd Armored and 104th Infantry Divisions.

Upon leaving, Priest reflected on the mission of the 120th. "We had done what they had wanted us to do. We had brought a certain stabilized living condition there. The prisoners were not dying wholesale, and the medical personnel in the camp, who themselves had been prisoners, were in a position with the medicine we could provide for them to take care of their own. So there was not the need for the kind of emergency role we were playing there. We were not actually medical people; we were people who were taking care of people in terrible conditions of suffering and near death."

Priest did not exactly take the easy way out of Buchenwald. He left with what appeared to be a very heavy cold, but as soon as he got to the hospital at Cham, he was diagnosed with typhus and bedridden for a couple of weeks. Without sulfa drugs, he would have died.

```
                      SHAEF
                 INCOMING MESSAGE


                 S E C R E T
                 P R I O R I T Y


FROM: TWELFTH ARMY GROUP SIGNED BRADLEY
TO: ETOUSA
PASSED TO: SHAEF MAIN FOR ACTION


This is a paraphrase of First US Army message.


BUCHENWALD concentration camp has been cleaned up,
the sick segregated and burials completed to such
an extent that very little evidence of atrocities
remain.


This negatives any educational value of having
various groups visit this camp to secure firsthand
```

information of German atrocities. In fact, many feel
quite skeptical that previous conditions actually
existed.

Suggest that further visits to this camp be
discontinued.

9 MAY '45

CHAPTER 9

GARDELEGEN

EVEN THE GOOD GERMANS HAD BLOOD ON THEIR HANDS

APRIL 14, 1945

GARDELEGEN, GERMANY

    25 miles south of Salzwedel

    125 miles east of Berlin

    130 miles north of Buchenwald

---

14 April—Evidence of mass Nazi atrocities is found at Gardelegen.
        —from U.S. Army Center of Military History, *U.S. Army in
          World War II: Special Studies Chronology: 1941–1945*

As part of the Ninth Army's rush to the Elbe River, units of the 102nd Infantry Division moved eastward on the right flank of the 84th Division, arriving in the town of Gardelegen, just thirty miles from the Elbe, on the evening of April 14. The ancient, moat-protected town was the site of an important airfield and a German air force replacement center, and it had been heavily defended.

This is the barn on the outskirts of Gardelegen where the local gauleiter organized townsfolk, members of the Hitler Youth, and local Luftwaffe cadets to assist a handful of SS in burning to death more than a thousand Dora-Mittelbau concentration camp inmates. They had been marched away from the approaching American troops after the trains they were packed into could go no farther. The mass murder occurred with American forces little more than a day's march away.

Some time before the fighting elements of the division arrived, several crews from the 102nd Signal Company laying communication wire had been captured, along with a liaison officer between the 102nd Division headquarters and the 701st Tank Battalion, Lieutenant Emerson Hunt. He pulled off a ruse and had the German commander convinced, according to the division's history, "that American tanks within the half-hour would blast Gardelegen from the face of Germany." Not knowing exactly where his battalion was, Hunt convinced the Luftwaffe colonel to surrender the garrison to the nearest American commander.

Unfortunately, the surrender came too late. On the morning of April 15, soldiers of the 102nd discovered a still-smoking grain barn on the Isenschnibbe estate a few miles outside Gardelegen. The floor had been covered with a foot-deep layer of gasoline-soaked straw; then

*Minnesotan Ed Motzko was one of the
soldiers from the 102nd Infantry Division
charged with forcing the resentful citizens of
Gardelegen to dig graves and bury the bodies
of those who'd been murdered in the barn.*

1,016 concentration camp prisoners on a death march had been
forced inside and deliberately burned to death.

Ralph J. Baringer, of Defiance, Ohio, was about to turn twenty
when the 102nd Infantry Division arrived at the still-smoldering barn.
And that is all he remembers. "I've been trying to forget it all my life,"
he said by phone from his Ohio home.

Elton Oltjenbruns, now of Holyoke, Colorado, was a medic with
the 2nd Battalion, 405th Infantry Regiment. He remembers seeing the
bodies, but mostly he remembers "the smell, the burning flesh." By
that time in the war, he says, "I'd had all the death that I could handle."

Edmund Motzko of the 548th Anti-Aircraft Artillery Automatic Weapons Battalion, attached to the 102nd, hasn't tried to forget it. He's do-

nated the pictures he took to museums in Washington, Los Angeles, San Francisco, New York, and Gardelegen itself. The barn was torched on Friday, the thirteenth, and the Minnesota native arrived either the following day or the day after. His commanding officer told the troops, "What you're going to see—you won't believe this could ever have happened." His CO was right.

The local German officials had enlisted civilians to help dig two trenches into which bodies that hadn't been completely incinerated were to be buried. The task was supposed to have been completed before the advancing Americans arrived. It wasn't. Motzko says, "Two piles of bodies were still smoldering when I got there, on the left side of the building by two huge doors. The people had piled up by the door, trying to get out. That was bad enough, of course, but there was all these dead bodies alongside the building that did get out, and they shot them. Then I went around to the back side of the building, and that's where they had dug a long trench for burial. I didn't know, but they had already five hundred buried under where I was taking pictures."

There are several accounts of what led up to the Gardelegen massacre. Most agree that approximately 2,000 prisoners, the majority of whom wore a red badge identifying them as political prisoners rather than as Jews, had been put on two trains from the Dora-Mittelbau concentration camp. The trains, like many of the death marches leaving concentration camps at this stage of the war, were to keep the prisoners from falling into the hands of the advancing Allies.

One of the trains arrived at the town of Mieste, seventeen miles from Gardelegen, on April 9. A second train arrived at Letzlingen, just seven miles away. They were unable to go farther because Allied aircraft had bombed the tracks. According to several accounts, the Nazi Party leader of the district of Gardelegen was thirty-four-year-old Gerhard Thiele. He had told his staff and other officials that he'd been ordered by Gauleiter Rudolf Jordan that any prisoners who were caught looting or tried to escape should be immediately shot.

Eventually, the U.S. Army investigators would report that Thiele had stressed to the Volkssturm and the citizens of Gardelegen that he would do everything possible to prevent escaped prisoners from looting homes and raping women and children, as was rumored to have happened in the village of Kakerbeck, some twelve miles to the north. This appeared to be their justification for the death march from the trains to the barn on the outskirts of Gardelegen, and for the massacre. The fact that within twenty-four to thirty-six hours, all the prisoners could have been made the responsibility of the onrushing Americans, and that they demonstrably could have been confined in the huge grain storage barn without torching it, seemed not to fit into Thiele or Jordan's equation.

One report says that roughly eight hundred prisoners on that death march either died or were killed before the group arrived at its final destination. Some prisoners watched as German civilians carted cans of petrol into the barn and stockpiled ammunition, including grenades and Panzerfausts, outside the stone building. When the remaining prisoners arrived, the sick and the lame were taken from wagons and carried inside. Then the others were herded inside, where they found the cement floor covered in gasoline-soaked straw.

The doors were shut, and those on the sides were held in place with stones. A pamphlet produced by the 102nd Infantry Division says, "The barn was then deliberately set on fire by German SS and Luftwaffe soldiers and boys from the Hitler Jugend [Youth], according to the survivors. Prisoners who tried to escape from the fire were machine-gunned to death by the Germans guarding the barn, including teen-aged boys in the Hitler Jugend."

There are numerous photos showing prisoners who died as they tried to claw their way underneath the walls and doors of the barn. Captain John H. Middlebrooks, who had been a company commander in the 1st Battalion, 405th Infantry Regiment, was among the first American soldiers at the scene. "When we opened the barn door, it was a horrible sight. Bodies were ten feet high at the door where they died trying to get out. Our division commander made all the town people go to see this sight. Made them take the bodies out of the barn and later bury them."

———

What makes this a horror among horrors is that to all of the Germans involved in the Gardelegen massacre, it was clear that the Reich had lost the war. There was no way the German army could hold back the advancing Americans. Local officials knew that the town would soon be occupied by Americans. The Luftwaffe cadets knew that American aircraft ruled the skies; their mission was over. The members of the Volkssturm, who had been recruited—or conscripted—no more than six months earlier, knew that there was no future in fighting for the Fatherland. Perhaps only the Hitler Youth—whose frenzied gunfire drove the prisoners back into the fire—still believed that victory was possible.

Six to ten of the prisoners managed to survive the ordeal, and Ed Motzko was one of the GIs assigned to protect them while they were recuperating in local homes, where the citizens were forced to feed and care for them. Motzko was able to converse with several of them, including a Hungarian Jew named Bondi Geza.

"He was my interpreter for the group, and I had quite a time talking with these guys. Bondi Geza was with another fellow, and they managed to get out of the barn. I didn't fully understand how he got out of the fire or why he didn't burn, him and this other fellow, but that's when they started crawling away from the barn. [Bondi] was ahead of him a ways, and an SS trooper—or not SS but this air cadet—come along with a dog and sniffed out the guy behind him, and he was shot. And he says he just curled up and played dead, and the dog never came to him."

Motzko said the Americans had a difficult time at Gardelegen. "We knew of some other atrocities, but we didn't know they were that severe. So it was definitely an eye opener. Our feelings of the German soldiers was bad, but this was the turning point, here. There was only one good German, and that was a dead German."

No sympathy was shown by the men of the 102nd when they were ordered to round up residents of Gardelegen and force them to dig graves and bury the bodies. Motzko says, "All able-bodied men had to come out one day—they marched them out there. They had to bury each one individually in graves, and that was supposed to be the duty of that family to take care of that grave site from then on. They had to go into the barn and pick up a body and carry it to the cemetery, which was a short distance away. And by that time, the bodies were in bad shape and quite slippery, and it was quite a mess. We put up infantry-

Under the supervision of 102nd Infantry Division soldiers, German civilians were forced to exhume bodies, dig graves, and carry bodies bare-handed from near the barn where prisoners had been murdered to a newly created military cemetery.

men along the way—the Germans had to move as fast as they could—and they had their bayonets on and they prodded them along to keep them going."

There's a memorial at the site of that massacre now. It honors the memory of the dead from Belgium, France, Poland, the Soviet Union, Italy, Yugoslavia, Mexico, Holland, Czechoslovakia, and Hungary. "Also Jews," as the English translation of the pamphlet handed out at the memorial site puts it. The pamphlet says that the commanding general of the 102nd, Frank A. Keating, "ordered: for every dead prisoner a grave has to be made." Each body had to be taken from the barn, from the mass graves, and properly buried by the "men of Gardelegen and surroundings." Buried properly by the "good Germans" who had helped murder them.

CHAPTER 10

BERGEN-BELSEN

A MONSTROUS SPECTACLE SET TO MUSIC

APRIL 15, 1945
BERGEN-BELSEN, GERMANY
   60 miles south of Hamburg
   200 miles west of Berlin
   165 miles north of Buchenwald

On the same day that President Franklin Delano Roosevelt was laid to rest in Hyde Park, New York, the Bergen-Belsen concentration camp was turned over to soldiers of the British Second Army, part of the Allied Twenty-first Army Group, a combined British and Canadian unit. The surrender of the camp had been negotiated over a period of several days. On the afternoon of Sunday, April 15, the first British units to enter the camp arrived in a van with a loudspeaker accompanying elements of the 63rd Anti-Tank Regiment of the Royal Artillery. One of the soldiers on the tanks was Chaim Herzog of the Intelligence Corps. He would go on to become Israel's ambassador to the United Nations and ultimately the sixth president of the State of Israel.

Just a week earlier, there had been more than 60,000 prisoners in the camp, nearly half of them recently arrived from other Nazi facilities. From April 11 to April 14, prisoners still able to work were forced to help the SS prepare for the surrender by burying bodies in mass graves. One report says, "While two prisoner's orchestras played dancing music, 2,000 inmates dragged the corpses using strips of cloth or leather straps tied to the wrists or ankles. This monstrous spectacle went on for four days, from six in the morning until dark. Still, there were 10,000 rotting corpses remaining in the camp."

The inmates who survived to see the arrival of the Brits were suffering from starvation, typhus, and other diseases. Circumstances were so dire that at minimum, another 14,000 of them would die *after* liberation.

The day after the camp was liberated, more than a hundred ambulances driven by American civilian volunteers departed in convoy from Italy to Bergen-Belsen to assist in saving the surviving inmates.

APRIL 15, 1945
SOUTHERN PO VALLEY, ITALY, NEAR BOLOGNA

While Allied forces were pushing their way into Germany from the west, units fighting on the so-called second front in Italy were driving north against heavy German resistance. The U.S. Army's 10th Mountain Division and 88th, 91st, and 34th Infantry Divisions, as well as the 1st Armored Division, moved up the center of the country, while on the Adriatic coast to the east, Polish, Indian, New Zealand, and British soldiers of the Eighth Army were surging northward. To the west of the attacking American divisions, the Brazilian Expeditionary Force also joined the fray. Fighting in dozens of small towns was often house to house. Allied air support was intense: on the afternoon of April 15, more than 760 heavy bombers of the Mediterranean Allied Strategic Air Force attacked enemy defenses around Bologna, as an additional 200 medium bombers and 120 fighter-bombers of the XXII Tactical Air Command hit targets in the Monte Sole area and the Reno valley.

Not far away, prepared for orders to move out, were several dozen civilian volunteers of the American Field Service (AFS) and their brand-new four-wheel-drive Dodge ambulances. A brief bit of history: in 1914, with World War I under way, American students in Paris organized the AFS to drive troops to the front in taxicabs. On the return trips, they picked up wounded and brought them back to hospitals. After the siege of Paris was over, the students decided that they wanted to continue what they'd been doing and got their parents to back them financially. They bought ambulances that were made by the Ford Motor Company in southern France and continued to volunteer until the war ended. In World War II, Americans who desperately wanted to serve but had been rejected by the U.S. armed forces volunteered with the AFS and, like their predecessors, drove ambulances in combat zones.

High blood pressure kept Texas-born Melvin Waters out of the Army, but he found his way into combat with the AFS. "We had several people like myself with high blood pressure. Rollins had a curvature of the spine. One boy that I was close to had an arm that was sort of withered—he'd been a bomber copilot in the air force and had been injured in a crash. 'Bama had a punctured eardrum. A lot of them were minor things you couldn't tell, and then some of them were apparent what was wrong with the person."

There were also a significant number of homosexuals in the AFS. These were men the Army wouldn't take but the AFS did. Wounded soldiers never seemed to care about the sexual preference of the guy who was saving their lives by driving an ambulance through enemy fire.

Waters had been a sixteen-year-old senior in high school when the war broke out. He'd wanted to join the Navy immediately, but his mother said she wouldn't sign the necessary papers—he'd have to wait until he was eighteen and drafted. Waters kept nagging, however, and she relented, allowing him to join the Marine Corps reserve at age seventeen. When he finally got called to active duty, he flunked his physical. It was just a couple of months before D-Day when he saw an ad in the local paper that read, "WANTED—AMBULANCE DRIVERS for immediate deployment overseas."

Waters signed up and was sent to a dormitory on Fifty-first Street in New York City for a two-month-long orientation period. He recalls that most of the training dealt with what *not* to do in combat: "Don't touch dead bodies, don't pick up any souvenirs, and don't walk anywhere that hasn't been cleared of mines. I was dumb enough not to worry about being injured or crippled for the rest of my life."

When he completed training, Waters received orders to go to Italy to serve with the British Eighth Army. His pay was $20 a month. By March he had joined the unit and was quickly put to work ferrying wounded soldiers down tortuous Apennine mountain roads to field hospitals. He'd been with his unit for only about six weeks when in mid-April, the lieutenant in charge came into their dayroom and said, "I've got an announcement to make. Company 567 is leaving Italy for an assignment. It's secret. We can't tell you where they're going, and they want ten volunteers to go with them." Eleven men volunteered. Waters and one of his friends were at the bottom of the seniority list. Both wanted badly to go, so the lieutenant had them cut a deck of cards. Waters drew a trey; his buddy drew a deuce. That's when the officer said that Waters had one hour to get his gear together—they were leaving that night.

Waters and the others went by truck to a base on the Arno River, where they met up with Company 567. The unit had been chosen for this mission because it had received 250 new ambulances the previous Christmas. Each one could carry two stretchers on the floor and two hanging, or it could accommodate eight to ten men sitting on pull-down seats. Ultimately, about 150 ambulances convoyed through Florence, past Pisa, and then to one of the ports on Italy's west coast. The first night, half the group was loaded on board an LST and sailed for Marseilles. Waters was in the second group, departing the next night. He recalls arriving in time to listen to President Harry S Truman deliver a relatively brief State of the Union Address to a joint session of Congress at around 6 P.M. local time on April 16, a day after FDR was laid to rest.

The next morning, the AFS ambulance convoy left Marseilles

heading north. It would be more than a week before they reached their ultimate destination: Bergen-Belsen.

APRIL 15, 1945
WITH COMPANY K, 395TH INFANTRY REGIMENT,
99TH INFANTRY DIVISION
Near Iserlohn, Germany

Roger Maurice got his Purple Heart from General Patton, but he doesn't remember the occasion. The nurses at the Second Evacuation Hospital told him about the general's visit after he woke up following surgery to deal with a bullet wound that entered the front of his left shoulder and came out his back. It happened just a week before VE Day, before the end of the war in Europe, and just a couple of weeks after his nineteenth birthday.

Maurice had joined the 99th Infantry Division as a replacement around the first of March, just a week before it crossed the famous Remagen bridge. He'd dropped out of high school in Leominster, Massachusetts, twenty miles north of Worcester, to help his family—there were five children—survive during the Great Depression. He was working as a fireman, tending coal-fired furnaces, when President Roosevelt sent him his invitation to join the Army.

In 1944, the Army was still putting together complete combat divisions as well as training thousands of replacements to ship to Europe. Maurice had completed basic training and received advanced training in communications, as a field lineman and switchboard operator, when he and hundreds of other troops at Camp Crowder, Missouri, were told that they'd volunteered for the infantry. They were shipped to Camp Livingston, Louisiana, for advanced infantry training and then sent to Europe on a seven-day cruise aboard the *Queen Mary* to Southampton. From there it was a boat ride to Le Havre, railroad boxcars to a point near the Belgian-German border near Liège, then the back end of a deuce and a half to Remagen.

The division was just finishing operations related to what came to be called the Ruhr Pocket and was near Iserlohn when it came across a barbed-wire-enclosed prison camp. Maurice is not sure exactly where it was, and he doesn't know its name, but the memory of it has stuck with him for more than six decades.

When they arrived at the camp, the German guards were fleeing across an open field. There was gunfire, and some of the guards were captured, while others got away. But the focus of the Americans quickly turned to the inmates of the camp.

"We came to this concentration camp, and the officers told us to guard the outside and not let the prisoners go, 'cause they wanted a firsthand look at them. We tried to keep 'em in, but some of them were getting out, whether we wanted to or not, and I was too civilized to kill a man that was starving. So the thing is, some of them got out and they went down to the village. And they brought back a hundred-pound— some potatoes in a cloth bag. And I helped them get the cloth bag into the camp, and some of them prisoners were so hungry that they were reaching through the wire and getting blades of grass to eat. And then another one, another prisoner came back, and he had a live sheep on his shoulders. So I helped him get the sheep into the camp, and that was, that was the end of the man I seen."

His squad stayed at the camp for no more than three or four hours and then moved on, leaving it to follow-on units to care for the inmates. At noon the following day, the town of Iserlohn surrendered. At Hemer, on April 17, the division liberated more than 20,000 Russian POWs kept in horrible conditions at a huge camp.

And then the 99th was sent to Bavaria, where it fell under the command of Patton's Third Army, entering combat on April 21 near Schwabach, with Salzburg, Austria, as its objective. The route would take the 99th through Munich and an area filled with subcamps of Dachau.

APRIL 21, 1945

HERSBRUCK, GERMANY

18 miles east of Nuremberg

110 miles north of Munich

Leo Serian tried to get into the war when he was seventeen, but his father wouldn't sign the papers, so he didn't put on the uniform until the end of 1943. By the time he finished basic training and got bounced around a bit, it was already late January 1945 and he found himself with the 65th Infantry Division at Camp Lucky Strike just outside Le Havre. The Battle of the Bulge was over, and Leo's outfit was high on gung ho and wondering if they'd get their chance to fight the Nazis. It wasn't until March, when they arrived at the Franco-German border, that they heard the distant sound of cannons.

Sixty-eight years after the event, Leo can still remember his first combat: "All of us were gung ho, but then as soon as we entered combat, actually, it was horrifying, because here men that we trained with and that we'd come to love as comrades, we saw them getting killed and wounded all around us, and nothing happened to me. Our company was headed towards a larger force, to engage in battle, and then we got word that on the way, there's a small town with a handful of Germans, and to wipe 'em out and then go on your way. Well, what a surprise we were in for; when we got there to that town, on the road in front of the town, we noticed that there were three American airplanes [flying] in a circular fashion. They had come down and machine-gunned the town, then go around and rocket the town, shoot rockets, and then go around and drop bombs. The three airplanes did that for about forty-five minutes or an hour, and then after they left, we got the order to spread out and to advance. No sooner than we got the order to advance, we were sprayed with machine-gun fire; we weren't very gung ho at that moment."

Less than two months later, now experienced combat veterans, his outfit experienced a very different kind of horror. They were walking down a road when, several hundred feet in front of them, two large gates opened wide. "Two German trucks pulled out, and a handful of

Private Leo Serian was with elements of the 65th Infantry Division when it discovered Hersbruck, a subcamp of Flossenbürg. More than six decades later, the image of a huge, unburned pyre of bodies is never far from his mind's eye.

Germans jumped in and fled. It was toward the end of the war, many thousands of Germans were either fleeing or surrendering. This handful decided to flee rather than confront us, because we were a couple of hundred men.

"We were on foot, and they were in trucks. We couldn't go after them. They disappeared before we could even raise our rifles. And then, slowly, we approached those open gates. We walked in, and the sight before our eyes caused us to freeze, like we almost were in a coma. To our left on the ground were dozens of bodies, like twigs that fell off from a tree. And most of them were dead. Some came crawling towards us."

Nineteen-year-old Private Serian and his buddies had known virtually nothing about concentration camps. Without warning, they'd walked into one.

"There was a pyre of human bodies about maybe eight feet high. They all appeared to be dead, but there could have been some alive on the verge of death. They didn't have any furnaces there to burn bodies, so I'm assuming they were going to just throw gasoline on them.

"Some came walking towards us, haltingly, and some came crawling on their hands and knees. You could almost see their bones protruding out of their bodies and wondered how they still remained alive. Some of them were completely nude. When they approached us, we didn't know what to say to them. Some of them spoke, but we didn't understand. Some embraced us and clung to us, standing and on their knees."

The camp they'd discovered was Hersbruck, one of seventy-four subcamps of Flossenbürg, later described by the Third U.S. Army Judge Advocate Section, War Crimes Branch, as "one of the worst . . . a factory dealing in death." On Easter Sunday, just three weeks before the Americans arrived, the Nazis had marched the prisoners still able to walk out of Hersbruck to Dachau, a hundred miles away. The survivors that Serian's unit found were the ones too debilitated to walk.

The image of the unburned pyre of bodies is never far from Leo Serian's mind's eye. In 1994, just prior to the fiftieth anniversary of the end of the war, with the country experiencing renewed interest in what World War II veterans had to say, Serian wrote to the U.S. Army Center of Military History. He wanted to know the name of the camp he'd helped liberate. After learning that it was Hersbruck, he got in touch with the U.S. Holocaust Memorial Museum and asked for help in finding survivors. Eventually he received a list of twenty-seven people and wrote to them; he's heard back from about a dozen who live in the United States, Israel, Prague, the Czech Republic, and South America. Each described daily life in Hersbruck; some told of the death marches to Dachau and beyond.

And Serian, who is motivated not only by his own family's tragedy during the Armenian genocide but by disgust with the Holocaust deniers who continually pop up to spread their lies, continues to speak often as a personal witness of the Holocaust.

CHAPTER 11

I START CRYING AND
I CAN'T TALK ANYMORE

APRIL 22, 1945

Near Rötz, Germany

75 miles east of Nuremberg

It was late on the night of April 22, and most of the remaining 169 American POWs from Berga were bedded down in a barn near the village of Rötz when word went from survivor to survivor: "We can't continue on this way." Morton Brooks says they reached a consensus: "When morning comes, we don't move."

Hours later, as the sun was rising, the guards began yelling, *"Heraus, heraus!"* (Get out!)

Brooks says no one moved. "We stayed still. And then we heard some shots, and the guards took off. We waited about ten minutes, fifteen minutes, and one of the fellows looked out the back end of the barn and saw the 11th Armored coming down the road. Tanks, trucks, whatever. And when they said 'Americans!' the door back there opened up, and we went down this hill and they couldn't believe who we were, and they pulled us up onto the tanks and trucks and the group went on to their destination."

Tony Acevedo, the former medic, recalls one of their German guards handing his rifle to an American and saying, "I am your prisoner now." He says the POWs immediately recognized the American tanks, but there was a tense moment when the American liberators couldn't comprehend what—who, actually—they were seeing. Acevedo says that moment didn't last long, and a tanker grabbed him by one arm and swung him up onto the tank as though he weighed nothing. Now in his eighties, when talking about the experience, Tony still has to pause a moment to grieve for the men he had tried to save in Berga and Stalag IX-B and couldn't. It's the curse of the medics in all our wars: they never forgive themselves for the men they weren't able to save.

Brooks, who'd been a POW and slave laborer for more than three months, says the liberators tried to give them food and water. "I remember I had a K ration—a cheese thing that was in this K ration, and I tried to eat it and I couldn't get it into my mouth, really. I was so hungry, and yet I couldn't eat. Which was lucky. Some guys ate and then became violently ill."

The 11th Armored Division brought them to the city of Cham, where they took over a building and quickly converted it into an emergency hospital. The POWs were deloused with DDT, put on stretchers, and given medical care. Brooks says that some Red Cross people came through with toothpaste and toothbrushes—he sighs, then laughs as he recalls the moment—"I mean, it was just so inappropriate to what our needs were."

Norman Fellman was with a different group of Berga prisoners on the death march. His memory of liberation two days earlier, on April 20, begins with lying at the side of the road, waiting to be lifted into the vegetable cart and pushed or pulled down the road. But he suddenly realized that the German guards had disappeared. "Next thing I know a tank comes over the hill, and there's a bunch of dirty, scruffy guys. They were members of the 90th Division, and they were the best-looking guys I ever saw." His liberators were most likely members of Company D of the 712th Armored Battalion, attached to the 90th Infantry Division.

It was only when he saw the reaction of the GIs on the tanks that he got a sense of how bad off he really was. "I never realized how bad we looked until I saw other people's faces when they saw us for the first time." When he was rescued, Fellman had cellulitis, a precursor of gangrene, in one leg. The problem had originated with bites from lice that had become infected at Berga. When he got to a U.S. Army field hospital, they weighed him: he was down to 86 pounds. He knew that death hadn't been that remote a possibility. "I don't know whether any of us that were in the carts—or even on the road—would've lived another week."

Mort Brooks wasn't able to get word to his family that he'd survived captivity until he arrived at a field hospital near Manchester, England. Brooks had an epiphany during his recovery there. "They saw I couldn't eat, and they started me on a liquid kind of diet, almost like milk shakes, that I could sip out of a straw. I would get food, and I would gag. And after a while, I was looking at myself in the mirror, and I said, 'You gotta do something about this. You've got to control it,' and gradually it improved. I learned what the power of thought was; maybe that's why I became interested in psychology. I could determine that I had to do something about that situation, and I would look in the mirror and say, 'Look, just calm down. And get over the gagging,' and I would talk to myself, essentially, and say that I had to improve, that this was not a tolerable situation. And gradually it improved."

Brooks spent about six weeks in the hospital and was then sent to London, where he and other former POWs were interrogated with an eye toward future prosecution of German war criminals. The commandant and assistant commandant of Berga were eventually tried, found guilty, and sentenced to death. The SS commander, Hans Kasten, was ultimately hanged by Communist authorities in 1952. His deputy, Erwin Metz, who had directly caused the death of many of the prisoners at Berga and had continued to cause deaths on the long march, was sentenced to death in 1946. The sentence was commuted, and he was released eight years later. To this day Brooks regrets that he was never called to testify against them formally at Nuremberg.

Shortly after his liberation, Norman Fellman was flown from a field hospital to Paris, where his leg required extensive treatment. But when he got to the hospital, a makeshift facility in a converted school, there were no rooms. "Casualties were coming in so damned fast, and the prison camps were beginning to empty out, the hospitals were just overflowing. They had me in a bed out in the hall, and people would come by, and kids would look at me and cry. So I felt like a freak.

"The care couldn't have been better, and the empathy was fantastic. They couldn't do enough for me. I lay in the bed, and I listened to a doctor, a lieutenant, and a chief medical officer, a colonel, and they were having an argument. The colonel is saying, 'That leg's gotta come off; we are loaded with people. We gotta move this man along.' And the lieutenant says, 'I think we can save the leg. We've got this new medication, it's working marvels. I'd like to try it.' And don't you know, the colonel finally decided, he said, 'I'll give you two days. If we don't see remarkable improvement, that leg comes off.' And he's talking about penicillin. And they gave me shots around the clock, every two hours. They had no idea how to dose it. There was twenty thousand units every two hours. You feel sorry for the poor sonofabitch who had to give me a shot, because all I had was bone. I had no fat. So he gave me a shot like you'd give it to a dog. He'd pick up the skin, which was loose, and you shot it under the skin. And then penicillin washes. I had these lice-bite holes in my ankle, and there were maybe six or eight of them going up my ankle and down into the foot. And you could take a medical probe and actually go from one hole to the other, like tunnels in my leg. And they would wash me—have the liquid penicillin go through, and in the end of two days' time, you could actually see the healing begin. It was a miracle, there's no question about it."

At the time, Fellman was indifferent to the discussions about his leg. He just wanted to sleep. "I was a bystander; I was divorced from the person who they were talking about. They were talking about cutting off my leg. They may as well been talking about squashing a fly. It just didn't matter to me. I just wanted to be left alone. I kept thinking to myself, Goddammit, go argue somewhere else."

A few days later, when it was clear that his leg was going to be saved, Fellman became interested in food. He remembers it as though it were yesterday. "They wanted me to have anything I wanted to eat. I told them I wanted eggs, and they said, 'How do you want them fixed?' I said, 'I want them every way you can fix one,' and I think they served me a dozen eggs. Two fried, two over easy, you know, two boiled, whatnot. And I ate them, every damned one of them. And about thirty minutes later I threw every one up. But it was good going down, I gotta tell you."

After about a month in the hospital, Fellman was put aboard a DC-3 and flown from Paris to Lisbon, then to the Azores, ultimately landing at Roosevelt Field on Long Island. Morton Brooks came home on the *Queen Mary*, sailing from Scotland to New York harbor. He still thinks one of the most exciting things he's ever seen was the Statue of Liberty as the ship came in. Fireboats were spraying water, horns were blaring, and a band on one of the boats greeted the former prisoners of war, the former inmates of a Nazi slave-labor camp, with one of the most popular songs of that year, "Don't Fence Me In."*

APRIL 22, 1945

SACHSENHAUSEN CONCENTRATION CAMP

ORANIENBURG, GERMANY

21 miles north of Berlin

Bernhard "Ben" Storch is an American, a veteran, a witness to the Holocaust, and a past state commander of the New York Jewish War Veterans. He saw things that no other American saw during World War II. That's because during the war, Storch was a Polish citizen, fighting first as part of the Polish army as a mortarman and then as an artillery sergeant, attached to the White Russian Front. As part of the Soviet forces moving west, Storch's unit was among the first at several of the Nazis' worst death camps, but Sachsenhausen was the only one liberated by his unit where there were still live prisoners to be saved.

---

* For the complete story of Berga and the Americans who were imprisoned there, read *Soldiers and Slaves: American POWs Trapped by the Nazis' Final Gamble* by Roger Cohen (Knopf, 2005) and *Given Up for Dead: American GIs in the Nazi Concentration Camp at Berga* by Flint Whitlock (Westview Press, 2005).

Storch was born in 1922 in the small town of Chorzów, Poland, not far from Katowice in Upper Silesia. His father had served in the Russian army from 1912 to 1919. When the Germans invaded Poland at the start of the Second World War, his family fled east, to Russia. And the Russians promptly sent them to Siberia.

In the spring of 1943, because he had to find some way to help support the family, he joined the army and was assigned to carry the tube in a three-man 82mm mortar squad. Their first engagement against the German army was on October 12. His unit was equipped with Studebaker and Buick trucks provided by the American Lend-Lease Plan.

Throughout the war, Storch offered morning Jewish prayers, laying tefillin, the small, square black leather boxes, one on the forehead, the other on the upper left arm and held in place by leather straps, that contain a handwritten copy of the Sh'ma, the sacred prayer that begins, "Hear, O Israel, the Lord is our God. The Lord is One." Despite his belief that anti-Semitism flows in the blood of the Polish people, he says it was not a problem in the Polish army.

By January 1945, there were two Polish divisions fighting alongside the Russians. In June, they'd pushed the Germans in their sector all the way back to the Polish border. A month later, they discovered their first death camp, Sobibor. Storch says, "We would have never found it, but there was this one guy telling us, 'Down there, in the forest, there is a camp. Follow the railroad track about five miles.' There was a railroad stop named Sobibor. The guy had simply said they were killing Jews there and Russian soldiers." Storch says when they got to the camp, there was nothing but an empty field, where they discovered mass graves and thousands of saplings that the Germans had planted to hide the evidence. The camp had operated for eighteen months, until an uprising in October 1943, when the inmates had been liquidated and the camp razed. In that short time, an estimated 250,000 people, the majority of them Jews, were murdered with carbon monoxide generated by a diesel engine in six gas chambers with a total capacity of 1,200 at a time. It was at Sobibor that the Jews of the Vilna, Minsk, and Lida ghettoes were killed. The camp had no crematoria; victims were buried in pits; some were ultimately burned.

Storch says his men were not quite sure what they were seeing at Sobibor. "We had no idea then about concentration camps."

Their next objective was Lublin, about sixty miles to the southeast, which they took on July 23, 1944, in what he says was a horrible massacre. About two miles outside the city they discovered the death camp called Majdanek. Storch was now a sergeant in an artillery unit, traveling in a truck towing a 122mm howitzer. When they arrived at the camp, they simply drove in. "This camp was complete. The doors were not even locked, we didn't have to break in anything. We went in and saw the gas chambers. We had no idea what it is. We thought it was a factory. The gas chambers didn't look like anything special. There were about six of them; they had benches on the side but no marks, not even any blood on the floor. There was a skylight in the ceiling for the SS guys to check and see if the people were already dead. The sign said BATH DISINFECTION — FOR SANITARY REASONS. They had steel doors, showerheads. No lights; no electricity. We walked into them."

Storch and his men then walked about a quarter mile down the road, where they discovered six crematoria, and the horror began to sink in. "We saw some parts of human bodies, bones. We started to think about it, said, 'It couldn't be.' But in Poland, the Catholics don't cremate people. We said, 'What the hell is going on here?' Finally someone from the outside showed up, and he told us that this is a death camp. Nobody had told us to be prepared for it. At that point I was twenty years old." Storch has had this conversation with hundreds of American veterans of World War II who were blindsided by their own discovery of Nazi death camps in the spring of 1945. "The [U.S.] government knew about [the death camps liberated by the Russian army]. That was 1944. Those two camps were liberated, Sobibor and Majdanek, in 1944." Treblinka was also liberated in 1944; Auschwitz was taken by the Russians in January 1945.

By the time Storch got to Majdanek, his outfit had seen death on a wholesale scale, but they still had the capacity to be horrified. "It was terrible. You had the ovens, you had the bones, and you go over to the side and you have this huge mountain of ash, [but] you don't think that it is ash. One thing that struck me is that when I was walking through the grounds—our shoes were black shoes—all of a sudden the shoes became white. It was white, light grayish white. And for some reason we couldn't figure out what it is; we were told later. The wind was blowing, it was fertilizing the fields there. The grass was so gorgeous, fertilized with bone meal. The commandant had a beautiful garden there.

"Going back to the other side, we saw the magazines, the storage rooms. First came the suitcases; they had the names on it. Then they had utensils, little pots, whatever, that the people had been told to bring. Little children, my God, those little dolls. We were pretty hard soldiers to that point; we knew what's going on. Every one of them— we were only nine Jewish guys in our battery, the battery consisted of eighty-eight people—it was absolutely horrible. Then they had the clothing, men's and ladies', then they had the shoes, sorted out neatly, men's, women's, and children's. They had eyeglasses." At this point Ben Storch pauses briefly, then whispers, "Thousands of pairs. The room with the shoes is huge, a warehouse. In my head and the other guy's head, my God, I hope my brother's shoes is not there, my mother's dress is not there, my grandmother's dress, and my grandfather and my uncles and my aunts."

Storch spent about forty-five minutes in Majdanek. He says there was "no time to think. You went here and here, you made a U-turn, and go out."

Was there time to cry? "Oh, yeah. We did. I said Kaddish. The gentile guys kneeled on the floor and prayed. On that big pile of ash, that's where we said our prayers. Yeah, the tears came to my eyes. I saw so many grave sites in Russia, [yet] that's the first time in my life during the war I cried."

At Majdanek there were no survivors. The only people they discovered were six SS who were hiding in one of the barracks. They learned from the prisoners that as the Russian army was approaching, the Nazis had sent all the concentration camp prisoners to Auschwitz, where some of them survived. Storch says, "The mentality was that 'we have to move these people somewhere else to kill them.' All those people in Auschwitz were to have been killed, but they couldn't do it. So they moved them to Sachsenhausen, to Buchenwald, to Bergen-Belsen, to Austria, to Czechoslovakian camps."

Storch recalls that he and the soldiers he was with were perplexed on their march west by the strange priorities of the German high command. "German soldiers fell in our hands because they didn't have any transportation. The transportation was strictly designed for the Jews; the Jews is the priority. Now, it's mind-boggling. Usually you'd try to save your people first. But no, for the Nazis, that was the main subject: the Jews have to be destroyed."

Leaving Majdanek, the Russians and Poles headed a hundred miles northwest, winding up in August 1944 in a town called Praga Warszawa on the right bank of the Vistula River, opposite the Polish capital city. There they paused because their supply lines were overextended, and also to deal with casualties. Ultimately, the battle for Warsaw ended on September 17, when they crossed the river. The city had been demolished.

They moved on, heading northwest about 150 miles to the town of Chelmno. In late 1941, it became the first city in Poland where Jews were systematically murdered. They were taken to a church, where they were forced to undress, and then loaded into sealed trucks, the so-called gas vans. Seventy-five Jews were killed in each load by the carbon monoxide gas piped into the van from the truck's exhaust. Storch says they could find nothing in Chelmno but graves. There were no crematoria; 350,000 dead Jews had been buried; then they were dug up, burned, and buried again.

They moved on to Zlotów, about seventy-five miles south of the Baltic, the first German city they took. (Today Zlotów is well inside the Polish borders.) The fighting grew ever more intense, with tank battles and Storch's artillery unit laying down barrages against Panzer brigades as they moved southwest to Paulsdorf, just sixty miles east of Dresden. At that point, American and Russian forces were separated by less than fifty miles.

On April 15, 1945, an announcement was made that the Russians and Poles would launch a new offensive in the middle of the night. "Forty thousand artillery cannons were firing; night was like day, honest to God," Storch remembers. "By seven o'clock, my battery was across the Oder River on pontoons, no bridges." They were heading north to capture Berlin, where Hitler remained in his bunker.

On April 20, in the face of the advance of the Soviet Forty-seventh Army, SS guards began the evacuation of some 33,000 prisoners from the Sachsenhausen concentration camp, just twenty-one miles north of Berlin. The plan was to march them north to the Baltic in groups of four hundred and load them onto ships, which would then be sunk.

Two days later, Storch's unit liberated a section of Sachsenhausen. "It's the first time we liberated human beings—they hardly could walk. The section I came across were mostly women. Everybody was crying. They didn't know who we were; our uniforms were different than the Russian uniforms or the German uniforms. All they know is we were soldiers.

"There was no resistance at all; we didn't have to break nothing, just open up the door. We caught two SS people; two of my guys just shot 'em. It was too horrible to see, because when we got there, people were still hanging on the hooks. In the camp, on the walls, in view. Hanging by their throats. I had no idea who they were. Just men, not naked. We would not remove them; can't put our hands on it, it's not our mission. Couple bodies laying which were shot."

He says most of the women were Hungarians who spoke some German. They were in bad condition and crying uncontrollably. The women were shabbily dressed; nobody had any hair, which made it hard to recognize people. A quick tour turned up a huge infirmary, but people were still dying. They weren't buried but processed in the two ovens the soldiers found.

The experience at Sachsenhausen was unique for Storch and his men. Until then, they'd liberated civilians, who'd realized they were free and could go home. "But all of a sudden you come to a camp. Those people have absolutely nothing in their pocket—not even a pocket. No hope at all. Absolutely no idea if anyone from their families is alive. It's very traumatic. And it's traumatic for people like us to see that finally we did something for people which had absolutely no power of doing anything, because their dignity was taken away from them. There was nothing. The only thing we left with those people, which is very important, is hope. You are now safe. You will have all the care, you will get all the clothes you need, all the food you need, all the medication. And they did. Even the same day we left, they did. That was a very, very strong moment for me, and for the other guys."

It took the Russian army twelve days to take Berlin. Storch's artillery unit fired its cannon from April 30 to the middle of the night on May 2, when they fired the last salvo. A week later, his division packed up and left by train for Poland, to a town fifty miles from Warsaw. He was discharged from the Army in September 1945. On November 18, in Katowice, he married Ruth, whom he'd known as a child. They both saw Jews who managed to survive the war killed by Polish citizens and knew they would not stay in Poland.

APRIL 23, 1945 (NINE DAYS BEFORE THE RUSSIANS TOOK BERLIN)
NEAR THE FLOSSENBÜRG CONCENTRATION CAMP
70 miles east-northeast of Nuremberg
140 miles north of Munich

In U.S. Third Army's XII Corps area, CCB and CCA of the 11th Armored Division drive quickly from Naab River to Cham, which CCB clears with ease, completing current mission of division. Roads in division zone are clogged with thousands of prisoners and slave laborers . . . 358th Infantry, 90th Division, overruns Flossenburg—where large concentration camp and an aircraft factory are secured—and Waldthurn.

—from U.S. Army Center of Military History, *U.S. Army in World War II: Special Studies Chronology: 1941–1945*

PFC Tarmo Holma had come to the United States from Finland as a child. He was drafted from his hometown of Milton, Massachusetts, and ultimately assigned to the tank platoon of Headquarters Company, 41st Tank Battalion, of the 11th Armored Division. On April 23, Holma was sitting behind his .50-caliber machine gun, scanning the road ahead of the tank convoy through binoculars, when he saw movement in the distance. "I could see this activity on the road, and the road was filled with people. I assumed they were soldiers, and

PFC Tarmo Holma was manning a .50-caliber
machine gun on one of the 11th Armored
Division tanks when it came upon the tail end of
an SS death march of prisoners from
Flossenbürg to the killing camp at Mauthausen.

I said to my commanding officer, 'The whole German army has to be
out there waiting for us.' "

And his CO responded, "No, we're arriving at one of the concentration camps." Until that moment he had heard only vague descriptions of the Nazi death camps.

They were traveling in single file on a beautiful spring day down the
narrow road near Flossenbürg, which, along with Buchenwald, Sachsenhausen, and Dachau, was one of the original concentration camps
inside Germany. What they'd happened upon was the last throes of a
death march that was to take the inmates to the killing camp at Mauthausen, Austria, about 190 miles to the southeast. By the time the
tanks arrived at Flossenbürg, all the SS guards had either run away or
had been killed by the prisoners. "We were trying to proceed on the
dirt road to continue the combat mission that we were on—to follow
the remnants of the German army. But we could hardly move. Where

they [the prisoners] were still coming out of the camp onto the main road, we were just standing still. They were so excited; they appeared to be dying as they ran out to greet us.

"I saw them fall down and not [get up]—I assumed they were dying because they were walking skeletons with a little skin on them." His voice breaks, and he begins to cry, "It bothers me to this day. I'm surprised I can talk this much about it; usually, I start crying and I can't talk anymore.

"They were just waving; they appeared to be so glad to see us. I don't remember hearing any language, because I'm sitting on top of the tank, I'm eight feet high above their heads. We were going to give them our rations, especially the K rations, they were very good. Because I'm the radio operator, too, I got the message right away: 'Don't feed the prisoners, they can't stand that kind of food that we have.' They said people coming behind us will take care of their health problems. So we had to keep going as best we could, very slowly."

Postwar research determined that approximately 14,000 prisoners had been driven from the camp by the SS in the days preceding the arrival of the Americans; in just three days, more than 4,000 of them died or were killed by the SS. Records show that more than 73,000 prisoners died in the Flossenbürg camp system.

After passing through miles upon miles of recently freed prisoners, the 11th Armored continued pushing eastward, becoming the first unit to arrive in Austria. Just two weeks after their encounter with Flossenbürg, the unit would come to an even worse hellhole, the Gusen-Mauthausen camp complex.

APRIL 25, 1945
BERGEN-BELSEN, GERMANY
    60 miles south of Hamburg
    200 miles west of Berlin

After leaving Marseilles on April 16, the convoy of 150 American Field Service ambulances plus a handful of accompanying support vehicles headed north. They camped overnight about twenty

Melvin Waters was deemed unfit to be drafted, but he still wanted to serve in the war. He became a volunteer combat ambulance driver with the American Field Service and eventually helped British and Canadian forces evacuate the survivors of the Bergen-Belsen death camp.

miles from Paris, continuing the next day into southwestern Belgium, where they stayed for four days at the town of Waregem. Then they headed north through Brussels and into southern Holland to Eindhoven, where they turned east and drove about twenty miles to a vacant seminary.

The convoy was split into three platoons, and the next morning Melvin Waters's group of about forty ambulances with sixty drivers was told to load up equipment and personnel from the British 9th General Hospital. They drove into Germany, seeing destruction on a massive scale for the first time. Waters recalls going through a town where, from one end to the other, there wasn't anything but rubble and bricks pushed off the road by bulldozers. They crossed the Rhine River on a pontoon bridge, traversed the northern part of the Siegfried Line, and, after two days of zigzagging to miss pockets of German troops, arrived at Bergen-Belsen in the afternoon.

Waters can still recall the moment. "As we came out of this forest, a little bend, all of a sudden the ambulances in front of us slowed to a crawl. And then, as we got into the opening, we could see the prison or the concentration camp over to our left, and the front gates were open, and people were just milling around. We were just looking at it with our mouths open. We didn't know it at the time, but we were looking at the women's section. They were just skeletons."

The convoy went on, passing an SS barracks and continuing about a mile and a half to the edge of a forest, where they made camp. They'd stay in this location for the next seven weeks. Initially, they slept in the ambulances but eventually they opted for tents after becoming concerned about the diseases and vermin carried by the people they were transporting.

The sheer numbers of inmates inside the camp were staggering. At liberation on April 15, the census was set at approximately 60,000. About 7,000 Jewish prisoners whom SS Reichsführer Heinrich Himmler thought he could use in negotiations with the Allies had been evacuated from the camp by train before the British took over.

Waters's first day inside the camp was eye-opening. "We had to drive to the north end of the camp and then down and out the front gate. And we would drive right by a big hole that had been dug, and what was taking place was that flatbed trucks were being used, and they were going through the camp picking up corpses and bringing them up to this big common grave. They were putting one thousand to two thousand people in these graves. They had Germans, either prisoners of war or people they conscripted from some of the nearby towns, down there stacking these bodies. Some of the bodies, you'd look at them, and the eyes would be open and they were looking, just staring."

In those early days after liberation, more than five hundred prisoners a day were dying. Their bodies, as well as the ten thousand that had been piled around the camp, were buried in the mass graves. Photos distributed at the time showed British army soldiers using bulldozers because it was the most efficient way to move large quantities of bodies quickly. All told, about 13,000 inmates died after the camp was liberated, many of typhus, which was at epidemic levels.

How does one erase those images from one's memory?

Waters says he wasn't as badly affected by the horrors as some of his coworkers. He attributes this to some of the combat time he'd had in Italy, where he'd picked up a reputation. "I got criticized when I was in Italy for being sort of hard-hearted, for not being friendly to the patients. And I said, 'I'm getting them down the damned mountain, don't I? What else can I do? I'm getting the job done.' And they said, 'Well, you can talk to them and offer them cigarettes and do this and that.' And I guess that I just had hardened myself and that's the way I got by. I don't mean [the sights in Bergen-Belsen] didn't bother me; it did bother me. But I guess it's like a doctor: you got to the point that you felt for them, but you couldn't feel for them so much that you couldn't do your job."

Later on the first day he went into the women's section of the camp working as a stretcher bearer. "These women were laying in bunks, they were so weak, and they couldn't walk, they couldn't get out of the bunks. Some of them were delirious.

"A medical doctor said, 'Take this one, leave this one, take this one, leave this one.' There was a unit of English medics, they had their masks on and everything, all their special gloves, and they were stripping these women of their clothes. The ones that were chosen to be carried off, they'd wrap them in a blanket and put them on a stretcher. We would help them. They would strip them off, and we'd put the blanket around them and put them onto the stretcher.

"I remember we had one woman that fought us like a cat because she thought we were taking her to the crematory. She was completely out of her head. The medics were telling her, 'We're here to help you. Don't be afraid, we're going to help you.' But they looked like men from Mars to start with, with all these masks on. We didn't have that equipment on. They dusted us, and that was about it. Some of us had on gloves, some didn't." Waters says he was dusted with DDT powder so often that for a month he looked as if he had gray hair.

Near the women's barracks, Waters recalls seeing what passed for latrine facilities in the camp. "The toilet was nothing but a slit trench with a board over it with holes in it. There was filth all over where someone went to the bathroom. Women would come up and get on one of these planks and pull up their dress. They wouldn't have any underwear on. I saw so many naked women that I thought I'd never care to see a naked woman again. And they had no modesty whatsoever."

The British medical units had turned the former SS barracks about a mile and a half beyond the camp into a hospital. These were four- and five-story brick buildings. In the center of the area were smaller buildings that had once been stables for a cavalry outfit but more recently had been used by the SS as a training area for Panzer divisions. Waters and his fellow AFS drivers would take the inmates from the camp to the stable buildings, where English orderlies and nurses would scrub and bathe them, cut their hair, delouse them, and do whatever else was necessary before they were taken to one of the brick dormitories. Some of the buildings were used for people who could care for themselves; the others were fully staffed hospital wards. Patients who recovered enough were turned into nurses' aides. "Everybody had a job there; everybody was doing something all the time."

By the third week in May, the camp itself had been emptied of prisoners. The survivors either were still in the hospital barracks or had already been processed and sent elsewhere. The Swedish government offered to take 7,000 survivors.

On May 21, many of the AFS men had gone to Paris on leave, and Waters had stayed behind in the hospital compound with just a few others. "I saw smoke. The blackest, biggest column of smoke going up in the air with flames. We were about a mile and a half away and somebody said, 'They're burning the camp.' I climbed into my ambulance and drove down there, and what remained of Belsen was being burned."

Melvin Waters served fourteen months as an ambulance driver with the American Field Service during the war, voluntarily exposing himself to enemy fire and to the diseases and vermin that were rampant in one of the Nazis' most horrific concentration camps. And he did it all for twenty dollars a month and a lifetime's worth of satisfaction.

CHAPTER 12

LANDSBERG

THE KAUFERING CAMPS

APRIL 23, 1945

DILLINGEN AN DER DONAU, BAVARIA, GERMANY

   31 miles northwest of Augsburg

   75 miles northwest of Munich

On April 22, the Hellcats of the 12th Armored Division captured the bridge over the Danube River at Dillingen, an act that had a profound effect on the course of the war in its final weeks. According to the division's newspaper, a light tank platoon "swept into town with guns blazing, routing more than 1,000 disorganized defenders and shooting up a retreating mechanized column. Surging on to the bridge, the unit captured a handful of demolition men and drove other Nazis away with tank fire before the span could be blown."

The Germans had planted six 500-pound aerial bombs and a significant quantity of dynamite around the bridge, but the Americans were able to cut the wires. While not as well known as the bridge over the Rhine River at Remagen, the capture of the Dillingen bridge allowed the Americans to continue unimpeded south of the Danube in their push toward Munich and the supposed Nazi redoubt in the Alps. It also meant that they would discover and liberate the Kaufering slave-labor camps near Landsberg and the huge Dachau concentration camp more quickly and, as a result, save more lives.

The Germans attempted to destroy the bridge using artillery as well as fighter planes, but accurate ack-ack fire from division half-tracks brought down half a dozen enemy aircraft and the counterattack was rebuffed.

St. Louis native John Critzas was a gunner on an M-4 Sherman tank in the 714th Tank Battalion, which meant that his view of the Danube, and pretty much all the territory they'd raced through since coming up the Seine River in September 1944 on a landing ship tank (LST) to Rouen, France, was what he could see through his targeting telescope. By the time the unit got to the Danube, the twenty-year-old Critzas had already had three tanks blown out from under him, destroyed by German antitank guns fighting a rearguard action against the onrushing Americans.

"As a gunner, I didn't know where we were, which direction we were going. I just got a slap on the head from the tank commander. He would say, 'Target two o'clock,' and I traversed that area and tried to find out what he was talkin' about by looking through the telescope. If we were rolling, it was very difficult to shoot accurately."

In spite of having been in the war since the fall of 1944, Critzas knew nothing about concentration camps or the Holocaust. And he's emphatic about that. "Zero. Zero. Zero. Absolute zero. We didn't know about that until April of 1945, after we crossed the Danube."

From the Danube, Combat Commands A and B of the 12th Armored Division began moving south from the Dillingen bridgehead. Twenty miles to the west, units of the 10th Armored Division, augmented by the 71st Infantry Regiment, 44th Division, cleared the city of Ulm in a coordinated assault and continued pressing on toward Munich, followed by cavalry units of the 103rd Infantry Division. The effect was that of a storm surge rolling across the Bavarian terrain, but instead of raging waters pushed by hurricane winds, it was hundreds of thousands of American troops, motivated by a desire to destroy the German army and put an end to the long and costly war.

By late on the twenty-fifth, several of the advancing units were within twenty miles of the eleven slave-labor camps at Kaufering.

APRIL 25, 1945

KAUFERING IV, BAVARIA, GERMANY

> **6 miles north of Landsberg am Lech**
>
> **40 miles west of Munich**
>
> **43 miles west-southwest of Dachau**

Israel Cohen knew the Americans were coming. At night he could see flashes of light from artillery shells reflected on the clouds, and he could hear explosions, which seemed like giant exclamation points to his prayers. The nineteen-year-old Chasidic Jew had been in various camps for more than six years, and his weight had dropped below 70 pounds. In 1939, Cohen had been confined in the Lódź ghetto in central Poland; he'd survived the evacuation of the ghetto; he'd survived a death march from Auschwitz. And now he was hoping to survive the final days in Kaufering IV, the *Krankenlager,* the sick camp, which was filled with roughly 3,000 inmates suffering from typhus, typhoid fever, tuberculosis, and dysentery.

There were eleven camps named for the nearest railway station, called Kaufering. They were all subcamps of the oldest concentration camp established by the Reich, Dachau, which was just north of Munich. The Kaufering camps had been built to house prisoners who would be used as slave labor to build three underground bunkers where parts for the ME-262, the Messerschmitt jet fighter plane, would be manufactured.

The first prisoners to arrive came from Auschwitz in June 1944. By the time the Kaufering camps were liberated, just under 29,000 prisoners had been sent there, and half of them had died, some of illness, the others worked to death. Israel Cohen was determined not to be one of them.

On Wednesday, April 25, Cohen came out of the barrack he slept in to discover that the SS guards had disappeared from the towers placed at intervals along the barbed-wire fence. The inmates took it as a sign that the artillery explosions they'd seen and heard the previous night were more than just meaningless sound and fury; they signified freedom. A group of the inmates broke into the camp kitchen and took potatoes, flour, cabbage, and bread—a virtual feast and a crime for which they would have been shot immediately just a day earlier.

What they had no way of knowing was that even though elements of two American armored divisions and four infantry divisions were heading toward the Kaufering camps on their way to Munich, the nearest GIs were still roughly seventeen miles away. The Germans, however, figured it out: liberation was not imminent for their prisoners, so they returned. The guttural voices of the SS cut through the air: "Everyone in a row! Roll call!"

The onrushing force of American infantry and armor was not yet close enough to stop the killing in the camps. It would go on for two more days until units of the 10th and 12th Armored Divisions and the 63rd Infantry Division were at the gates and, a day or so behind them, the 101st Airborne and 36th Infantry Divisions.

If he and his group of young friends, all Gerer Chasidic Jews from Łódź, were to survive, they'd have to find the strength to live by their wits until the GIs arrived.

APRIL 25, 1945
LEIPHEIM, GERMANY
19 miles southwest of Dillingen
40 miles northwest of Kaufering

While the 12th Armored Division was coming down from the north, the 1st and 2nd Battalions of the 254th Infantry Regiment of the 63rd Division crossed a damaged bridge over the Danube near Riedheim and moved two more miles to the southeast, taking the town of Leipheim and repelling a tank-supported counterattack by the Germans.

Irv Schlocker had left his high school in Philadelphia with half a year to go and joined the Army, ultimately being assigned to the 254th. He says every kid wanted to do his duty, and it was a common thing for kids to lie about their age to get in. He personally knew one fifteen-year-old and one sixteen-year-old in the division and seemed surprised that they weren't found out because they looked "so damn young."

Schlocker's outfit arrived in the European Theater of Operations (ETO) in time for the Battle of the Bulge. The stories he enjoys telling are about getting there from Marseilles in 40 and 8 railcars. "Did you know how men went to the toilet?" the former staff sergeant and squad leader asks. "In their helmets?" ventures the interviewer.

"No, no," he says, a broad smile creeping into his voice because he knows what he's about to say will gross out well-mannered civilians. "They had big, open sliding doors. And you extended your arms in each direction, your right and your left, and a big, hopefully strong guy held each arm and you squatted and did your business while the train was moving. Picturesque, isn't it?" The vision of American infantrymen mooning the French countryside from a rolling freight train is worth a smile. It becomes a full laugh with Schlocker's next instance of providing too much information: "And if you had to urinate, that was easy. They had a big bucket in there. And they waited until the train slowed down to empty it out, or else the guys in the car behind you got sprayed." By now Schlocker is in full-throated laughter as he adds, "It was unbelievably filthy."

He saw combat in Alsace-Lorraine, including action in the Colmar pocket, and recalls being "as frightened as you could be and still do your duty," but he was never told about the concentration camps. He did, however, run into anti-Semitism in his own unit. "There was one guy who was an extreme anti-Semitic sonofabitch. I'm Jewish. And he had the same stupid fucking dumb joke all the time. He used to tell this story before I got a couple stripes. 'What's the fastest thing in the world? A Jew riding through Germany on a bicycle.' You know what I mean? This was his humor. As a matter of fact, when I first made corporal, my first duty was to take him out on what they call prisoner watch. You went to the stockade at the base, in Camp Van Dorn, picked the sonofabitch up, and we stayed with him all day—he had to do everything the company did—and at the end of the day, we had to take him back to the stockade. They worked their ass off up there. I was a prisoner chaser, they called it. And they gave me a loaded weapon. And he said, 'You wouldn't shoot me, would you, Corporal?' I said, 'Nick, I got a loaded fucking carbine, I don't like you to begin with, and if you make one fucking move, I'll put a bullet in you. Whether I'll kill you or not, I don't know; but I will shoot you, I guarantee that. I'm not going to lose these stripes over an asshole like you.' That's exactly what I said to him, and he shut up. If he's still alive, he's got to be the head of the local Ku Klux Klan somewhere. He got in a fight later on with a nice old Polish guy in our outfit who was maybe thirty, thirty-five years old—and he was ten years younger than the Polish guy. And afterwards, we threw a blanket on Nick and every noncom in the company kicked the shit out of the guy."

On April 26, Schlocker's 63rd Division unit established contact with Combat Command R of the 12th Armored Division at Günzburg and began a forty-mile sprint to the Landsberg area, where the next day they would discover the Holocaust firsthand.

APRIL 27, 1945
SOMEWHERE NEAR LANDSBERG-KAUFERING, GERMANY

For more than twenty-four hours, the 63rd Infantry Division had been leapfrogging its line outfits toward Landsberg, closely following tanks of the 10th and 12th Armored Divisions. The 254th Infantry Regiment was somewhere in the area of the eleven so-called Kaufering camps when they came across their first slave-labor/death camp. Irv Schlocker says there was always somebody in every company who could speak Polish, Russian, Ukrainian, Yiddish, or German, and they were able to learn that the strange people they'd begun to see along the road were prisoners who had just gotten out of a camp.

"There they were," Schlocker recalls, "sittin' on the road. Some of them had bags with them, some of them had no shoes, some had little or no clothes on. Our officers came around—especially the medical officers—they begged us not to give them food. They said, 'They will die if they eat it.' While we're marching there, a jeep came down flying a Red Cross flag, and they kept saying, 'Don't feed 'em; give 'em candy if you want, cigarettes, but don't feed them.' We couldn't understand that at all. We saw how emaciated they looked. We were reasonably intelligent young kids. Can you comprehend it today if you saw it all of a sudden? Okay, same thing for us."

They figured out that the starving prisoners were civilians, and though they couldn't feed them, the Americans felt they could at least get them something to wear from the abandoned homes or apartments in the German towns. Schlocker says, "I remember kicking a door in for one of them, and I brought in a few of his buddies with him. I went to a closet—you've seen where a guy takes a suit and holds it up to someone and says, 'This is your size'? I gave them stuff that was in that closet—anything they wanted, just take it. That's how we outfitted them."

And as he and his squad members helped the recently freed prisoners, he found his hatred for the Germans intensifying. "I couldn't even comprehend it, to tell you the truth. I hated the fuckin' Krauts, being Jewish. But we had no idea about these atrocities. [Though] we knew there was concentration camps, we had no idea what they were like, no concept of what they were."

Schlocker never went into the camp they came to. His unit kept moving, but they were able to see quite a bit from outside the fence. "It was horrible. There were fires. And I also saw one Kraut—a couple of the prisoners grabbed him, and they actually drowned him in a horse trough. Just held his head in there until he drowned. And we didn't even bother to stop them." Asked how emaciated prisoners could pull down and kill a well-fed German soldier, he matter-of-factly says, "We saw what the places were like. We were probably assisting them, maybe shot the guy in the arm or the leg, or even shot 'em full, killed 'em. We gave them any assistance that they needed, unquestionably. I seen a German guy killed with his own helmet. They just beat him to death with it. It was the only weapon they had."

Any shooting that was going on at the time came from the Americans. He says there was no enemy fire at all. "They were hiding. A lot of them—what you would do is find German uniforms all over the place. They just got out of their uniforms and got the civilian clothes."

And while the survival rate of former SS camp guards was fairly low if they were discovered by their former prisoners, it was no higher if they were captured by the Americans. Schlocker says, "We were looking for German stragglers. We knew enough to look under the left armpit of the Germans to look to see if he was an SS guy. You know what I'm talking about? That tattoo they had? Some tried to escape, shall we say. And they were executed, right on the spot. We knew enough from fighting these bastards, if they looked young and full of pep and piss and vinegar, we made 'em take off that tunic; we looked under their armpit. If it was that [SS blood-type tattoo], they were shot. No questions asked. It was cold-blooded killing, but it was overlooked. This was done. There's no way of denying it."

———

Inside the turret of their Sherman tank ten miles from Kaufering, T/5 John Critzas and his four crew members began to smell something they couldn't readily identify. "We knew the odor of combat and we knew the odor of dead soldiers, but we didn't know the horrendous odor of a concentration camp." They kept trying to find the source as they continued down the road, but the smell only got worse and they could find nothing to explain it. "You don't see anything. You don't know where it's coming from. And we saw these things that looked like prisons, but we didn't know what they were. And, of course, we're looking for the enemy, and there wasn't any enemy to be found. As we approached, the odor got even worse, and there were no people around to talk to and ask."

Critzas's crew did what any self-respecting tank crew would do when faced with a mystery behind a stone wall about ten feet high. "We just went through it. I was instructed to turn the gun around because the 76 protrudes beyond the front of the tank. So I was told 'traverse 180 degrees,' and I did that. There wasn't an impact when we hit the wall. We just went through it and we stopped on the other side and looked at all of these people, maybe two thousand of them. We saw all these emaciated prisoners with striped suits on that looked like two-hundred-pound men starved down to about eighty pounds, the vast majority of them being Jewish. And we found out pretty quickly what it was. They all came up to the tank, and several of them knew English and welcomed us, and they were asking for food."

The prisoners quickly explained that their German guards had fled but that some of the inmates were still locked in their cells with 500-pound bombs on timers ready to explode. Critzas says they called for the nearest explosives ordnance disposal squad to deal with the problem. Questioned about his seemingly nonchalant attitude toward the possibility of large bombs exploding nearby, he said, "We had stuff exploding all around us all the time, and one bomb was like another. Under that kind of pressure and at that age, you don't feel anything. You don't know if you're going to live another day or not. And you just don't think about that stuff, that's all."

His tank unit wasn't given the opportunity to wait around and learn more about the camp or to help with the survivors. Orders came down from General Patton telling them to "get out of here and keep chasin' Germans—don't stop. We've got 'em on the run, we don't want them to stop and regroup and set up their defenses." So they left, heading toward Munich.

———

Many of the men of the 255th Regiment of the 63rd Infantry Division were riding on tanks from either the 10th or 12th Armored Divisions as they moved into the Landsberg area, not knowing what to expect but fearing the worst due to the stench. Staff Sergeant Wayne Armstrong, a rifle squad leader in Company C from Westerville, Ohio, says they were coming down a road when they reached a set of open gates. "We saw all these people in what we called blue-and-white striped pajamas. It was just unbelievable. The tanks stopped, and we're staring at these people. They looked like they was walking dead. And corpses piled on flatcars. We didn't know what to make of it.

"These people looked like they was starving, and we started giving them stuff out of our K rations, and it was not too long, word came down not to give them food. We couldn't figure out how anybody could treat people like that. We'd heard rumors that they had slave labor—but the slave labor they had was in factories and they fed them enough to keep them working, you know. We'd run into a lot of that."

Domenick Pecchia had been drafted less than six months earlier from the Chicago area, and he was just eighteen when H Company of the 255th found itself at one of the Kaufering camps. His squad was on foot when they came to open gates with prisoners in striped uniforms pouring out. "We kinda hesitated for a moment, but my squad leader said, 'Get your butt going,' so we went in. I was horrified. Their condition is what stuck in my mind more than anything else. They were all gaunt and stooped over, and you had the feeling that they were not as old as they looked, you know what I mean? It was a short stay at that particular place, but I can remember it vividly, seeing the little old hats without a brim and the striped uniforms."

None of the prisoners approached him at that time. "No, no. They were moving. We were going, like, to the left, past the gates over there, and they were streaming out and going to the right. Where they were going—I'm sure somebody else was going to start picking them up and seeing if they needed immediate attention. But we went right on."

Sergeant Vincent Koch (Kucharsky at the time), a New Yorker, was head of the mortar platoon in Company M of the 255th as they approached one of the Kaufering camps. He'd been in Europe since the previous November and had fought in the Battle of the Bulge. Koch wasn't aware that there was any concentration camp in the Landsberg area until he and his men were walking down a small dirt road and nearly walked right past one. The gate was open, the Germans were gone, and his squad just walked in, the first Americans to see this particular camp.

"I opened up the doors. The odor coming from there was absolutely unbelievable. And I walked in [the barracks] and they picked their heads up, some of them, they were in a horrible state. They were like double-deckers, some were on the top, others on the bottom. I was able to speak German, so I spoke with them, thinking that it was pretty close to Yiddish. They really couldn't do much talking, though.

"About three days before that, I received a huge package from home, and there were groceries. And it was in the jeep that was with our outfit. And when I started opening some of the packages, those that were able to got out of their bunks, and they started to walk toward me and the package that I had on the floor there. And that was a big mistake, because they started to claw at each other trying to get to the food. I didn't realize that that would happen. There was crackers, there was honey cake, there was all kinds of things that they had seen.

"I walked out, and then the captain came back in with me and he said, 'The smartest thing you can do is take that package out, because they're going to tear each other apart to get to it.' We tried our best."

The discovery of the camp happened in late afternoon. By the following morning, Koch says, ambulances started to arrive.

By the time M Company got to Landsberg, Koch was the only Jew in the outfit. There had been three when the company had been formed in Mississippi, but the other two had been killed. "I was the only survivor with that background, and knowing what the story [of the Nazi persecution of the Jews] was, it was a devastating experience that you remember forever, as you can imagine.

"When we got into the town of Landsberg itself, we started to see the German people, civilians. And I started to discuss it with them, and every single one of them denied that they knew. It was so hard to believe because the stench in that area was so strong that they would have had to know something was going on there. And we took some of the civilians, and we brought them in to show 'em this particular segment of the concentration camp, and we walked them into where these bodies were lying—you know, the trench. They were horrified, too; whether they put it on or not, it's very hard to say."

Tom Malan was a twenty-three-year-old 60mm mortarman with the 63rd Infantry Division on the day it arrived at Landsberg. He'd grown up in Centralia, Illinois, and worked in the oil fields before being drafted. His first combat had been on the Maginot Line, and he had been with the division at the Colmar Pocket. But Kaufering IV—the camp that Israel Cohen was in—was the first concentration camp he saw.

"I will never forget, I ran across a Jewish fellow, I gave him a piece of bread. All he could eat at one time was a little piece, about the size of the end of my finger, because he was thin and had been starving." The man he fed was outside the camp. The scene that awaited Malan once he walked through the gates and into the camp was also something he'll never forget.

Tom Malan, a mortarman with the 63rd
Infantry Division, tried to find survivors among
the charred bodies in Kaufering IV, one of the
Landsberg camps.

Before they left in the face of the American onslaught, the Nazis
had used the last of their gasoline to set all the barracks in Kaufering
IV afire with the inmates locked inside. The Kaufering barracks were
about fifty feet long and about fifteen feet wide. They'd been built by
first digging a rectangular hole in the ground, perhaps three feet deep.
A triangular wall was built at each end, with a door no more than five
feet high in the wall at the front. A peaked wooden roof, often covered
with dirt, covered the minimalist structure, its eaves going all the way
down to the ground. There were no provisions for drainage, so the
slightest bit of rain created a mess inside. A central aisle ran from the
door to the far end of the structure, and on either side were wooden
shelves, usually two decks high, on which the inmates slept.

When Malan came into the camp, all but two of the buildings were
still smoldering. Charred corpses were everywhere, some arrested in

the act of trying to crawl out beneath the walls. He recalls, "They were burnt from the neck on down—or depending on how far they got out, from their waist on down. They tried to dig out underneath, and they didn't make it."

He and his buddies went into some of the barracks that hadn't been totally consumed by the flames. They were looking for survivors, and he acknowledges that they didn't go into any more than they had to. All that was left to see was dead bodies.

Malan's response was to try to get through the camp as quickly as possible, to try to help the survivors who were wandering the camp, one of whom could very easily have been Israel Cohen.

In the final days, it's estimated that as many as 12,000 prisoners were marched away from the eleven Kaufering camps. Thousands were loaded into boxcars at the nearby railway station. It's unclear how many of them survived the war.

Cohen says he and his friends saw what was happening when the Germans returned after having run the first time, and they made a decision. "I said, 'I'm not going to go anymore, I've had enough.'"

On April 26, they decided to hide among the sickest prisoners in the camp, people who could be talking one minute and dead the next. "We didn't care about the consequences, that they were contagious. We were hiding the whole day, the whole night, and then the next day, we didn't see the Germans. We thought the Germans left. And then they came back. We were hiding there in the belief that the Germans wouldn't come into those tents. But they did come in, and they evacuated the rest of the people and put them on trucks, these people that couldn't move. And we were on the trucks. I weighed about seventy pounds, I was skin and bones. We had no strength. But we tried."

He and one of his friends rolled off the truck when the Germans weren't looking. They went back into the hut and hid, and they were caught again. And once again they managed to get off the truck and back into the hut. It was nighttime, and Cohen turned off the single light in the hut, and they hid again. Once more the SS came to the door, but this time, they didn't come in. They stood at the opening and called for anyone inside to come out. Cohen and his friend didn't move.

The next morning they thought the Germans were gone for good. Some of his friends wanted to celebrate, but he said, "No, we can't celebrate until the Americans come. Don't show that we are alive here." They posted a guard outside to keep watch, and in a short time, he came back in and said that things were not good.

"The Germans came back with dogs, and we're hiding again, under *shmatas*—rags—and other people were hiding in the straw. They came in, and there were shots and shots and shots. And our luck, one of the people which were hiding in the back by the window got up and they wanted to shoot him, but their gun jammed."

Several of the prisoners then jumped out the window and hid in the ditches that had been dug behind the hut in preparation for the mass burial of hundreds of bodies. There was more shooting, and Cohen could hear people moaning. Once again, the SS came into the hut and began poking through the straw. Moments later they left and set the structure on fire.

Somehow Cohen and his friend were able to crawl out the door unseen. Nearby was a pile of corpses that had already been soaked with gasoline and burned. They burrowed in among the bodies and lay there. After two hours, he was ready to surrender. "Yeah, then I gave up almost, lying there, and I see that the Americans are still not here, and I said, 'We can't go another time, to hide and run around. We're not able to do it.' So my friend encouraged me again. He said, 'Now, you told me in Auschwitz we should not give up, never give up.' So we lay down."

They were hiding in the kitchen, a brick building that had not burned, when they heard another inmate shouting, *"Yidden, zaynen frei!"* "Jews, we are free, the Americans are here."

Cohen remembers thinking about the date—one month after Passover. "I said, 'It's Pesach Sheni.' We are liberated the same day as the second Passover." (Certain Chasidic Jews recognize a second Passover as an opportunity given to persons who were unable to offer the Passover sacrifice to do so one month later.)

One man whom Israel Cohen wanted to talk about was a friend who had been part of a block of thirty French prisoners. When the Germans left the first or second time, the French inmates took over the kitchen and were boiling potatoes and singing. Then the Germans came back, lined them all up against the wall, and shot them all point-blank. His friend, who spoke German and had the temerity to ask the SS why they were doing that, was also shot, but the bullet went in one check and out the other, and the man pretended to be dead. He was lying on the floor with his mouth open when one of the SS saw that he had gold teeth. Cohen says the SS man took pliers and tore out his teeth, together with the gums. And all the while the man pretended to be dead. "When I came, he stood there with the gums down and the teeth on the gums, and he was bleeding badly." Cohen says that when the Americans arrived, they rushed the man to a nearby German hospital and in no uncertain terms told the surgeons that if the man died, they would die, too.

The GIs removed the remaining survivors, putting those who were too weak to walk, like Cohen, in a wagon. They were taken to a nearby farm, and it was made clear to the farmer that nothing bad had better happen to the survivors. Cohen says the farmer, who'd been doing the "We didn't know, *nicht Nazi*" routine, was very scared. "They thought that the Americans are going to do to them what they did to us.

"When I came to the farm, they wanted to give me [something] to eat. I said, 'No, I don't want to eat. I need a hot bath.' And I took off my clothes, and the clothes were full of lice. They would walk away themselves. And then I took the tub in the stable. My skin was burning from the bites of the lice, but I relaxed so much. And then they came and fed me."

Israel Cohen was bounced among several different hospitals until his medical conditions were controlled and he began putting on weight. He tried to reconnect with family members, only to learn that they'd all perished in the Holocaust. He spent three years in a TB sanatorium in Switzerland. In 1951, he moved to Canada, where he lives today with his wife, five children, grandchildren, and great-grandchildren.

He never lost his faith in God. "I talk to people, and they ask me, 'Why did it happen?,' and I say, 'I don't know, and nobody knows.' Hashem [God] wanted him to be saved. I know that someone lately had a video and said he was rescued by chance. I got up, and I said

*Monroe "Monty" Nachman at home in Skokie, Illinois, with the
103rd Infantry Division yearbook showing pictures at the Landsberg
area camps. Note the triangular, semiunderground barracks that were
unique to the Kaufering camps.*

that 'You win the lottery, it could be chance. You win twice the lottery,
it could be chance. But if you win the lottery seven, eight times in a
row, it can't be chance.' I was seven, eight times just before being
killed, and I was saved at the last minute, and this can't be chance."

———

Five-foot, five-inch Monroe "Monty" Isadore Nachman was a tough
kid from Detroit who, just before Pearl Harbor, joined the National
Guard's 6th Cavalry unit because he had a low draft number and didn't
want to be in the infantry. He was in the twelfth grade when he got
tossed out of high school for fighting in class. "A guy called me a
sheeny, and I hit him." His mother wanted him to go back, but he was
tired of fighting. "I lived in a half-Jewish, half-gentile neighborhood,
and every day I had to go by St. Mary's Church, and every day I was
fighting. My mother called me a *vilde chaya*—a wild animal—but she
didn't understand. It was 'Here comes the Jews, or here comes the
kikes.' [My friends and I are] the type of guys who don't take that kind
of stuff, so every day, we would fight."

Anti-Semitism wasn't a theoretical concept for Monty Nachman.

They listened to Father Charles Coughlin's broadcasts on Detroit radio—"he was a *mamzer* [bastard] from the first go, he was a bad guy"—and they paid attention to the headlines from Germany. He knew about Kristallnacht, about the Jews being killed.

He ultimately found himself enrolled in OCS and doing well, but the Army wanted him in the infantry, and he said no. So he was tossed from officers' school and sent to Camp Claiborne, Louisiana, to join E Company, 2nd Battalion, 411th Regiment, of the 103rd Infantry Division. It's where he found out how the Army works. He'd made it all the way up to sergeant, only to get a new commander, an anti-Semitic captain, and he ended up being busted back down to private.

In October 1944, the 103rd went to Marseilles, rode boxcars north, and was committed to action at Saint-Dié, near Strasbourg. They lost fifty-five men, wounded and killed, the first day. Though Monty was aware of Germans' mistreatment of the Jews, the Army had never told the troops about concentration camps. His introduction was much the same as most other combat soldiers': the smell. On April 27, his outfit was walking near Landsberg. He was carrying the burp gun he'd traded for; it's a tanker's weapon, but an armored guy had wanted a carbine, so they'd swapped. "All of a sudden, when we're approaching this place here, it started to smell like a different smell, a terrible, terrible smell. And it never goes out of your nostrils. You always remember that smell, you can never forget what you see. And we came into this place, and, my God, it was horrendous. A few of my guys threw up.

"These underground huts, and bodies are lying all over the place, filthy, and the stink around there was unbelievable. I talked to some people there in Yiddish, and they said that whoever could walk, the Nazis were taking to Dachau to kill off. So we left, we got in our jeeps. We caught up with them."

It took his company about forty-five minutes to come upon the death march. "We saw a line of people, walking if they could walk, stumbling all over the place. The guards were around, and we caught up and killed them. They threw down their arms, and I just plain shot them. There were about a dozen or so. And the other guys shot them, too. We didn't take any prisoners." They turned the forty or fifty surviving inmates over to another outfit, "and we went back to our task, because we were way into Germany now."

His hands-on contact with the Holocaust lasted less than half a day, but, as he said, the memories don't go away. Flashbacks happen without warning. Nightmares occur. "I used to get crazy, you know. It'd come back. You see the bodies. We were living with my in-laws in [Chicago's Albany Park area], and they had this party to introduce the new son-in-law. Now, I never lacked for words in my life. I'm talking, and all of a sudden, I'm seeing bodies laying all over there. I felt like a *shtumi* [mute]—you know what I mean? I couldn't talk."

Monty Nachman never spoke about what he saw at Landsberg until 2003, when a veteran at one of their reunions urged the men to go on the record. Since then he's been outspoken, taking on the Holocaust deniers, including the tenured professor at nearby Northwestern University whose book made big headlines in Skokie, Illinois, where Nachman and his wife live. He recognizes the bookends of his life—fighting anti-Semitism as a high school kid and now again as a ninety-year-old. He quotes his mother, who used to say *"Shvertz azayan Yid"*—It's hard to be a Jew.

APRIL 28, 1945
LANDSBERG, GERMANY

Jack Kerins was born on March 30, 1912, making him the oldest veteran interviewed for this book. In fact, he was one of the oldest draftees in the 63rd Division on its last day in Landsberg. Kerins was thirty-one when he was drafted; he'd had deferments because he was the sole support of his mother in the tiny town of Farrell, Pennsylvania, about seventy-five miles north of Pittsburgh, but when the Army got desperate for bodies, the deferments were taken away, and in late 1943, he was shipped to Europe with just part of his division—no artillery, no support units. They were thrown into combat without really being ready and took on the 17th SS Panzers while units farther north fought in the Bulge. After a year and a half of combat, he'd earned a

Jack Kerins was thirty-one years old when he was drafted and ultimately served with the 63rd Infantry Division, which liberated the Landsberg camps. At age ninety-six, he is the oldest veteran interviewed for this book.

Purple Heart at the Siegfried Line for a concussion from an incoming oversized German artillery round that killed his company commander and by all rights should have killed him. He was also awarded a Silver Star and an unwanted battlefield commission from tech sergeant to second lieutenant and platoon leader.

April 28 was a beautiful, sunny day, and from the jeeps of the 2nd Platoon of D Company, 255th Infantry Regiment, they had an incredible view of the Bavarian Alps' snow-covered peaks. Kerins's unit was assigned to antiaircraft defense for the column—"only a show," he says, because the .50-caliber machine guns were not likely to be effective against planes like the Luftwaffe jet that had buzzed them the day before. They had gotten to the far side of Landsberg when a messenger stopped them, saying, "Hold up, don't chase the Germans any farther than right here." They disembarked from their jeeps, and that's when he saw them.

"I saw these pajama-clad prisoners coming down the little streets. They were holding each other. A lot of them could hardly walk. And the boys were directing them to go where there'd be somebody to take care of them. Suddenly one of the DPs [displaced persons] bolted from the line and ran over to me, grabbed my hand, kneeled down, and began kissing my hand, saying '*Danke, danke,*' over and over again. Apparently he picked on me as I was the only officer he saw as he rounded the corner. The physical condition of the man was inconceivable. I took hold of him by the arm and raised him up and could not believe what I saw. He had no flesh on his arm, only skin and bone, his eyes were sunken, he had very little hair and only two teeth visible on his upper jaw. His smile, though, was contagious, and the boys around me started calling him Joe and began to offer all of them rations. All of them dug in their pockets and were giving them chocolate bars and K rations—loading them up. I told them, 'Be careful, boys, they'll be sicker now than they were before.'

"I said to my jeep driver, Morgan, 'There's a nice house right there. Go in and see if you can get some clothes to put on them. Take those pajamas off them.' He went in there, and I went on up to the camp, toured it, and came back. And here Joe was: he had a tall silk hat, like when you dress with a tuxedo, and he had a long-tailed formal black coat and striped trousers. No shoes and no shirt. I turned to Morgan, who spoke fluent German, and asked him, 'What kind of a joke is this?' I wanted to know if he was making fun of him. He assured me apologetically that the house he entered was that of an undertaker. These were the only items of clothing that fit Joe, and he insisted on taking them anyway.

"By now Joe had regained some strength from our rations and was smiling broadly with his two widely spaced front teeth showing. He took off his high silk hat and again kneeled down and began kissing my hand and mumbling thanks in German. I gently raised him up by his arm and steered him over to the stragglers' line. As he passed from our sight, he was still looking back and waving to us."

Kerins was, perhaps, fortunate that his visit to Landsberg ended with a happy moment, because what he had seen inside the camp was soul-destroying. "I went into the camp and looked it over. It was a terrible thing. I saw prisoners that were dying from starvation. I went into the little kitchen they had, and there was a half a barrel of sawdust and a half a barrel of flour, and they were mixing flour and sawdust to feed them, and mostly sawdust. And there was a big trench there with an array of bones, dead people, they just threw them in the trench. They hadn't had time to cover them up. And the GIs, some of the GIs were crying, and I had tears in my eyes. I couldn't help it. The GIs, they were swearing revenge if they would let them go on and catch some of those guards that got away."

They wouldn't have the chance, because shortly after he came out of the camp he received word that the 36th Infantry Division would be going through the 63rd and chasing the Nazis all the way to the Alps. For his unit, combat was over. They were assigned to occupation duty at a town back north called Bad Rappenau.

———

As the 63rd Infantry Division prepared to head back north for occupation duty, the 36th Infantry Division T-Patchers were ordered to move through and capture the hard-core SS thought to be hiding in the Reich's so-called National Redoubt in the Bavarian or Austrian Alps.

The assignment was an honor for a division with a significant record in the war, including four hundred days in combat, fourteen Medal of Honor recipients, and the ninth highest casualty rate of any Army division in the Second World War.

On April 1, the 36th had moved from a rest-and-relaxation (R&R) break in the Saar to occupation duty in the city of Kaiserslautern in the Rhineland. The assignment was described by 36th Cavalry Reconnaissance Troop Sergeant Don Latimer, now a resident of Albuquerque, as a safe chore with nonlethal hazards—mostly the nonfraternization policy, which prohibited American soldiers to even speak to German civilians without an officer present.

Three weeks later, the 36th was given its final assignment and moved to the Danube and then on to the Landsberg area, where the 63rd was still involved with the survivors of the Kaufering camps. To that point in the war, the T-Patchers had seen small groups of Jewish prisoners in striped uniforms but had never been confronted by the Holocaust on a large scale. That changed around April 28. Latimer's recon outfit was in its armored cars, leading the division down the highway through a little town, when they spotted people walking toward a train of perhaps six to eight boxcars. In quick order, soldiers got to the cars and yelled back, "There's people in the train."

Latimer lowered the hatch and remained on the radio as his car was maneuvered close to the tracks. "I remember seeing these boards. This is before anyone came out of the thing, when we first saw the train. The boards [were] maybe one-by-sixes or two-by-sixes nailed across the train doors. [The Nazis] closed the doors and nailed the boards on them from the outside, where it'd be practically impossible for a person to get out. By that time, a lot of other 36th Division companies were up there, too, and started prying the boards off the doors."

When the soldiers began helping the prisoners out, he saw that most were wearing the familiar striped uniforms, but some had on ragged civilian clothes. He never got a count of the number of people on the train but estimated it to be many hundred to perhaps a couple thousand Jews. "A lot of them were dead and many were seriously ill, and there were several babies that had been born while on the train.

They had no water, no food, and had had to perform all bodily functions in these boxcars, with only a little hay in them. By the time we got there, the German army train guards had disappeared."

The division brought up field kitchens, tents, and medical personnel to tend to the survivors. "Later on, we discovered that some of the healthier Jewish males were entering the German village and were attempting to kill the civilians. We rightfully put a stop to this and ended up putting them inside a field cage made of barbed wire, where we continued to feed them until our rear-echelon troops came forward and took over."

In a memoir written long after the war, Latimer says, "This encounter with the trainload of Jews was one of the most traumatic events of the war to me, and it left many of our troops in an ugly mood, which they demonstrated when they later came into contact with German troops."

———

Bernard Schutz has lived his life since the war surrounded by art. His apartment is above a Skokie, Illinois, art gallery; his apartment *is* an art gallery, where he still practices his violin. Bernie was never supposed to be in combat. He lived on the West Side of Chicago and played violin with the Works Progress Administration (WPA) Orchestra. He also had a birth defect that excluded him from combat duty. So when he was called up for his induction physical, the doctor agreed that, with one ear closed, being near explosions would be problematic. Nevertheless, he was accepted by the Army and classified 1-A limited service.

"What does that mean?" Bernie asked the doctor he'd been talking with for nearly an hour.

"Well, you won't go overseas because of your situation."

Which pretty much explains how Bernie wound up in North Africa, Italy, France, and ultimately Germany with the 20th Special Services Unit of the Fifth Army. He earned four battle stars yet never fired a weapon. The entire unit of 109 men and five officers was infantry trained in case something untoward occurred, but their primary job was to break up into small groups, travel around the battlefield picking

Bernard Schutz of Skokie, Illinois, was the master of ceremonies with a Fifth Army special services unit entertaining the troops during the war.

up additional players from the line outfits, rehearse in the afternoon, and put on a show at night. For a short time, Tony Bennett, a member of the 63rd Infantry Division, was their vocalist.

Bernie, who was born in 1917, was the master of ceremonies, the joke teller. He'd stand there with his fiddle and do intros for the acts. He was doing Jack Benny's television act long before Benny. "Someone would always holler, 'Hey, Sarge, you gonna play that fiddle?,' then at the end of the show I would play it off with a straight semiclassical number. It worked like a charm."

Schutz's outfit was not far from Landsberg when they heard that a camp had been liberated, and he felt compelled to see it for himself. That evening, the day he'd seen the horrors at Landsberg, the day he'd seen recently freed prisoners lynch one of their former guards while his cries for help were spurned by an American captain who said, "They know what they're doing, leave them alone," Bernie had to entertain the troops. He says the atrocities he saw changed his life. Yet even in combat, the show must go on. So with what he'd just witnessed etched in his mind and knowing that perhaps that day, more than any other, the troops needed to laugh, he took the makeshift stage, did a couple of flourishes on his fiddle to loosen the audience up, and told this joke:

> Fellow was living in a semirural district and was talking to a neighbor, and he says, "How's things going?" The neighbor replies, "I can't believe it. Here we live in a dairy country, and dairy products are so high priced. I never saw such prices." Fellow says, "Well, why don't you do what I do?" "What is that?" "Buy a cow, and I'll teach you how to function with a cow." So he buys a cow, and things are working out fine. Sometime later, they meet again, and he says, "How you doing?" He says, "Oh, I'm doing fine." He says, "Would you like to even do better?" He says, "Sure, what?" He says, "You buy a bull, and you'll be in the business. You'll be able to have calves and even make some money with it and have a nice existence with it." So he buys a pedigreed bull for a lot of money, he puts the bull out to pasture, and nothing happens. Every time the bull approaches the cow, the cow waltzes away. So he goes to the vet, and he says, "Listen, I've got a problem here. I've got a lot of money invested in a bull, and we're hoping they mate and I get calves. But every time the bull approaches the cow, the cow walks away." So the veterinarian looks in his book and thinks awhile and says, "Wait a minute. Was that cow bought in Wisconsin?" The man says, "Well, how in the heck would you know that?" The vet says, "Because my wife is from Wisconsin."

"We got a million of 'em!" Bernie Schutz says with a grin.

—

Because there were eleven different Kaufering camps in the Landsberg area, and because even at the time, low-ranking combat soldiers didn't necessarily know precisely where they were, it's virtually impossible to know which Kaufering camp the soldiers interviewed in this chapter were at or even whether some of them were in the same camps. The exception, of course, was Kaufering IV, the *Krankenlager*, which stood out because it had been burned.

The newsreel footage available at the U.S. Holocaust Memorial Museum Web site shows American soldiers compelling local German civilians not only to view the Kaufering camps but to dig graves and respectfully carry the dead to those graves and give them a proper burial. In one division record, a soldier is quoted as saying, "They were real nice Germans—the wealthy ones. Let me say here that no one has money unless he is a Nazi. These people were fat and well dressed." And, as has been mentioned, the Germans impressed into burial duty didn't hesitate to invoke the mantra du jour: "We knew nothing."

And on this April 29, the same day as the U.S. Army units at Landsberg were moving out, some to continue chasing the Germans across Bavaria and into Austria, others reversing course in preparation for occupation duty in cities and towns already captured, men of three other American divisions were about to come face-to-face with Holocaust horrors that would stay with them for a lifetime. Just forty miles to the northeast in the suburbs of Munich, they would discover Dachau.

CHAPTER 13

DACHAU

SHOCK BEYOND BELIEF

KZ DACHAU
By Dee R. Eberhart

Company I, 242nd Infantry, 42nd Infantry Division (Rainbow)
Written four decades after the liberation

Nazi dawn—Dachau's gate opened wide,
Swallowing prisoners for a dozen years,
Incubator for the Holocaust.
Long hard roads and a collision course;
For victims in their gray/blue stripes;
For gray SS; and American soldiers,
Rainbow 42nd; Thunderbird 45th,
All of their dead pointing the way.

Explosion for the world to see.
Skeletons, alive and dead.

Liberators' tears of rage.
SS sprawled, in the coal yard, in the moat.
unmourned by those behind the wire.
Grill iron work gate swung open.
Crematorium doors clanged shut.
Nazi twilight at the end of April.
One final plume of oily smoke,
in the outer yard of the Berlin bunker,
pilot beacon for the fires of hell.

APRIL 29, 1945
DACHAU, GERMANY

12 miles northwest of Munich

41 miles northeast of Landsberg

"All of their dead pointing the way," wrote Dee Eberhart, but he could have written "*our* dead." Five months earlier, he'd come over with them as part of a task force named after Henning Linden, the Rainbow Division's assistant division commander, on the USS *General Black.* In less than a month, the three infantry regiments, the 222nd, 232nd, and 242nd, found themselves in the middle of a tank battle near Gambsheim, France, where entire rifle platoons ceased to exist. At Hatten in Alsace, along the Maginot Line, they faced the tanks of the 25th Panzer Grenadier Division and the 21st Panzer Division as well as the German 7th Parachute Division.

"I had three foxhole buddies picked off right beside me," recalls Eberhart, "one after the other." They took heavy casualties, from 88s, mortars, from a huge railroad gun, and from the Nebelwerfers, the "Screaming Meemies" that sounded like a freight train going overhead, which were firing high explosives. Their squads were reduced from ten and twelve men down to four."

Eberhart says, "I didn't know how bad it was. I didn't know how bleak it was. I thought this was the way it always was. Well, it wasn't. After things turned around, it was a totally different war. We had not been trained for defensive warfare; yet we were on the defense. The

*Scout and sniper Dee Eberhart of the
42nd Infantry Division.*

Germans were on the offense, and so, psychologically and tactically, none of us had any training. From all that infantry basic [training, what I learned was] fire and movement and lay down a field of fire and try to do a flank attack. And we were good, or we thought we were, at least in training. Later on, we were good at it."

Later on, when the war was going the Americans' way and everyone could see an end to it, they were headed for the supposed redoubt where the Nazi dead enders were to hole up and fight to the last man. His outfit crossed the Danube in assault boats and became part of the great race for the glory of capturing Munich. But on April 29, a bright and sunny morning, at a point past Augsburg on the Autobahn, they were diverted onto secondary roads and eventually were ordered to "detruck and go in this direction."

"We kind of fanned out, and we'd been through this so many times it was nothing new. We moved toward what I thought were a bunch of factories, an industrial area of some German town." He was about to

*Dee Eberhart of Ellensburg, Washington,
has published two volumes of World
War II poetry. He was instrumental in
organizing the 2008 reunion of the 42nd
Infantry Division (Rainbow) Association
in Mobile, Alabama.*

discover Dachau, first built of the German concentration camps, ostensibly for political prisoners.

Dachau was opened by the Nazis in March 1933 on the grounds of
a former munitions factory about ten miles northwest of Munich.
Over the life of the camp, more than 200,000 prisoners from more
than thirty countries were sent to Dachau, a third of them Jews. More
than 25,000 died in the camp, and at least another 10,000 died in the
many Dachau subcamps. Alongside the prisoner compound, the Nazis
built a training center for SS concentration camp guards.

The prison camp, which is actually inside a larger area that is also
part of the concentration camp, consisted of thirty-two barracks, including one reserved for medical experiments. On the western side of
the prisoner compound there was an electrified barbed-wire fence,
outside of which was the water-filled Wurm Canal, which joined the
Amper River just north of the complex. On the northern, eastern, and

southern sides of the prisoner enclosure the barrier was a masonry wall about twelve feet high. About ten feet inside the outer wall and fence were two dry moats, about three feet deep and ten feet wide, and on the outer side of the moats was a grid of tanglefoot barbed wire about a foot off the ground.

The crematorium building was actually outside the prison camp walls. Nearby were two types of gas chambers, one used to fumigate clothing and a second, which could have been used to murder inmates, but Holocaust scholars don't believe it was ever put into operation. Nevertheless, mass murder was a daily occurrence at Dachau. Some prisoners, mostly Russians, were used as moving rifle range targets, others were killed in experiments, still others were tortured and hanged, and more were euthanized.

If you visit Dachau today and pass through the Jourhaus gate archway, you'll find a plaque provided by the 42nd Infantry Division commemorating its liberation of the camp on April 29, 1945. There's also a plaque honoring the 20th Armored Division. What's missing, in part because the German organization that runs the Dachau museum didn't want to get into the middle of a dispute between U.S. Army veterans, is any remembrance of the role played by the 45th Infantry Division in the liberation of Dachau.

Both the 45th "Thunderbird" and the 42nd "Rainbow" Divisions had troops inside the outer walls of the camp by midday on the twenty-ninth. Who got there first has been disputed for sixty-five years, but it is a pointless dispute whose resolution will bring no additional honor to the unit declared the winner. Dee Eberhart, in his role as chairman of the board of trustees of the Rainbow Division Veterans Memorial Foundation, wrote a letter about the situation to the U.S. Army Center of Military History. In it, he said, "Bill Clayton [one of the first Rainbow Division soldiers to enter the Dachau prisoner compound] sets the tone that it would be well for all of us to follow. There was no glory for anyone during the liberation. A major battle did not take place. . . . For those present, probably no other single event of the war made such a profound impression as seeing or hearing the firsthand accounts of the condition of those 32,000 victims of Nazi brutality imprisoned there."

One memory that weighed heavily on Eberhart's mind as he wrote that letter was what the GIs saw even before they entered through any of several gates into Dachau. It was a sight that previously couldn't have been imagined, even by hardened infantrymen who had been through multiple hells in their fight to liberate Europe. They called it the death train, thirty-nine railcars of dead bodies parked on a siding mostly outside the boundaries of the camp.

———

Had Russel Weiskircher known that his combat tour was going to end with the sight of the death train and Dachau burned into his brain, he might not have tried so hard to get into the Army. In 1942, he volunteered for the draft but flunked the physical four times because his urine test results were off due to a hereditary condition. Finally, he says, he cheated. "I slipped a guy a fin—that was big money—and he filled the bottle, and I got to wear a uniform."

His five bucks would eventually buy the Pittsburgh native three Purple Hearts and a Silver Star, as well as a ticket to Dachau and the lifelong nightmares that went with it. Of course, after the war he might not have become an ordained minister, a PhD, a retired brigadier general, and the vice chair of the Georgia Commission on the Holocaust, a state agency that runs a public institution wholly devoted to training teachers to teach the Holocaust.

Weiskircher had carried a flamethrower and been a sniper and an assistant squad leader with the 157th Infantry Regiment. Wounded for the third time, he came back from the hospital just before spring and was assigned to 3rd Battalion headquarters as the acting operations sergeant, working for Lieutenant Colonel Felix Sparks, at age twenty-seven one of the youngest battalion commanders in the entire Army. On the morning of April 29 the job was pursuit: catch the fleeing Germans in Bavaria. They had a feeling that by the time they got to Munich, the war would be over. They were chasing along in trucks when they got an ops order from the regiment that said, in effect, "Somewhere up there is a concentration camp. The first unit that gets there should seal it."

"The reaction was nil," he says. "We didn't know about a concentration camp because Eisenhower had deliberately downplayed a lot of it up until that time because he had a control problem with men going nuts and reacting like assassins, to put it bluntly. And nobody believed anybody could be that inhumane."

Weiskircher was in a jeep from the HQ motor pool with two or three other soldiers; they stayed close to Sparks, who was in the command jeep with his driver, radio operator, and runner. "We got to the town of Dachau," recalls Weiskircher. "It was a little old Bohemian artist's colony; at one time it was the Greenwich Village of Europe. Nobody knew anything about a war. It was all Hitler's fault. You know the story. Until we met an old guy who pointed to his nose and told us to follow it. So we went about two kilometers following our nose, and the smell is indescribable." The source of the odor was a field full of bodies along-side boxcars and open-top gondola cars loaded with corpses. They had started out alive but had been locked in the railcars without food, sani-tation, or water. "And the irony of it," notes Weiskircher, "is they were being taken to Dachau to be done away with while Hitler was trying to hide the evidence."

The train was parked on tracks that led into the camp. The SS had marched the survivors into the camp across a small bridge over a canal. Some of the survivors, dying of thirst, dived into the canal and drowned.

Sparks's battalion broke up into three sections, each approaching the camp at a different entry point. Weiskircher, who has done signifi-cant postwar research on the subject, thinks of capturing Dachau as like trying to occupy a golf course. Others have described it as taking a sprawling college campus. No matter the metaphor, the upshot is that each man's Dachau experience was different, depending on his time and place of entry. So what was Russ Weiskircher's experience as he approached the train of thirty-nine cars somewhere in the middle?

"Well, first of all, the smell would gag you. Then you realize these are bodies, and after you get through vomiting, you start looking in the boxcars and ripping them open to see what you've got. You think, 'Oh, my God.' We don't know what a concentration camp is, and one of those people had an old Army OD [fatigue] shirt on. Now, this was a DP who picked it up somewhere, but immediately [one of the soldiers] said, 'My God, these are GIs.' You know what the reaction was? Chaos. I mean, absolutely almost uncontrollable chaos."

Some of the soldiers had leaped to the conclusion that the bodies were those of American POWs, a not unreasonable conclusion considering that none of them had ever seen a concentration camp and most didn't know about them. They were well aware, however, of the German stalags, the notorious POW camps. Weiskircher explains the confusion this way: "We did not know what to expect about a concentration camp. Now, clearly, Sparks was no fool and we weren't fools either, but you just don't read the paper every day. You don't get *The New York Times* in a foxhole, and the *Stars and Stripes,* when we did get it, could be a week, maybe a month old. We'd get our news mostly from Axis Sally, and we also got news from the tankers from their radios— they'd pick up some broadcasts, both British and American."

With his soldiers going crazy, at about noontime Lieutenant Colonel Sparks ordered the commander of I Company to lead his men into the camp. Weiskircher went with the battalion commander to a gate, where some of the troops scaled the wall, then removed the four-by-fours on the inside and opened the gate. At that point, there was no shooting going on.

Among the soldiers moving with Sparks was PFC Karl Mann, his interpreter. Mann had been born in Königsberg, the capital of East Prussia. He moved to Cologne when he was two and at age eleven moved with his family to Chevy Chase, Maryland, where his father worked at nearby American University. He finished two years of college before being drafted at age eighteen and became a citizen during basic training in Alabama. After the war, he would get his doctorate in industrial labor relations at Cornell, eventually teaching at Rider University near his home in Yardley, Pennsylvania, until he retired in 1994.

In early 1943, he was sent to Europe as a replacement and wound up in Sparks's 3rd Battalion. Mann recalls Sparks as being an exceptional person, highly intelligent and an outstanding soldier who was very highly regarded by all his men.

Mann remembers that Sparks had been given a heads-up about a day earlier that they were going to be sent from the town of Dachau to the concentration camp, but that information wasn't widely shared.

On the morning of the twenty-ninth, Sparks's command group was walking with I Company. "I noticed some commotion ahead of us, and it turned out that here was this German in a black SS uniform. I think he had a red cross armband. And he was getting pushed along by the GIs, and all of a sudden, he seemed to be running off to the side, and I heard a bunch of shots. They shot him, and that took care of him. A little later, in the sequence of things, we saw this train that carried all those dead bodies."

The story of what's become known as the Buchenwald-Dachau Death Train is important not only because of the impact it had on the hundreds of American soldiers who were confronted by it but because it is an example of what the Nazis did to their prisoners even when they knew the war was lost.

That particular train is the one that left Buchenwald—more precisely, Weimar—on April 7, just days before that camp was liberated. It carried 4,500 inmates and was supposed to go to the concentration camp at Flossenbürg, a distance of about 125 miles. Instead, it ended its journey at Dachau, roughly 250 miles due south. The actual trip covered 471 miles over twenty-two days as the train meandered north to Leipzig, then east through Dresden and south into Czechoslovakia, passing through Pilsen, then into Austria, and back west through Munich, all to avoid bomb-damaged tracks and advancing Allied forces.

The details of that particular Nazi atrocity are known because of a vast amount of research done by a former political prisoner at Buchenwald, Pierre C. T. Verheye. Now an American citizen living in Tucson, Verheye is no longer willing to talk about the concentration camp years, but in a phone call he did say that it took him twenty-five or thirty years of painstaking research, mostly by mail in pre-Internet years, to come up with the full story of the death of 2,310 prisoners.

In 1999, he provided his complete manuscript to 157th Infantry/Dachau veteran Dan Dougherty, who published an edited version in his newsletter *Second Platoon*. What follows is a summary of Verheye's work.

At 2 P.M. on April 7, 1945, the 4,500 Buchenwald inmates who had been rounded up for the special transport to Flossenbürg left the camp escorted by 130 SS enlisted men. An additional 90 SS accompanied them to the train station in Weimar, a march of just under six miles, during which 60 weak, sick, or handicapped inmates were shot to death. Each inmate had been issued fifteen small boiled potatoes, 5⅔ ounces of bread, and less than an ounce of sausage.

When the train left Weimar, it consisted of fifty-nine open and closed freight cars, each jam-packed with as many as 80 prisoners. In the early hours of April 19, after twelve days of meandering, the train arrived at Nammering, about 110 miles east-northeast of Dachau, with only fifty-four cars. Verheye writes, "It appears that, as the number of survivors decreased, some of the freight cars were abandoned." At Nammering, Verheye determined, a mass killing of about 900 inmates took place. More would die during the remaining days of the horrible odyssey. "Most of the victims died from exhaustion, exposure, disease, dehydration and hunger, the latter two causes being the major ones."

Verheye's interviews with survivors determined that "some inmates [were] drinking their own urine, others lapping water from rain puddles on the floor of the railroad cars—floors which were the resting place of dead bodies, bodily wastes, and dirty clothes crawling with lice—and still others who, upon arrival at KL Dachau and due to their eagerness to quench their thirst, fell into and drowned in the canal that ran along the fence of the 'Schutzhaftlager' (Protective Custody Camp)."

Verheye's report concluded with two questions:

1. Why did these atrocities happen and how could these barbaric crimes against humanity have been approved—sometimes tacitly but often enthusiastically—by the people of Germany, a nation which had achieved such great advances in cultural, artistic and scientific fields?
2. Why were these infernal "Death Trains" sent on their way at a time when the Third Reich was already on its knees and the end of the war only a few weeks or even a few days away and why did the Germans carry on with their extermination programs and mass executions until the very last minute?

"These questions have never been answered," he states.

While the men of the 157th were still going through the train cars, four German soldiers wearing medic insignia, which, under the circumstances, did not necessarily mean they were medics but could have been SS posing as such, attempted to surrender to Lieutenant William P. Walsh, who was commanding I Company. According to a report of the investigation conducted by the Seventh Army inspector general, Walsh ordered the four into a boxcar, "where he personally shot them." Private Albert C. Pruitt "then climbed into the boxcar where these Germans were on the floor moaning and apparently still alive, and finished them off with his rifle." Witnesses say that before shooting the men, Walsh had screamed at them about being medical personnel and allowing the horrible things he'd just witnessed along the train tracks. The IG recommended that the two men be tried for murder, but his report was "lost" and never acted upon.

Amid the horror along the length of the death train, there was one, just one, positive moment. It involved Tech Sergeant Tony Cardinale, Jr., from Pittsburg, California, who was a month shy of his twenty-fifth birthday when his outfit, the 222nd Regiment of the 42nd, got to Dachau. The rail-thin soldier, who would entertain his buddies with his Italian tenor voice, was the radio operator for the unit's commanding officer, Colonel Henry J. Luongo. He was riding in the backseat of his jeep, communicating to HQ on the radiophone or in Morse code, as they drove past the death train. The colonel ordered his driver to stop so they could get out and take a closer look.

Cardinale, who now lives with his son in Royal Palm Beach, Florida, remembers walking alongside the train. "We'd peer into each car, just disgusted with all the dead bodies. And as I'm walking along, I see something move, see a hand waving like this, back and forth, like that. The boxcar was open, and he was towards the end."

The nearest officer happened to be a battalion commander, Lieutenant Colonel Donald Downard. Cardinale called out, "Hey, Colonel, we got a live one here." Downard and another officer ran back to the car, more of a gondola with no roof and sides that swung open, jumped into the pile of bodies, lifted the survivor out, and handed him to Car-

42nd Infantry Division soldiers rescue one of the few survivors they discovered in the Dachau Death Train on April 29, 1945. Carrying the emaciated Polish man is Sergeant Tony Cardinale, who spotted movement amid corpses in one of the railcars.

dinale. The man, a Polish prisoner, said only one word to Tony. *"Frei?"* The American soldier responded, *"Ja, du bist frei"* (You are free). A French photographer caught the moment on film, just before the survivor was placed on a stretcher and driven away as rifle shots could be heard coming from inside the walls.

Cardinale, now approaching ninety, says, "That particular scene is embedded in my mind all these sixty years. The sun never sets on any day that I don't think about when I found that man. But at that particular time, what was going through my mind, you know, that we had to stop this. Somebody had to be there to stop all this crap that these Nazis were doing."

It's possible the rifle fire Cardinale heard came from members of the 157th Infantry, 45th Division, who had walked past the death train on the way into the camp just before noon. The late Ralph Fink of Hershey, Pennsylvania, who was active in the 157th Infantry Association, sent a letter to the membership in 1994, describing that afternoon. As they walked past the train, he recalls, the reaction of the men varied. "A few cried, some cursed in anger, but most seemed almost in a trance-like state."

They moved through the Jourhaus gate into "a bedlam type situation. The prisoners were milling about, shouting and obviously expecting to be given freedom immediately. . . . I would say hundreds and possibly a thousand or more. I do remember two ranks of bodies, mostly unclothed, piled near the entranceway, as if placed there earlier to be hauled away."

Once inside the prisoner compound, they learned that their assignment was to work their way from front to back, down the road that would take them past sixteen or seventeen barracks on either side. Fink wrote:

I think we went down the center roadway, clinging to the left side and using the barracks for protection from any possible sniper fire or any other resistance we might encounter. We were trailing the riflemen who were cautiously leap-frogging ahead, two or three at a time, always using the next barracks for immediate cover.

As this was going on slowly, there were no prisoners to be seen outside but we did notice emaciated people peering out at us from doorways, with those haunting, deep-set eyes. We were later to learn that these captives were so weak and non-functional that they could not work their way up to the Jourhaus entrance area prior to our arrival.

About half way to the rear, this one brave man came forth with the intention of coming down the street toward us, but he would fall down, crawl, regain his feet, fall down again, and so on. When he finally reached us he was hysterical—laughing, crying, hugging, kissing. This prompted others to come out, many just able to crawl along the ground, others clinging to each other for a bit of support.

This was easily the most poignant experience of my life and to this day the scene plays out in my mind as in slow motion, probably because of the extreme and total weakness of the people.

PFC James Dorris had finished his freshman year at the University of Chattanooga in his hometown when he was drafted, and turned into

James Dorris in 2008

a BAR (Browning automatic rifle) man with the 222nd Regiment. Like most of the others in his outfit, he'd never heard anything about concentration camps until Dachau.

Leaving the site of the death train, Dorris and his platoon came to a wide avenue and started down it. He says, "I think they called it SS Strasse, this big, wide road leading to the camp, and we were marching single file, one file on each side of the road. And all of a sudden we could smell the crematory. And immediately I realized what it was. It was a horrible, horrible odor that was so bad that first I tried not to breathe, and then you can't go very long doing that, so finally I started breathing as lightly as I could until I more or less got used to it."

Dorris's platoon entered the camp through the nearest gate, and once inside, his lieutenant ordered him to take his BAR and position himself between a high concrete wall and the barbed-wire fence that had, until the Americans turned the power off, been charged with enough electricity to kill on contact. His only instruction: don't let anybody out. The rest of the platoon headed into the camp while Dorris walked about a hundred yards toward one of the now-abandoned guard towers.

The young soldier was almost immediately confronted with the brutality of life inside Dachau. "There was a man, a body, lying there between the fence and the wall—well, he looked like a rag doll that'd been thrown down, arms and legs all different positions, and one of his eyes was laying out on his cheek where he'd been beaten so badly. I couldn't imagine how this body got there unless they'd thrown it over the fence. Right at that point, I looked inside, and there was a long row of naked bodies lying on the ground, about maybe fifty feet from me, and on the other side, toward the prison houses, was about two hundred, two hundred fifty prisoners standing there, just looking at me. [They were wearing] all kinds of rags that supposedly were uniforms, prison uniforms, and some of them in real bad shape. Not saying a word. Doing nothing but looking at me.

"Right about that time, one of the guys jumped over the bodies and ran towards me and leaned over and picked up, like he was picking something up off the ground and held it up. I couldn't see anything there to pick up, but he acted like that and started running with it, back towards the houses. Well, three more guys left the group and started chasing him, and they tackled him and knocked him down and were on top of him, kicking him and hitting him, trying to get his hands open to see what he had. Well, I thought, 'They're gonna beat this guy to death, gosh, they're all crazy, going through what all I imagined them having gone through.' "

Dorris was about to fire a burst from his rifle over their heads but stopped when he realized the bullets might go into the nearby barracks. So he did nothing. "I just stood there and looked, and I thought, 'This is what Hell is like.' That's the only thing I could think. And in my condition, mental condition, I thought I even saw the Devil coming out of the ground. It's a horrible-looking man with a real red face. I was imagining all this, and I looked up in the sky and said, 'God, get me out of this place.'

"Well, right at that point, when I looked back down, another prisoner had left and come over to the fence where I was, and he said, '*Haben Sie einen Zigarette?*' Do you have a cigarette? I thought, I've got four or five packs on me, but seeing all those people, if I bring those out, I don't have enough to give all of them, and I'd have a riot on my hands, so I said, 'No.' He said, *'Ein moment,'* and he turned around and ran back towards the houses.

"Then I looked back where these people were on top of that man, and they've gotten his hands open, and there was nothing in them. So in disgust, they got up off of him and went back with the other prisoners. Well, by that time, the man that had run off past me for a cigarette ran back to the fence, and he stuck his hand through the wire fence, and he had a little tiny rusty can. Took the top of off it. Inside was a cigarette butt about, oh, maybe three quarters of an inch long. It was all water-stained, and he handed that to me, and he said, I can't remember the exact German words, but 'This is in thanks for rescuing us.' Well, that just really got to me. Tears came to my eyes, and I had a complete different change from the way I had felt just two minutes before, and I thought, 'I'm really doing some good here.' And I felt that was God answering my prayer, because I felt like I was really despairing when I said, 'God, get me out of here,' and this fellow coming over and giving me that cigarette butt that he'd been saving. That was his treasure. No telling how long he'd been saving that.

"I took it and thanked him profusely, shook his hand, and I looked out at the other prisoners—they were still all standing there, and I waved to them, and they all waved and started smiling and laughing and talking. And this guy that handed me the cigarette butt was standing there smiling. He turned around and went back into the prison."

Russ Weiskircher had entered the camp with the command group of the 3rd Battalion, 157th Infantry. When they got inside, they found themselves in an area that was still free of all but a handful of prisoners.

They quickly surveyed the administrative buildings near the gate, including one that contained an entire IBM keypunch system that identified every inmate, but were struck by the fact that they weren't seeing a mass of living prisoners. Weiskircher says, "We didn't see anybody. It was eerie, and you know why we didn't? 'Cause the Germans told them that the Americans were coming, and when they got there, the Americans would kill everybody in the camp. And since they'd already suffered from the bombing right outside the camp, they probably were ready to believe anything.

"Then some people crawled out from under the barracks, the crawl spaces. Hollow-eyed people that you couldn't believe. They crawled out of there and crawled toward the gate and called out, and the GIs ran toward the [internal] gate. Now, the gate was locked. We got orders we could not go in and we could not let them out. They had every disease known to man, and we weren't inoculated for anything."

He and the other soldiers had what by now had become an almost ubiquitous experience of giving chocolate or rations to the starving inmates, with almost immediate, disastrous results.

Now an ordained minister, Weiskircher acknowledges an upgrading in the adjectives he uses to describe situations back then. But he still can feel the anger—and express it. "Listen, I'm still profane as I ever was, except then I spoke a barracks language. I'm amazed. I'm shocked. I'm nearly out of my gourd. And it was real hard to keep your cool."

Peter DeMarzo of Annapolis, Maryland, a rifleman with Company L of the 157th Infantry, had seen the death train, a sight that caused what he calls "complete shock." The shock was magnified once he got into the camp. "I never saw so many dead people in all my life. There were stacks of bodies."

Contact with surviving prisoners was also shocking for DeMarzo. "Oh, my God. This poor guy came over and kissed me. He must've weighed about seventy pounds. I thought, oh, God, it was terrible." Yet he recalls that he managed to kiss him back. "What'm I gonna do, you know?"

DeMarzo heard shooting inside the camp and became aware that inmates were tracking down and killing their former guards or kapos who hadn't escaped when the SS evacuated before the Americans arrived. He says the prisoners "would point them out, and somebody would walk over and shoot them." DeMarzo also recalls seeing inmates throw a suspected camp guard into a fire, burning him alive.

He's reluctant to talk about an incident mentioned in the inspector general's report on events that took place during the liberation of Dachau. The report describes an inmate asking DeMarzo to lend him his rifle, which he reportedly did. The inmate presumably used the weapon to kill one or more Germans still hiding inside the camp and then returned it to DeMarzo. While from the perspective of sixty-five years later, it may seem a strange thing for a soldier to do, the fact that similar incidents have been reported by GIs who were at several other concentration camps tends to give credence to the notion that it wasn't an unreasonable response under the circumstances, even though Army brass might not have endorsed it.

Early in their exploration of Dachau, Lieutenant Colonel Sparks had become aware that the anger level of the men of I Company was off the charts, and he'd ordered Weiskircher to contact higher head-quarters and ask for replacements before the place exploded.

Sparks's fears were realized not long afterward at an area near the SS hospital that was the coal yard for the Dachau power plant. It was there that SS prisoners from the nearby hospital, the NCO school, and finance center were being collected and guarded by soldiers under the command of the same Lieutenant Walsh who'd shot the German medics at the death train.

Walsh ordered a young machine gunner and other soldiers to train their weapons on the SS prisoners and shoot them if they made a move.

Karl Mann remembers Sparks disappearing around a corner near the coal yard, and when he did, "the I Company officers decided that they were going to shoot these Germans." Mann's memory contradicts the inspector general's report, which says that when the machine gun-ner placed a belt of ammunition in the gun and cocked it, the Ger-mans thought they were about to be executed and moved forward, at which point he opened fire. Seventeen Germans were killed before Lieutenant Colonel Sparks, firing his .45 in the air while shouting "Cease fire!," kicked the gunner away from the weapon and the shoot-ing stopped. The incident has generated controversy for years, with troops from the other division inside Dachau, the 42nd, insisting that as many as 350 German soldiers who had been patients in the SS hos-pital were lined up and executed, by the men of I Company. The IG re-port says it didn't happen, and there's no photographic evidence supporting it, unlike a significant number of photos and bullet hole forensics that tend to confirm the IG's conclusion that no more than seventeen Germans were killed at the wall.

The incident does give credence to reports that I Company was out of control, which led to its men being withdrawn from inside the camp and replaced with soldiers from another battalion.

For Russ Weiskircher, there was one moment inside Dachau that was memorable because it was just plain goofy. He was deep inside the camp when "Some dumb sonofagun who put on lederhosen and an Alpine hat and got a walking stick came strolling by. Said he was on his way to the mountains, trying to convince people he was a Dachau [town] citizen. He was someplace hiding, and he decided to dress up like he belonged to *The Sound of Music*. And the prisoners were yelling in German, "The captain!" He was desperate. He also had been educated in the United States; spoke better English than I did."

Herbert Butt of Company A, 222nd Infantry, 42nd Infantry Division, is fairly controlled when talking about the horrors he saw in Dachau, but when asked about the crematorium, a look passes across his face that gives pause. "Early on, I could break down just bigger than shit. Outside the crematory I can remember—and the thing that stuck with me the longest was all of those shoes laid there from these prisoners outside, and they were all killed. And that vision, I can see that almost to this day. That was just something that jarred my whole reserves."

Butt has another memory as well. "I got the smell. There was a stockyard area between Kansas City, Missouri, and Kansas, and it was a stink that you noticed as you drove by. It just plain stunk, and I made the statement that I couldn't see how people could live in that area. While we were there, they brought people in from the city of Dachau itself and took them through. And they didn't know anything like that was going on." The look of disgust on his face says it all.

Corporal Eli Heimberg was a twenty-eight-year-old assistant to the 42nd Division's Jewish chaplain when Dachau was liberated. He'd gotten the job because he could sort of play the organ, and the brand-new chaplain, Captain Eli A. Bohnen, was desperate for a reasonably observant Jew who could drive a jeep, pour wine into a Kiddush cup, and handle an M-1—sequentially, not simultaneously. They were in Salzburg when word came to them about Dachau, and they immediately drove to the camp to try to minister to surviving Jewish prisoners.

The South Dartmouth, Massachusetts, veteran, now in his early nineties, says, "I remember very vividly, it remains as a nightmare sometimes. Crossing the moat on a bridge, enough for one car at a time. And on the other side of the bridge, several big piles of clothing. Lots of clothing. Quite a few piles about three feet high and ten feet square." He also saw shoes piled fifteen feet high.

They were very quiet driving through the gate, just observing. They found someone to direct them to what he calls "the Jewish section." That may have been just one or two barracks, because at liberation, there were just 2,539 Jews, including 225 women, out of a population of just over 31,000.

Heimberg says, "Chaplain Bohnen announced in Yiddish, 'Ich bin ein amerikaner Rabbiner.' At that moment, it was as if all the pent-up emotions of the years in misery were unleashed in that room. There was a burst of wailing and crying. We stood there for a moment, unsuccessfully trying to control our emotions as the victims, who were able to, surged forward to kiss our feet and hug our hands. I felt humble and uncomfortable, for it was I who should have been hugging and kissing them."

The first group they found didn't number more than twenty-five, many of whom said they had relatives in the United States and wanted the chaplain to contact them. "People said, 'Look, just ask for—he lives in New York, my uncle. His name is Sam Cohen. You'll find him.' So we took the names anyway, and where we could get a telephone number, we'd take a phone number."

The Jews they met with were Polish and had come from other camps. He remembers them talking about Bergen-Belsen in Germany and Birkenau, part of Auschwitz, in Poland. And after just talking with the survivors, Rabbi Bohnen held a brief memorial service, chanting the traditional memorial prayer, El Moleh Rachamim, as the newly freed inmates sobbed.

The next day, Chaplain Bohnen wrote a letter to his wife, Eleanor, describing the experience. "Nothing you can put in words would adequately describe what I saw there. The human mind refuses to believe what the eyes see. All the stories of Nazi horrors are underestimated rather than exaggerated. . . .

"The Jews were the worst off. Many of them looked worse than the dead. They cried as they saw us. I spoke to a large group of Jews. I don't remember what I said, I was under such mental strain, but Heimberg tells me that they cried as I spoke. Some of the people were crying all the time we were there. They were emaciated, diseased, beaten, miserable caricatures of human beings. I don't know how they didn't all go mad. There were thousands and thousands of prisoners in the camp . . . and as I said, the Jews were the worst. Even the other prisoners who suffered miseries themselves couldn't get over the horrible treatment meted out to the Jews. I shall never forget what I saw, and in my nightmares the scenes recur. . . . No possible punishment would ever repay the ones who were responsible."

Chicagoan Morris Eisenstein had already earned two Silver Stars for gallantry with the 42nd Division by the time his outfit got to Dachau. But the concentration camp terrified him in ways that combat did not. Now ninety-one years old and dealing with the aftereffects of a severe stroke, the Delray Beach, Florida, resident remembers walking into the prisoner compound and being swallowed up by 10,000 or more people. "I figured I've got to identify myself, so I fired a clip up in the air to quiet everybody down, and I remembered a prayer I learned in Hebrew school. I said to them, '*Barukh attah Adonai eloheinu melekh ha-olam, shehecheyanu v'kiyemanu v'higianu laz'man hazeh.*' It's the Shehecheyanu prayer, said on special occasions, that translates as 'Blessed art thou, Lord our God, Master of the universe, who has kept us alive and sustained us and has brought us to this special time.'"

The prayer had the desired effect. Eisenstein—they called him Ike—says the prisoners began whispering in Yiddish, *"Ehr ist ein Yid"* (He's a Jew), a reaction of surprise that was common at liberation. After talking with him in Yiddish for a while, some of the prisoners took Eisenstein on a tour of the camp. As he was about to leave, he stumbled over a man who was sitting on the ground. "He looked like he was dying, he looked like he was dead, and I didn't know what to do, so I figured maybe I can help him out. I wanted to make sure that he stays there, because I knew our rear echelon had medics and everybody else would be coming up soon. I said to him, '*Ich bin amerikaner yiddisher* Soldat,' and he looked at me.

Morris Eisenstein outside his Florida home, proudly wearing his Jewish War Veterans cap displaying his two Silver Stars and Combat Infantryman Badge.

"At that time, I got down on my knees next to him, and in my pocket I had about twenty thousand marks. We killed some SS in a firefight the week before, and we got some loot. I took it out and I put it in his hand. And he grabbed my hand, and he said to me in Yiddish, 'I cannot take this. It's not proper. I must give you something in return.' Here's a man who was absolutely emaciated, just about dead. You think philosophically about what he just said. So I kept looking at the Star of David pinned to his uniform, and he saw me looking. He unhooked the pin and gave me the star." Eisenstein left Dachau in tears. That star is now on display at the National Museum of American Jewish Military History in Washington, D.C.

Dallas Peyton came to Dachau with the 70th Armored Infantry of the 20th Armored Division and is more than a bit cynical about the ongoing battle of who got there first, the 42nd, the 45th, or the 20th. He's clear that the three divisions had elements that hit the concentration camp at roughly the same time, certainly on the same day. He's also clear that the argument will end when there's only one man left standing who can claim the honor because there'll be nobody else to argue about it.

Peyton has blocked out most of what happened at Dachau on April 29, except for two things that he's seen in his mind's eye for the last sixty-five years. "One of them was that train. At first I thought it was people in there, and then I realized, no, that's not people. They're just thrown in there like little logs. I don't know what I thought. Shock beyond belief. And the other's when we got inside the camp and saw two of what I call 'walking skeletons' shuffling along, one in front of me and the other coming towards us. And those two guys stopped, stared at each other for a few minutes, then screamed and ran together, hugging, kissing, hollering, and crying. Up until that moment, neither knew the other was still alive, and I can see that right now."

As darkness settled over Dachau, Jim Dorris and the men of Company A of the 222nd Regiment were told that they would be spending the night inside the SS garrison barracks, in the building where the on-duty SS guards had eaten and slept. Dorris says the building was about seventy-five yards inside the main gate, and their cook had come in to prepare a big meal for the American troops. "The building had a nice kitchen in it," Dorris recalls, "and a big part of it had bunks. Everybody was just kind of numb from what we'd seen. You couldn't describe. I mean, everybody had seen something so bad that they just didn't want to talk. We just sat there eating and not saying a whole lot.

"After we ate—we'd had a hard day of it—we went in and picked out different bunks. They all looked like maybe the guards had been awakened, hearing that we were coming, and they'd just thrown the covers back and jumped up and took off to resist us or whatever they did. And I remember getting in that bunk and thinking, 'What kind of guy was laying here in this bunk last night?' I thought about that for quite a while."

APRIL 30, 1945
DACHAU, GERMANY

By the next morning, other outfits had come in, bringing food and medical care for the prisoners. Dorris's company got something to eat around dawn and then loaded onto tanks and headed for Munich, about fifteen miles away. They expected a battle but were surprised. "The people were lined up on both sides, cheering us, and we were completely taken aback by that. That was the first time we'd had that happen, but they were giving us bottles of champagne and throwing flowers on us. And we were wondering how much they knew about what was going on out there at Dachau."

Jim Dorris never had a chance to find out. He'd made it through the war with nothing more than some minor shrapnel wounds, but while he was sitting in a house with three of his buddies, one of them pulled out a .38 revolver, gave the cylinder a twirl, and pulled the trigger. The bullet went into the top of Dorris's leg and out the back, leaving powder burns. The guy with the gun asked if he'd shot him, and Dorris claims that all he said was "Hell, yes!" He was taken to the hospital, where they took his clothes. The cigarette butt in the can that he'd been given by the Dachau prisoner was in a pocket. He never saw it again.

Dee Eberhart was also one of the 42nd Division guys riding tanks on their way from Dachau to Munich. It was a memorable morning, not only because of what they had left behind at Dachau, but because the ugliness continued. "We were in the outskirts of Munich, and I was on this lead tank, nobody ahead of us, and maybe three or four other guys on the tank, and here was a German soldier who was running straight down the street, maybe a block ahead of us. And behind him, pounding along, was not one of the emaciated prisoners but one of the blue-and-white prisoners, a husky guy, and he caught that German and tackled him and then kicked him to death before we got there. And here was the tank with machine guns pointed forward and all of us with rifles, we didn't raise a damn hand, not a hand. We saw this premeditated murder, killed him dead. And that guy was just a bundle of dead rags when our tank rumbled by, and the other guy was standing around, looking at the man he'd just killed. So there was a lot of residual violence, on both sides, during that day."

New Yorker Jerome Klein was part of the 48th Tank Battalion of the 14th Armored Division when, on April 30, his outfit was told they were being taken to see a most unusual sight. The sight was the concentration camp at Dachau, and, just as he had with Ohrdruf and Buchen-

*Jerome Klein with his mother, Bessie, in Brooklyn,
shortly after he completed basic training. After
the war, at Jerry's request, she would help bring
Holocaust survivor Sidney Glucksman to live
with them.*

wald, Eisenhower had ordered that as many American soldiers as possible should be given time to see the horrors firsthand.

Klein's arrival happened to coincide with another instance of the
inmates discovering a guard hiding inside the camp. He describes the
scene as upsetting. "I didn't realize at the moment what it was that was
happening, but these wasted inmates had ganged up on somebody and
were stoning him and killed him. Then I learned it was a prison guard
who had not gotten out and had put on civilian clothes and thought he
could escape, but they recognized him." Klein watched from no more
than ten yards away, listened to the "enormous amount of noise," and
noticed that other Americans were doing the same thing he was
doing—gaping. "I don't think anyone tried to intrude on it. We had already had some explanation of what this was all about. I took a photograph and walked on."

The camera he used was one he'd been given a few days earlier by a German army doctor he'd captured in a small town. The doctor had asked if Klein would permit him to say good-bye to his wife before taking him to a POW camp. Klein agreed, and to thank him, the doctor took him down in the cellar of his home, removed bricks from the wall—an act that made Klein briefly wonder if he'd made a huge mistake and was about to be shot—and withdrew an unusual military camera from its hiding place and gave it to him.

After leaving the scene of the killing near the Dachau gate, Klein went inside the prisoner compound and began walking around, saying hello to some of the inmates. Initially he spoke German, but when he met a Jewish inmate, the language swiftly morphed to Yiddish. At one point in the camp, he met a sixteen-year-old boy, a Polish Jew named Stashek Gleiksman, who had survived in the camps as a tailor. "He was extremely friendly. He was much more alert. He seemed to be less damaged than the other inmates."

Klein remembers Gleiksman as being slender but not emaciated. "He hadn't been in Dachau all that long. He'd gone through a succession of other camps, and I have a feeling since he was valued as a tailor, they probably kept him in somewhat better shape."

The boy Klein connected with had been taken from his home in the small Polish town of Chrzanów, near Auschwitz, in 1939, when he was twelve and a half. He, along with the other Jewish boys in his school, had been loaded onto a truck and taken to a Nazi SA camp several hundred miles away, where the brown-shirted guards made them build the barracks. While they were constructing the foundations, a bag of cement fell on him and broke his arm, and he was sent to another camp to stay until it healed.

From there he was sent to the death camp known as Gross-Rosen, where he stayed for three years working on construction of barracks. It was while he was there that he learned the fate of his family. "They brought in some more people from my town, and I asked them how my parents were, how's my brother doing, how's my sister doing? They just put the finger in front of their mouth and said 'Shh!' like that, and since then I never heard from anybody."

About a year and a half before the liberation, Gleiksman and other prisoners were taken out of Gross-Rosen and set on a death march to Dachau. "One day they took us out, we were young, we were able to walk. But every night when it got dark, they put us on the field where it was nothing there, no trees or anything, and we had to lay down like an animal on the grass until daylight came. Because they were watching us. But there was no way to go away, to run away. If you had to pee, you had to pee right there where you were. We didn't have anything to eat. A lot of people died during the march.

"Once we got to Dachau, there we had to again line up. There were chairs and tables and SS, a woman and an SS man, sitting on one side. And I remember they called out 'Next!' to come over. I got to the table, and I remember [from previous camps] when they say, 'Jews on one side, every other nationality to stay where you are,' and I could smell the stink from the crematorium, you saw the smoke coming out. It stunk like terrible, you know, when flesh burns and the bones. So I said to myself, I'm going to take the name of my friend who we lived together in the same building, so I gave them a Polish name. And they brought me over to the other side where I was with the Polish people."

After being put in a barrack with young people from different countries, he became quite ill. "I got sick, typhoid, because an epidemic broke out. And I don't remember anything what happened, I just remember that I fell down while I was talking to somebody, and that was the end. How I survived, who put me up in my bunk, I don't remember. I don't know. I woke up after that, maybe my fever left me. I wasn't able to walk at all. Just to try, you know, you didn't care at that time. Just that you wanted to live. So somehow I was holding on to the walls and tried to walk, to look for some water to get washed. I must have been laying there in filth without washing myself, without taking a drink of water, even. I still don't know how I survived."

He recovered from the typhoid but still had to survive months of hard labor until liberation. "I just put on my striped *shmata* on myself and the shoes with the wooden soles, which you could hardly walk, and they put us in trucks. And what we had to do is clean up after the bombardments, you know, bigger towns like Munich or any other place. If they bombarded during the night, that was like being on vacation, in paradise, because there we were able to find some kind of food. If it was a rotten potato or even a dead cat or whatever. Just to eat. At that time, I was weighing about eighty-seven pounds."

At 6:30 on the morning of April 29, in the dark, Gleiksman and the other inmates had lined up outside as they did every other day before being taken to work. "That day, we were lined up, waiting for the SS to come and get us, to count us up and get to work. They didn't show. It was very quiet."

The kapos—the inmate guards who got special favors from the Nazis in exchange for being overseers and goons—never showed up. When daylight came, the prisoners saw white rags tied around the machine guns in the guard towers, but they still had no idea what was going on. He says somewhat matter-of-factly, "You know, I didn't see a newspaper for six years. We don't have radio. We didn't know what day it was. At nine o'clock in the morning, it was really bright, and those guards are still staying in the towers. Shaved their heads off. They didn't have any helmets on, and they had uniforms on from what we wore, striped uniforms."

Shortly, the prisoners heard shooting—Gleiksman believes tanks were firing, but he may have actually been hearing explosions and seeing rising smoke to the northwest when the Germans blew the bridge over the Amper River in the face of the advancing L Company of the 45th. When the gate was opened and soldiers in jeeps and trucks poured into the camp, "Whoever was able to walk, you know, was not sick anymore, they started to run towards the gates. We saw a color green, and German tanks were dark gray, so we knew that something happened. We saw a different marker on the truck, a white star, and the jeeps' white stars, and they started to surround the whole camp, staying on guard.

"And they started to go in deeper into the camp, and the people were laying there, half dead all over the ground, with flies all over the bodies, maybe rot even. People were still with typhoid, and they were not able to stand up, they were too weak. They were breathing, but that's all. And some soldiers I saw, when they bend down, they started to cry like children. That's how bad it was. It stunk terrible. And they still found bodies in the crematorium, in the ovens, and there were bodies laying in the front to be burned with those big pliers to be picked up and thrown in the fire. Those things I do remember."

And what did he do? "I just sat down. I was too weak to go back to the barracks."

There's some confusion as to whether the man now known as Sidney Glucksman of New Haven, Connecticut, met his future lifelong friend, Jerome Klein of Manhattan, on liberation day or on the day after, as Klein recalls. What the former inmate does clearly remember is his own disbelief that the American soldier was a Jew. Sidney says, "I myself, I couldn't believe it. But I didn't know that he's a Jew, because all the Jews in the whole world are dead. I didn't know that Jews were still alive when I was liberated. I thought the Germans killed all the Jews, because in so many years, what I saw [them] bringing in, hundreds of thousands of men, women, even children.

"It's sometimes so hard to talk about it, but in Gross-Rosen when I was there, I remember when they brought in trainloads of women with children on their hands. They were lined up. I was already an old-timer there, and they made the women get undressed and the little children, set them down on the ground. And the women were all naked, and they told them they have to go in to get showered up, and they already had new clothes on their hands, like going to take a shower. They never came back. And the children were on the ground. We had to go over there, you know, all the younger prisoners, and undress them, shoes take off, take off the clothes, whatever they had on, and take off eyeglasses, and bring all the stuff into the barracks.

"The children, I cry whenever I start talking about it. They threw them in bags and hit them against barracks until you didn't hear a child cry anymore. When I start talking about it, it makes me sick. So many years after."

MAY 2, 1945
DACHAU, GERMANY

Second Lieutenant Charlotte Chaney, all five feet, 1½ inches of her, had been told by the first nursing school she applied to in New York that she was too short to be a nurse. Too short to move patients, to change the bed, to do everything nurses had to do. So she went back to New Jersey, to Beth Israel, which gladly accepted her in its three-year course. She went through all the rotations but fell in love with surgery. She graduated at the age of twenty-one, and in 1943, having seen most of the doctors and nurses at the hospital leaving to join the Army, she did the same. She shipped overseas as part of the 127th Evacuation Hospital in January 1945 but managed to get married first, to a soldier.

After landing at Le Havre, they were shipped to northern France, near Reims, where they lived in what had been a children's boarding school. In April—she remembers because it was after Passover—life changed for the 127th. "We suddenly got orders that they're coming to pick us up, and we're heading south. They put straw on the bottom of the truck, and we slept foot to foot. We finally got orders to go into Germany, cross over, and that's what we did. We had orders to go to Munich, and then we still didn't know anything about the Holocaust. Nobody said anything.

"We got into Munich, and they told us we had to go ten miles past Munich, and they said there's some kind of a camp there. Some camp. We went into the courtyard, they had something above the entrance." She's talking about an enormous Nazi eagle with outstretched wings, a swastika in its talons, mounted over the main entrance.

Their arrival came three days after the liberation of Dachau, and she doesn't remember seeing a huge number of GIs when the 127th arrived. The combat units that had freed the camp had moved on. "When we went in, we were told the Army had been right before us. And they said, 'You'll probably find some dead bodies around.'"

As the trucks drove into the center of the compound, she got her first glimpse of the horror. "We looked to the right of us, and we saw all these people, you know, behind barbed wire. So that's the first time we saw them. I thought to myself, where in the world am I? What happened here? How could this happen?"

They took over the four-story SS barrack that was inside the administrative area of the camp. "We were told to be careful, because if you touch anything, it may explode."

Not long after their arrival, the nurses were assigned to go into the prisoner enclosure behind the barbed wire. They were warned that

Nurse Charlotte Chaney married her late husband, Bernie, in 1944. A few months later she went to Europe with the 127th Evacuation Hospital, which eventually was assigned to care for survivors of Dachau. In one of her letters home she wrote, "Our job was to separate the living, the half-living and the dead."

reprisals were still being taken against German guards or kapos found in the camp; they were being killed. "And we were told just to—don't even bother with it—let them do what they want."

The prisoners who were outside the barracks were apparently those in the best physical condition. It's when she went into the buildings that she was confronted with the ultimate in horror on bunks stacked three high. "We'd walk into a barrack, and there you saw what it was. They were like skeletons, so close together. We started to go in and clean out. We took them over to where the German GIs stayed, it was on the other side of the camp, and the Army came in with beds and linens, and we would delouse them. We had sprays, we shaved them, put on clean clothes. We had to do it for some of them. We set up like a triage, and then we realized we were going to need help, lots of help, because there were so many people there."

When the Americans first came to Dachau, they reported that as many as three hundred or four hundred inmates died each day. Chaney remembers fifty to one hundred dying daily, for several days. Their job was to separate the living from the half-living from the dead. "We couldn't stop to even think, because there's so many hundreds and hundreds of people. There were children there that we tried to get to. And then to feed these people, we couldn't give them regular food right away, we had to start off with a gruel because their digestive systems were shot, you know? And even if we gave them a crust of bread, they would hide it under their pillow. We'd try to tell them, 'You'll get more, you don't have to do that anymore.' But . . ." her voice trails off, her eyes misting, the scene playing over in her mind.

The fact that she spoke Yiddish helped somewhat in communicating with her patients, many of whom were suffering from typhus and TB. To try to avoid succumbing to the diseases they were treating, the doctors and nurses wore long gowns and masks, had their heads wrapped, and wore rubber gloves. And they were regularly sprayed with DDT powder.

The odor is still with her. "It was a distinctive smell or odor that you got—you know, if you walk into a room with a lot of people that are ill, they have a distinctive odor. This was ten times worse."

Their priority was to get the inmates out of the barracks and into the rapidly expanding hospital as quickly as possible. "We would just get 'em out of there, get 'em cleaned up, put them in clean beds, and start giving them food, gradually increasing the diet. Those that couldn't even eat gruel were given IV feedings. And that was all that we could do at the time. We worked practically day and night." She says the nurses were overwhelmed, "always, every day. There were so many, and the children. These kids with the bloated bellies from starvation."

She saw the bones and the bodies behind the crematorium that the Germans had not had time to bury and was there when they brought civilians from Munich to dig graves. They were asked, "Didn't you see anything? Didn't you smell anything? Didn't you see the smoke? Nothing."

And then they went to see the boxcars, the death train.

Sitting in her Hollywood, Florida, apartment sixty-four years later, holding the boxes of letters she wrote home from the war, she knows that she'll never forget her experiences at Dachau, and she doesn't want others, especially today's children, to forget either. "It's always in the back of my head, even when I go out and speak to schools, to the children, I try to make them understand what happened, and to this day, we still don't know—because for people to follow a crazy man, you know, he should have been put away."

And God? She questions where God was. "If there was a God above, why did this happen? To let this happen—my belief in God went way down. Even to this day, I still can't understand. They say there is somebody up there looking after everybody. I say, how? In the Holocaust, there was nobody, nobody."

Shortly after the 127th Evac had set up operations at Dachau itself, arrangements were being made to transport some inmates in dire need of medical care to the 120th Evac, which had moved from Buchenwald to Cham, a town about a hundred miles northeast of Dachau. Within days the 120th was treating more than nine hundred former prisoners hospitalized in five different buildings.

Len Herzmark, who was a medic, not a doctor, has one very precise memory of his time with the unit at Cham. "I had a patient whose hands were paralyzed for whatever reason, and while we were working the inspector came through from Army headquarters somewhere, a medical inspector, just wanted to look at what we were doing—you know, visited with some of the patients and so on. And after he left, this one patient who had the paralyzed hands, he said, 'Did the doctor give you any recommendation for my paralysis?' And I knew that this guy wasn't really paralyzed, you could tell, you know? So I said 'Yes,' and I'd probably be shot for this today, but I got a syringe of saline, sterile saline solution, and I gave him an injection, a muscular injection in the back between the shoulder and elbow, the muscle there. And you know, the next day, he was folding blankets. I cured him."

Two days after the liberation of Dachau, the 45th Infantry Divi-

Leonard "Pinky" Popuch, later Leonard Parker, sang Yiddish songs to the Jewish Dachau inmates, who had a difficult time believing there were Jewish soldiers in the U.S. Army.

sion's Leonard "Pinky" Popuch, who after the war became Leonard S. Parker, an acclaimed architect who designed the Minneapolis Convention Center, the State of Minnesota Supreme Court Building, and the U.S. Embassy in Santiago, Chile, wrote a nine-page letter to his family at home in Milwaukee. In a bold hand, he assured them of his safety and assessed his life and the world around him. "I am still well and trusting in God. A little tired and worn out perhaps, and maybe a little older, now, than my 22 years—but well, never-the-less."

He'd last written when his company was at Nuremberg. Now he wrote, "Many times since I have come overseas, while miserable in a wet foxhole, or sweating out a Jerry artillery barrage, or lying out in the rain pinned down by enemy small arms fire, I have asked myself what it is all about. Why am I here—why! why! why!"

Dachau answered his questions, and he tried to help his family understand. He described the death train and the bodies and said, "We took no German prisoners that day . . . they are no better than swine and we treated them as such. We saw and smelled the crematorium where they cremated the dead bodies after removing the shoes and any other valuables the people might possess . . . we heard from the lips of the prisoners themselves as to how they were beaten and starved and made to work anywhere from 12 to 18 hours in one day. We listened to countless stories of cruelty and the inhumanity of the Nazis and it made one want to tear the eyes out of the next German soldier you saw."

He went on to describe the first prisoner he heard speak—of all things, a U.S. Army captain who had parachuted into France before D-Day and been captured by the Gestapo and sent to Dachau. And he wrote about the prisoners who kissed the Americans, crying for joy:

> They fell on the ground at our feet and kissed our boots and grabbed our hands and kissed them, and these suffering, crying Jewish people yelled, "*Dank gott was ze haben gekumen—yetzt zenen mir frie*" [Thank God you came—now we are free]." There were women, children and men alike—those that were able to walk—all crying, half mad with happiness.
>
> A Jewish man came up to me and asked me if it were true that there were Jewish soldiers in the American army. When I told him that I was a Jewish "unteroffizier" he nearly went mad. Soon I had about 50 Jewish men and women around me hugging and kissing me. They were starved also for "das Yiddishe giest" [Jewish spirit], and I wanted so much to make them happy. I sang some "chazonish shticklach" [Jewish cantorial music] for them, and all, "A Yiddishe Mama."
>
> I saw firsthand the things that I have heard about and which I had never quite believed. Now, I know what this war is all about. Now I know why we are fighting. To me, all the suffering and misery I've had to put up with these past 8 months has been well worthwhile. Just to see the joy on the faces of these tortured, suffering people repaid all of us that saw, a thousand fold. . . . I'm proud to be one of the many who finally helped free those poor souls who have

been through a hell that the decent mind cannot imagine possible here on God's own earth. . . .

. . . I wanted to let you know of how our people have suffered and that we're (I mean the Americans) are bringing light in their hearts and maybe in the homes they may have again some day. I have hopes that you'll feel as I feel, that the anxiety and worry and heart suffering you are going thru is for something. To stamp out the poison Hitler and his kind have spread over the world.

I will write again when I can. I love you all and miss you very much.

Still your same devoted Sammy.

CHAPTER 14

THEY'RE KILLING JEWS—WHO CARES?

MAY 2, 1945

AMPFING, GERMANY

52 miles east of Dachau

35 miles southeast of Moosburg

Coenraad Rood lay in the hole in the ground the Germans had assigned to him and roughly a dozen others when he had arrived at the Waldlager V concentration camp five days earlier. There were only two facts the twenty-eight-year-old Dutch Jew thought relevant at that moment: the Americans were coming, and he would not live to see them.

Just three days earlier, those Americans—the tankers and infantrymen of the U.S. Army's 14th Armored Division—had liberated Stalag VII-A, the POW camp at Moosburg near the Isar River, freeing an astounding 110,000 Allied prisoners of war.

Nathan Melman was part of a mechanized cavalry reconnaissance platoon attached to the 48th Tank Battalion when Moosburg was liberated, and the twenty-three-year-old enlistee from Trenton, New Jersey, was one of the first Americans into Waldlager V—it means Forest Camp 5—at Ampfing. The 48th didn't even know the place existed until they stumbled across strange-looking people in striped uniforms. Melman was driving a jeep convoying with a couple of tanks and armored cars traveling down a dirt road through the woods when they happened upon the camp.

He recalls some shooting, but mostly, he says, the Germans "were trying to get the hell outta there, and the prisoners, as weak as they were, they got hold of"—he pauses briefly, then continues, "I think there were five Germans they captured that were guards, and two of them must've been so mean and rotten that as weak as the prisoners were, they beat them to death with their bare hands." This happened after the Americans arrived. "And the other three, they told us they were half decent, not to hurt them, so we let those three go. They just left the bodies of these two lying near the front gate, and when the officers told them, 'We let you kill them, we didn't stop you. Now pick them up and take them some place and bury them, we don't want them laying there.' Bury them? They all lined up, the ones that were able to walk, and they urinated on them."

Melman recalls that the gates to the camp were open when the GIs arrived, and some of the prisoners walked out of the gate, then walked back in, just to see if anybody would harm them.

As the Americans made their way through the camp, they discovered a mass grave containing as many as two thousand bodies. It was identical in construction to one found at Buchenwald. Melman says prisoners were made to dig a trench perhaps thirty or forty feet long; then a removable barrier was placed at the end. Bodies—some still alive—were tossed into the trench. When more space was needed, the trench was extended beyond the barrier, which was then pulled up and moved.

Melman's small unit stayed in Ampfing overnight, as did C Company of the 62nd Armored Infantry Battalion. Robert Highsmith, now of Las Cruces, New Mexico, was not quite twenty-two years old when his unit made an overnight stop at Waldlager V. He has just one vivid memory of that moment. "There were about four or five of the prisoners that were standing there. They spoke German, and I spoke English only. Four of them were tall. Their hair was unkempt. They were very, very, very, very skinny. They'd lost a lot of weight, with one exception: there was one of the persons there, he had a haircut, was shaved, skinhead. He was fat. When he smiled, you could see a stainless-steel tooth there in his mouth, and I know to this good day that he was a collaborator, because his physical appearance was so much different from all the others that were there."

Highsmith, who got a commission after the war and retired as a lieutenant colonel in 1967, recalls moving through the Ampfing camp, his rifle at the ready. "When you're infantry and on the attack like that, you're always at the ready, because you don't know what you're gonna get when you get into there. Only a few days before we had gone to another prisoner-of-war camp [Moosburg]. We went into that camp, and there were German guards there." Highsmith chokes up as he recalls finding a soldier from his company in the POW camp. The man had been captured two or three months earlier and had lost almost 40 pounds in the interim. So as he walked through Ampfing with twenty-five or thirty members of his platoon, he was remembering his buddy. "I'm thinking that if there are any German guards there, that we're going to do everything we can to eliminate them."

But they found no guards, just prisoners who were nearly dead. "Most of them were emaciated, starved, ill, and as I understand, a lot of them died later, because they had been maltreated, malnourished, and then no medication."

Karl Pauzar of Dayton, Ohio, was a sergeant in Company A of the 62nd Armored Infantry Battalion when his outfit came upon Ampfing. "We didn't know anything about it being there. I was in a half-track, come up upon this town, said, 'Ampfing,' and there's this camp. There's not a guard or anything around it, so I drove around to the right side of it and I saw—this is the only individual I remember—this elderly gentleman, very emaciated. Emotionless. The only thing was a shuffle, blank stare, striped uniform. And he come up to the fence. And I kept going; we were instructed not to give them any food or anything else because of this-and-this. I understand that they dropped some medics off, and they were there about six weeks doing what they could with them."

Pauzar, who also stayed in the military and retired as a lieutenant colonel, says that staying to help out at the camp just wasn't their priority at the time. "Oh, no, no. Go, go, go, we had the Germans on the run. We didn't give them a chance to set their defenses. We just run, run."

But while some units kept going, the outfits that stopped, even for a few hours, saved lives. Consider Coenraad Rood. Ampfing was his tenth concentration camp since he'd been arrested by the Nazis on April 25, 1942, in Amsterdam. Speaking from his home in White Oak, Texas, between Dallas and Shreveport, Rood recalled that most of the moves from camp to camp were part of the effort to keep prisoners, especially slave laborers, from falling into Allied hands. A week earlier, he'd been at another of the Dachau subcamps, Mühldorf. Asked to evaluate his five days at Ampfing, he says, "They were not too bad compared to what I already experienced." Here, then, is what he calls "not too bad":

"We lived practically on the ground, in holes in the ground, with a movable roof over it, and we lived ten to twenty in a ditch, you could say. We came there from several camps, and Ampfing was one of those places where they could place us. We had two camps next to each other; I had to work in Camp Six, but I belonged to Camp Five. Six was already evacuated because the Americans came too close. We were waiting to be evacuated, and at the last moment, that all went into smoke, you can say, because the American Army was faster."

Coen and his new friend Maupy were assigned to walk each day to Camp Six, where they were to whitewash empty prefabricated huts. The walk gave them a chance to find food along the way, usually potato peels in an adjacent field, which was more than anything being provided to the inmates of Camp Five. During his captivity, the five-foot-eight Coen's weight had dropped from 143 down to 60 pounds at liberation. They walked between camps without a guard, which, Coen explains, did not offer them an opportunity to escape. "Where should we go, anyway? We were prisoners, we wore prisoner clothes, we were tattooed, we had numbers. The danger outside the camp was very great that we should be detected as prisoners, especially if you were a Jewish prisoner, you know, that's the end of the day for you." He said it obliquely, but the danger he refers to is from local German civilians—the same people who would soon protest, *"Nicht Nazi."*

Just a couple of days before the 14th Armored arrived, Coen learned that the Germans were intent on liquidating almost the entire camp population. "There was a roll call early in the morning. It was just as daylight came through, and we had to line up along a rail track that went across the camp from one end to the other. We were about 1,100 or 1,200 men standing there. And the camp commander, which we had barely seen before, talked to us. He said, first, all the Jews from Western Europe have to stand on the side. So we had about sixty men, and he talked to us in German. He explained that he expected that the Americans are coming, and he would leave us. The camp will be evacuated; all the people from East Europe would be removed. And he said, 'You know what's going to happen to them.' He talked openly about it. 'And you stay here.' And then the Americans—he talked about the enemy, you understand that? When the enemy was coming, we had to report that we were handled humanely. And if we should tell them how it was, he called it, 'Where you start lying, we know how to get to you, so you better don't tell them what actually happens at the camp.' "

Coen said the thousand or so Eastern European prisoners were marched down to the gate. "And they went through, out the gate, and then we heard suddenly like a motor. We heard *tat-tat-tat-tat,* and we thought, 'Oh, my gosh, they shoot them already. They didn't even wait until they have them in the woods.' But it was a motor sound, a motorcycle, and it was the commander and a German officer. He came into the camp and said, 'Close the doors. The enemy is surrounding the camp. You cannot go nowhere.' " After being sent to a big tent and then a warehouse tent next to the kitchen, they were ordered back to their so-called buddahs—the below-ground hovels about the size of a single carport.

"And we went back," he recalls, "and I lay down. A few days before, I had lost a very good friend in the camp, and that was tremendous on my mind. He is called Nico, and we were very close. We took always care of each of us in kind of choosing to go to another job; we took care that we were together always. We helped each other, with food and with friendship, mostly. And I had lost him in Mühldorf, where we stayed two and a half days before we reached Ampfing. During an attack from American airplanes."

Coen tells of being in a truck with many other prisoners when the planes attacked, saying, "I'm the only one not wounded on that truck, although I felt like I was wounded. And that's when I lost my last friend, together more than two years. And that was still on my mind. When we had to go back to the buddahs and I lay down, I thought, 'Well, this is the end of it. They are shooting, they are fighting.' And I was very sick, also, and I felt I was dying. And in that situation, I was liberated.

"I was laying down, losing my conscious. I had the feeling that I was floating through the air, and I knew that this was the end. It was my turn, now, to go, to leave everything."

That's when he heard Maupy, who spoke English. "They're here, they're here, they opened the gates!" Others yelled, "Americanski are komen!"

More than sixty years later, Coen can still re-create the experiences, almost second by second. "I had a feeling I was floating through the air, looking at myself lying down, and I was yelling at myself. I thought I was yelling, but I don't think I made any sound. It was like a séance that I float through the air, that I saw myself laying and yelling at myself, 'Stand up! Go by the people outside.' And I couldn't; I couldn't move. And suddenly I heard, outside the buddah, my friend Maupy, I heard him talking English, saying, 'Go in there. My friend is dying. He should know that he is free now.' There was a little trapdoor entrance of the buddah with a hole in it, like a window. And that got dark, and then it opened up, and there was an American soldier there.

"He opened it up, it got lighter inside—I was laying in the dark, in the dirt, and he told me, 'Come, comrade. You are free now.' And then I start crying. I try to get to him, but I was, like, paralyzed. So I remember I was crawling over the ground, trying to get to the door. And then he picked me up by the collar of my little jacket, and he hurt me, and he was holding me. I remember I thought, 'Man, is the man

This is the photo that Nathan Melman took of prisoners at Ampfing shortly after their liberation. Coen Rood is in the striped uniform (second from right).

strong.' And then he looked so clean and well taken care of, and he was full of weapons. And he told me, 'You are free now, it's over.' And I was just laying against him. He was holding me, took me outside, and then he repeated again, 'You are free now. You understand? You are free.' As dirty as I was, that soldier, the American solder, kissed me. And I kissed him back, and he was holding me and took me outside and said, 'See? You are free now.' And he cried, too."

There were roughly a dozen American soldiers in the recon squad that discovered Ampfing V. One of them was Nathan Melman, and when Coen and his fellow survivors lined up near one of the jeeps from which the Americans were handing out packages with food, Melman snapped a photo of them that ultimately led to their reunion in the United States.

Coen never did find the soldier who lifted him out of the hole in the ground, but he does tell one amusing story about him. "While he was holding me, he pushed my head back, and he had a bottle with

*Nathan Melman (left) and Coen Rood, reunited in
1996.*

some whiskey or whatever was in there, and he opened up my mouth
and poured whiskey in there. And that shot me back. And I could
walk." It was a double shot for Coen, who in the Netherlands had been
a member of a youth organization that believed "in pure living, clean
living, no alcohol, no smoking. Everything that young people do on
street corners, we stayed away from. So I was not used to alcohol."

Shortly after liberation, Coen Rood and Maupy raided the SS
kitchen and the homes of their former guards for food and little things
like a hairbrush and a pocket knife. They managed to avoid the fighting
that broke out between the ex-prisoners and were taken in—certainly
with some urging by the Americans—by a local farmer, where they
stayed for almost the entire month of May. Eventually, he found his
way back to the Netherlands, and in 1959, with the help of a friend
who had preceded him, he and his wife—they'd lost their young son in
an accident—moved to Shreveport, Louisiana. Eventually they and their
two daughters settled in Longview, Texas, where Coen owned and operated his own tailoring business for forty-three years until he retired.

MAY 4, 1945

GUNSKIRCHEN, AUSTRIA

> 150 miles east of Munich
>
> 70 miles east of the Austro-German border
>
> 130 miles west of Vienna

The war in Europe had been ending in piecemeal fashion for almost a week. On April 29, representatives of the German military signed surrender documents for their forces in Italy, effective May 2. On April 30, with the Battle of Berlin raging above and around him, Hitler committed suicide in his bunker. On May 2, the commander of the Berlin Defense Area unconditionally surrendered to the Soviet army. And on May 4, British Field Marshal Bernard Law Montgomery took the unconditional surrender of all German forces in northwest Germany, Holland, and Denmark. (On May 5, Admiral Karl Dönitz would order all U-boats to cease offensive operations and return to their bases.)

Despite these signals that the end of the war was near, American forces in the U.S. Third Army's XII Corps area came under heavy enemy fire in Linz and Urfahr, Austria. The 71st Infantry Division's three regiments—the 66th on the left, the 14th in the center, and the 5th on the right—sped southeast by foot and in vehicles to the Traun River, where they took Wels and Lambach as well as the bridges at both cities.

Late on May 4, the cavalry reconnaissance group of the 71st discovered the Gunskirchen concentration camp hidden in a young pine forest so dense the site was almost invisible from the main highway as well as from the air. The camp was relatively new; it had been built by four hundred Polish and Russian prisoners transferred from the Mauthausen concentration camp just five months earlier. At the time of liberation it had eight or nine partially completed buildings used as barracks and was surrounded by an eight-foot-high barbed-wire fence with guard towers positioned along the perimeter. The area inside the fence was wooded.

In the last two weeks of April, three columns of prisoners had been marched from Mauthausen to Gunskirchen to relieve overcrowding caused by the flood of Nazi prisoners arriving from camps farther east. Those who had come from Hungary had been force marched more than 150 miles over mountains and winding roads. The ones who couldn't keep up were shot. There are reports that somewhere between 15,000 and 17,000 Jews had been crammed into Gunskirchen; barracks that had been built to hold 300 were housing nearly ten times that many prisoners.

In the final days before liberation, food in the camp was minimal, and water was almost nonexistent. Once a day, a fire truck carrying 1,500 liters of drinking water came to Gunskirchen. There was only one latrine for all the prisoners, and the SS guards decreed that it could be used only six hours a day. Prisoners had to line up to use the facility. Diarrhea was rampant. The Germans warned that prisoners caught defecating outside the latrine would be shot on sight.

Shortly after the war ended, the 71st Infantry Division published a booklet titled "The Seventy-first Came . . . to Gunskirchen Lager." In it, Captain J. D. Pletcher of Berwyn, Illinois, wrote:

Of all the horrors of the place, the smell, perhaps, was the most startling of all. It was a smell made up of all kinds of odors—human excreta, foul bodily odors, smoldering trash fires, German tobacco— which is a stink in itself—all mixed together in a heavy dank atmosphere, in a thick, muddy woods, where little breeze could go. The ground was pulpy throughout the camp, churned to a consistency of warm putty by the milling of thousands of feet, mud mixed with feces and urine. The smell of Gunskirchen nauseated many of the Americans who went there. It was a smell I'll never forget, completely different from anything I've ever encountered. It could almost be seen and hung over the camp like a fog of death.

PFC Delbert D. Cooper spent the night in Lambach. The Dayton, Ohio, native, whose extended family had seventeen men serving in uniform, was twenty-two years old and a member of Headquarters Company of the 14th Infantry Regiment. He'd joined the 71st as a replacement when the division was still on the other side of the Rhine

Twenty-two-year-old Delbert Cooper
near the end of the war and sixty-three
years later.

River. Sixty-three years later, he remembers quite clearly the day he came to Gunskirchen lager.

"I was looking for some coffee, really. I had spent the night in Lambach, and I went down to the railroad station the next morning, relatively early, and I spotted my captain. I went through the railroad station, just a small place, and I stepped through the door and, going out into the railroad yards, something moved—and I reflexed real fast. I saw a young fella, like a kid, sitting against the wall there, and he was all scurvy-looking. I walked back into the building, and I said to Captain Swope, 'What is that out there, sir?,' and he says, 'There's a camp, one of those concentration camps, about five klicks down the road.' A klick was a kilometer. And he said, 'There's a truck going to be coming up here with a couple guys. We captured that train out there last night. It's a German supply train. Would you go out and break open a boxcar and help those guys load?'

"The captain's talking—I'm a PFC—so I said sure." Cooper got into the boxcar, which was filled with food, helped load the truck, and figured he'd go along to help them unload. There was Cooper, the driver, a major, and one other GI.

"As we were going along the road past Lambach, we started smelling something and also seeing a lot of people along the road. And they were throwing their hands in the air and prayin' and all that. We got out where we turned off to go in these woods, and people were just about to mob us, I tell ya. We went on back into the woods—I don't know how far—a pretty good ways—and people were laying around dead." What he saw were prisoners who had come into the woods to relieve themselves and dropped over dead.

Cooper was in the camp for several hours, giving him time to explore.

"I remember one old man sitting on a big boulder, farther back from where we were, and I can see right now, throwing his arms up, or his hands up, into the sky and praying. They were saved, and we kept telling 'em, 'Look, you're gonna be safe, we got food, medics will be coming.' We've got to go on—the war was still being fought."

Cooper, whose father had worked on a railroad, went back to the train station and climbed into the engine that was still hooked up to the captured supply train. He discovered that there was an Austrian woman in the cab, a member of the train crew, and there was still a good fire burning. So he went back to Captain Swope and suggested that rather than running trucks to the camp, they could just move the train down the rail siding that went out to the camp, which is what was done.

Two days later, Cooper had time to write a letter to his wife, Joan. Sitting on an ammo box and using his mess kit as a desk, he told her about Gunskirchen.

Morning Blondie,

Here's that pest again. Guess it's been a couple of days since I wrote you. Can't keep track of the time any more, you know. Just days and nights now. The weather has been pretty bad for sometime now. Rainy and cold, but I'm inside most of the time so it's not so bad. I have seen the Alps mountains for the past couple of days. . . . You should see my clothes this morning. I rode on a jeep over these muddy roads yesterday and we didn't have any top on it. . . . Incidentally, I helped capture 8 Germans and one SS man yesterday. They are really beginning to give up. (4 hr. break.)

Yesterday I was to a concentration camp. From what I saw with my own eyes, everything I ever heard about those places is absolutely true. . . . I'm going to tell you now I never want to see a sight again as we saw when we pulled in there. 1400 starving diseased stinking people. It was terrible. Most of them were Jews that Hitler had put away for safe keeping. Some of them had been in camps for as long as 8 years. So help me, I cannot see how they stood it. No longer were most of them people. They were nothing but things that were once human beings. As we pulled off of the highway into the camp, we had to shove them off of the truck. We had the first food that had been taken in there for a month. The people for the most part were dirty walking skeletons. Some were too weak to walk. They had had nothing to eat for so long. Some of them were still laying around dead where they had fallen. They would fall as they tried to keep up with the truck. . . . You could stand right in front of them and wave your arms for them to move over and they would just stand there, look right in your face and cry like a baby. It was really a pathetic scene. Finally we took out our guns and pointed them in their faces, but they still stood there and bawled. They were past being afraid of even a gun. We fired a few shots up in the air and still we couldn't clear them. They just couldn't believe that we had food for everyone.

While we were standing outside the truck, any number of them came up and touched us, as if they couldn't believe we were actually there. Some of them would try to kiss us even (They must have been bad off.) Some of them would come up, grab you around the neck, and cry on your shoulder. Others would just look and cry. Some of them would throw their arms up in the air and pray. They were mostly the ones who were too weak to stand. I recall one woman who could only cry and point at her mouth. One fellow must have felt that he should give me something. As he had nothing to give of value, he gave me his little yellow star that designates a Jew.

Someone had slipped 500 eggs aboard [the truck]. I took one of the [English-speaking] guys and told him to start with the children and give them one egg apiece and if he had any left over to give them to the women. He told us people were dying off at the average rate of 150 per day at this camp. They just stack them up in a pile if they died in the barracks. If they died outside they left them there. I know, I saw them. . . . There was human refuse everyplace. I had enough on my boots to be a walking sewer pipe. On top of all this, they had no water. . . . The young people who were in this camp will probably never get over it. They will be stunted for life.

There are two things about all this that I want to tell you:

1. I never again want to see anything like that happen to anyone.

2. I wish 130 million American people could have been standing in my shoes.

Delbert Cooper's casually tossed off line about helping to capture "8 Germans and an SS man" obscures a dramatic incident that took place less than an hour after he left Gunskirchen to catch up with his unit. He hitched a ride in a jeep, and after a bit, they stopped at a farmhouse to get something to eat. "We just walked in and ordered what they had—if they had anything, we'd just take it. You know how that goes, even in Austria, 'cause they were still the enemy—however, we did notice a difference in their attitude.

"And there were several German soldiers in there, sitting at the table, and there was a couple of French DPs. One of them said to me, 'SS.' I can't speak French or German, so I told these guys we was with, 'Hey, this guy says there's a couple of SS around here.' Anyway, the SS were the tough guys, and they'd just as soon shoot you as look at you. I had picked up a couple pistols earlier in the war, and I went out with this guy, and he pointed towards the barn.

"I peeked around the corner, and there's a guy, a young fella, standing out in the barn lot, and he's bare from the waist up and he's got civilian trousers on. And this French DP said, 'SS,' and I pointed and I said, 'SS?,' and he said yeah. So I put my hands behind me with the pistol and I started walking up toward him. He said there was two—there was only one—so I went walking up to this fella and I said to him, *'Deutsche Soldaten?'* And when I said that, he just kept looking at me, and I whipped the pistol out from behind me and put it right on his chest, and I started to squeeze the trigger. Thank God they were new pistols."

Cooper says he was hoping that the soldier would make a move, anything to justify shooting him. "I thought, raise your arm. Give me a real excuse to shoot him. Other than that I'm murdering. Anyway, one of the other guys came around the barn, and he said, 'Shoot the SOB, Cooper.' And I stepped back a pace, handed the pistol toward him, and said, 'You shoot him.' Well, he wasn't going to murder him either. So I says, 'We better take him with us.'" Cooper got into the back of the jeep, holding a pistol on the SS man, told the eight other German soldiers to head back down the road, and they left. A short way down the road, they turned their prisoner over to an American MP who was directing traffic and caught up with his unit close to Linz.

Stories abound of angry American soldiers taking no prisoners after they'd liberated one of the concentration camps. Many soldiers, both enlisted and officers, have said that the Geneva Convention rules against such activities were never mentioned. As one former first lieutenant, an infantry platoon leader, said, "It was war." His implication was that rules of engagement were irrelevant to the realities on the ground.

The life span of captured SS was especially short in GI hands. So why didn't Delbert Cooper retaliate? Why didn't he shoot when urged to do so by his fellow soldier? It's something he's thought about for years. "I think that you are either a murderer or a killer. And I can be a killer, but I discovered that day, I wasn't a murderer. And there is a difference.

"When I walked up to that fella in the barn lot, had he raised his arm to attack me—I walked right up and put this pistol right here, almost against his chest, and that man knew he was dying because I was going to kill him. I needed resistance; you just don't run out and shoot somebody. Even right in the middle of the war, even after you've been in a place like that the same day. I didn't anyway, and neither did these other guys, 'cause this other guy couldn't kill him either. But I was hopin'—in plain language, now, exactly what I thought—*raise your arm, you sonofabitch*. That's what was in my head. I wanted him to give me some resistance. And when he didn't, I'm not just gonna shoot him down."

It's impossible to adequately convey what both the rescued survivors and their liberators were feeling during those first hours in Gunskirchen. In "The Seventy-first Came . . . to Gunskirchen Lager," the public relations officer for the division, Major Cameron Coffman, describes it as best he could in a lengthy essay that was published shortly after the liberation. He wrote:

A little girl, doubled with the gnawing pains of starvation, cried pitifully for help. A dead man rotted beside her. An English-speaking Jew from Ohio hummed, "The Yanks Are Coming," then broke out crying. A Jewish Rabbi tripped over a dead body as he scurried toward me with strength he must have been saving for the arrival of the American forces. He kissed the back of my gloved hand and clutched my sleeve with a talon-like grip as he lifted his face toward heaven. I could not understand what he said, but it was a prayer. I did not have to understand his spoken word.

MAY 5, 1945

WELS, UPPER AUSTRIA

5 miles west-northwest of Gunskirchen

After elements of the 71st Infantry Division liberated Gunskirchen, they moved east toward Linz, meeting moderate resistance as they approached the village of Wels five miles away. The town's railway tracks and station had been destroyed by recent Allied air raids. What they didn't know is that they were about to discover another of the Mauthausen subcamps, this one actually a subcamp of Gunskirchen known as Wels II.

According to the *United States Holocaust Memorial Museum Encyclopedia of Camps and Ghettos, 1933–1945,* the camp was established on March 24, 1945, with the arrival from Mauthausen of about a thousand male inmates, the majority of whom were metalworkers. They were probably destined to be enslaved by the Flugzeug und Metallbauwerke Wels (Aircraft and Metal Construction Company, Wels). The next day, another thousand inmates arrived from the Ebensee subcamp. Initially, the inmates were used to clean up the damage at the train station. They were housed in a factory hall that was not fenced and lacked a kitchen and sanitary facilities. The slave laborers were guarded by SS and Volkssturm (home guard) soldiers.

As the Nazis were pressed by Soviet forces, they grew desperate to ship inmates from the easternmost camps to facilities in Austria and Germany. That's the likely explanation for the presence of Hungarian Jews at Wels on the day the 71st and Private Leonard Lubin of Miami, Florida, arrived.

Lubin, with the 609th Field Artillery Battalion, was not quite twenty when he walked into Wels. When interviewed, he was eighty-three and had recently retired as a solo practice attorney who spent years doing appellate law. He talked about his experiences on that nice spring day in early May 1945 and about how it affected him, as though he were representing clients before a panel of feisty judges. He spoke with precision and intensity, with the knowledge that overt emotionality could undermine his case. Pounding his fist on the lectern never

*Private Leonard Lubin of Miami, Florida,
was not quite twenty years old when his
outfit, the 71st Infantry Division, liberated
Wells II, a subcamp of Mauthausen. He had
one experience there that, at age eighty-
three, he described as "the content of my
nightmares."*

helped. Nevertheless, there was no doubt that what he saw had affected him at both a brain and a gut level—in the *kishkes,* as Jews of
his generation are wont to say.

There were things he didn't remember about that afternoon, and
even under persistent questioning, he wasn't inclined to fill in the
blanks. He was also aware that soldiers *know* only what's immediately
surrounding them. Rarely is a private in a position to have even a mod-
erately big picture. That said, Lubin recalled walking down a street,
perhaps the equivalent of a four-lane American boulevard with two-
and three-story brick apartment buildings on either side. There were a
few automobiles parked along the road, and every few yards saplings
had been planted.

"I heard sounds before I saw *them*. The sounds that I heard were
'Ungarischer Juden.' Hungarian Jews. I had a smattering of street German; I didn't know all that much but enough to know what it was. I got

behind a car, and I was able to identify three men coming toward me in obvious prison clothing, that kind of striped clothing, and they pointed behind them and said there was a '*Konzentrationslager,*' a concentration camp, down the street, very excited. I motioned them to continue going in the direction they were and told them in pidgin German with sign languages we all spoke that there were American soldiers behind me who would help them.

"The fact that they were ambulatory, they were not the skeleton kind of prisoners that the photography of the era shows us, the living dead, tells us they were more recent arrivals at the camp." Lubin's later study taught him that at labor camps such as Wels, "people went in the front door—new people who are normal people, recently captured— and they were put to work. Out the back door, if that's the way to put it, are the dead people when they died from work." But as he walked toward the *Konzentrationslager,* he knew next to nothing about what he would soon confront. (His unit had not been among the outfits from the 71st that had recently liberated nearby Gunskirchen.) "We knew that the Germans had been persecuting minorities, especially Jews; we'd heard some rumors about killing but had no concept whatever of this. The military had taught us nothing, told us nothing, had no training or expectations, and so much of this sounds crazy."

Within hours it would become clear to him that the Army knew, at least in general terms, what its men would be uncovering. His officers were to tell him that "We had to go, and they're telling us that there are units behind us to take care of these people. Well, if that were true, how come we soldiers weren't oriented to the proposition we were going to be encountering concentration camps? You would have thought if they knew as much to have units prepared to take care of these people, we would have known to expect it." The question is reasonable, considering that American forces had discovered the first occupied concentration camp almost a full month earlier.

To be precise, Lubin recalled knowing the words "concentration camp," but only in the same context that America's civilian population knew them—"a jail facility where you hold people, like we held the Japanese Americans in the United States in World War II. We called them concentration camps—that didn't mean that they're killing fields."

With his carbine at the ready, he continued down the boulevard toward a structure at the end. As he began seeing other American soldiers out of the corner of his eye, he realized that the street he'd been walking on was just one spoke of a wheel—fellow soldiers were converging from other spokes—and in the center of that wheel, inside the traffic circle, was a wall, perhaps fifteen or sixteen feet high. And in the wall was a big gate with two swinging doors. "As I got there, I saw that the doors were ajar and people were pouring out through the gates, out onto the street, into the circle—people of all descriptions, many who could walk. It wasn't until I got in I saw that there were many more who couldn't walk. And various degrees of debilitation, some in far better shape, like those three I first encountered a block or two or three up the street, who were the most recent arrivals and therefore the healthiest. And then some who were less well, and less well and less well diminishing in stages and degrees; some extremely feeble, probably close to falling down."

The sights and sounds rendered his mind blank. "I'm embarrassed to say it, I was stunned, and I can't tell you I was thinking of anything. It's like when [you come upon] an automobile accident, if you've ever been—I was stunned. I couldn't formulate much in the way of thought; I wasn't thinking as much as I was reacting. We soldiers shouted at each other—what to do? 'Grab them!' somebody says, 'Stop them, grab them.' While all of this was happening, more American soldiers were pouring in, and they started chasing down the people. The people who were escaping, we concluded later, were running from us like crazy in a panic. They saw our uniforms and may not have been able to distinguish us from Germans. That or freedom, I couldn't tell you, but they ran like hell."

Lubin stopped talking for a moment and audibly took a breath before continuing. "Here comes the big moment for me, which to me sums up the whole, the whole war, the whole Holocaust, which is the content of my nightmares. Not dead bodies; I've seen a lot of dead bodies. I wasn't in combat all that long, a few months, mostly chasing like crazy up the highway. But I'd seen plenty of dead bodies—theirs and ours. So it wasn't that. This was something different.

"Here was this guy, and he had found a food can, a tin can—the larger kind that tomatoes sometimes come in. It had been opened with one of those old-fashioned push-and-lift can openers. You punch a hole in it, and then you lift it all the way around, it creates a horribly jagged edge you didn't want to handle. You didn't take it all the way to the end, you would get it close to the end of the circle of the can and then push the lid back so it stands up, and you would empty the contents and then push the lid down and throw the can away so you didn't cut yourself, because it would make brutal cuts very easy.

"This man had found one of these cans and was trying to get the contents out of it. He had it with both of his hands jammed up against his face, trying to get his tongue into it to lick the contents and lick the top lid and the sides of the can, and the blood was pouring down his face, and he was acting totally insane, and that vision is what's in my mind. If I were an artist and could paint a picture, I would, but I can't. Didn't have a camera. So in my nightmares, that's what I see. And to me, that's what the Holocaust was. . . . It wasn't the death, it was a torment of the kind that can reduce a human being to subanimal status. To be willing to lacerate himself to get a slight bit of nourishment.

"My guy with the tin can, I tried to knock the can out of his hand, to stop him from doing that, and not let the can be there so somebody else can pick it up and do the same thing."

He saw other examples of the level to which the Holocaust had reduced civilized men—for he realized years later that all he had seen were men, no women, no children. "There were miserable puddles of water at the street edge, the corner of the curb, not large puddles—they must have been old, they were filthy, dirty puddles, and small. Some of the people were falling down on their face to lick up the water from the street. And others ran to the closest trees and were trying to rip bark off and eating the bark. And amid all of this was screaming and crying and carrying on. And American soldiers looking confused, not knowing what the hell to do."

Lubin remembered that mayhem going on for quite some time before any of the soldiers really entered the camp. "All the effort was concentrated toward attempting to grab these people. I don't know why. I didn't know what else to do."

Through interviews with the inmates of the camp, they later learned that the guards had left just minutes prior to the arrival of the Americans. "They knew we were coming, and they split. They went out the back door, lickety-split. They didn't want to be there. One minute they were there, and suddenly the guards were gone. And the people see the guards are gone, and those who were the healthier among them headed for the door. That's all pretty expected, pretty logical."

———

Lubin's time in Wels stretched to what he thought may have been a few hours, almost all of it spent outside the walls of the camp. A couple of times when the gates were opened, he could peer inside. All he could see was an anteyard, buildings. Other men were assigned to go deep inside. One time he got into the yard area, the compound. "It was crammed with people in all stages of debilitation. Some were relatively healthy-looking, like the first ones I saw up the street at that first encounter. Others were in worse shape, skinnier, more hollowed and hollow-cheek-looking. Others were on the verge of falling down, the bones sticking out of their chests, and others were on the ground. We were trying to pick people up or move them around from one place to another. It was during this time that some kind of order was restored.

"My instinct was to stay, although I didn't know what the hell I would do if I stayed. But someone's dying there . . ." He paused in his narrative; it had become difficult to continue. "My instinct was to help save. These were Hungarian Jews. For those dying, pick them up, hold them, recite the Sh'ma, a Jewish prayer. When somebody is dying you say, *Sh'ma Yis-ra-eil, A-do-nai E-lo-hei-nu, A-do-nai E-chad*—Hear, O Israel, the Lord is our God, the Lord is One. They told us we had to go. So we went."

Leonard Lubin had been just another nineteen-year-old kid from Miami. On that day, a day that lasted a lifetime, he became much, much more.

MAY 6, 1945

EBENSEE, AUSTRIA

    50 miles west of Salzburg

    30 miles south of Gunskirchen

    60 miles southeast of Mauthausen

L eaving the Buchenwald area on April 12, the three infantry regiments of the 80th Infantry Division—the 317th, 318th, and
319th—began what would be a leapfrogging three-week push into
Austria. Initially they moved rapidly to the east, taking Jena and Gera;
then, closely following the 4th Armored Division, the 319th cleared
Crimmitschau and Glauchau in Saxony, while the 318th prepared to
take over the bridgehead at Chemnitz, fifty miles southwest of Dresden.

On April 19, the U.S. Third Army was committed to chasing the
Germans into Austria, with XX Corps designating the 71st and 65th
Infantry Divisions as initial assault forces, with the 80th Infantry and
13th Armored Divisions in reserve. Two days later the 80th changed
direction and headed southwest toward Nuremberg to relieve the 3rd
Infantry Division. The 150-mile push took a week. On April 28, in
order to follow armor in the zone to the right of the 71st Infantry Division, the 80th was relieved in Nuremberg by the 16th Armored Division. Elements of the 318th and 319th once again turned southwest
toward Regensburg, passing through the 65th Infantry Division. At
this point, the 80th was roughly seventy-five miles north of Munich,
which would soon come under attack from divisions moving from the
west, rather than from due north.

On April 29, when Dachau was liberated by the 42nd and 45th Infantry Divisions, the 80th completed its crossing of the Danube and
elements advanced to Köfering in Bavaria. A day later, the 318th
crossed the Isar River over the railroad bridge at Mamming and moved
southwest toward Dingolfing. On May 2, with the 318th on the left
and the 319th on the right, the 80th Division reached the Inn River in
the vicinity of Braunau. The 80th was now midway between Munich
and Linz and due north of Salzburg.

On May 3, the 11th Armored Division took Linz, while the 80th overtook the 13th Armored near Braunau. The next day, the 71st Infantry Division, operating slightly south and east of the 80th, sped to the Traun River, taking Wels and Lambach, where concentration camps at Gunskirchen and Wels would be liberated. On May 4, final elements of the 80th got across the Inn, and the 317th attacked to the southeast toward Vöcklabruck. At that point, the division was less than twenty miles from the concentration camp at Ebensee. The five-hundred-mile advance from Buchenwald to Ebensee had taken twenty-two days.

Out in front of the 80th was the 3rd Cavalry Reconnaissance Squadron, which had landed at Utah Beach a month after D-Day and fought at Metz, France, the Siegfried Line, and the Bulge. Robert Persinger, now of Rockford, Illinois, was a twenty-two-year-old platoon sergeant in one of the 3rd Cavalry's M24 Chaffee light tanks as the end of the war approached. They took their last casualties on May 5, when they engaged a number of Hungarian soldiers fighting in the German army near Vöcklabruck, Austria. One American tank was destroyed, and two men were killed.

That evening they advanced to the town of Gmunden, Austria, at the north end of Traun Lake. The next morning, they were given the mission to enter Ebensee, about ten miles away along a curving, mountainous road at the south end of the lake, to outpost and hold the town until the end of the war. There were no Nazi soldiers defending the town, which Persinger recalls was one of the most beautiful places he'd ever seen. Within hours of arriving, their recon platoon discovered a concentration camp about two and a half miles up the mountain, concealed in a pine forest. His squadron commander ordered two tanks up the hill to the camp gates—one commanded by Persinger, the other by Sergeant Dick Pomante. It was a beautiful, warm, sunny Sunday afternoon as they cautiously went up the winding gravel road.

At about ten minutes to three, Pensinger remembers, he was struck by the smell of death. "We made a right-hand turn into this road, and there, a hundred, two hundred feet away, was this concentration camp. There were people standing behind the barbed-wire fences and the two towers there that were used for the entrance, guarding the gate." The gate was closed, but the inmates opened it to allow the tanks to drive inside. The Americans would soon learn that the SS had left the day before.

Ebensee was one of the sixty-plus subcamps of Mauthausen, the giant killing facility sixty miles to the northeast. Prisoners from Mauthausen began building Ebensee in November 1943, digging tunnels into the mountains and constructing the future concentration camp. A month later there were more than 500 prisoners in the camp, and the first deaths had already occurred. The SS designed the camp to be built in a thick forest in order to avoid detection from the air. By mid-1944, the crematorium was operational.

The camp was initially populated by Italians and French, but in June 1944 about 1,500 Hungarian Jews arrived from Auschwitz. Then came Soviet prisoners of war, followed by Poles from Auschwitz. Initially, prisoners had been selected for Ebensee who would work effectively digging tunnels into the mountains for various plants, including a gasoline production facility that the American forces would ultimately take over. But in the closing months of the war, prisoners were being sent in open cattle cars from the camps in Poland and northern Germany that were about to be captured by the Russians. Deaths at Ebensee resulted primarily from exhaustion and deliberate exposure to harsh winter conditions. It was the most economical way the Nazis had to kill their prisoners. Roughly 8,000 inmates died at Ebensee, and it's likely the toll would have been higher but for the fact that seriously ill prisoners were shipped to Mauthausen, which had a greater capacity for processing the dying and dead.

Though acknowledging the horror laid out before them, Staff Sergeant Bob Persinger wasn't emotionally traumatized by the sight. "We were combat veterans. I saw things I couldn't imagine on the way to getting there, so it wasn't too much out of line. It was a horrible sight, but we had been used to seeing horrible sights. We had been in Patton's Army."

They had stopped their tanks in the middle of the roll call square and just sat there taking in the scene. "We were looking at thousands of men who were skin and bones, maybe weighing around seventy-five pounds. They were standing in mud that was almost ankle deep, dressed in the striped garment, some with just the trousers, some with just the top, and some with nothing. However, there was so much singing and crying for joy that it was hard to take it all in. We passed out all the rations we had, so a few received a treat that they would never forget, and we felt bad when our supply was depleted."

Their mission had been to go up to the camp and see if there was any resistance; since there was none, they had no reason to stay. Persinger radioed his lieutenant to ask for orders. But in the meantime, the prisoners were shouting for them to dismount the tanks. What awaited them was difficult. "We knew we were getting into a bunch of filthy human beings, and they were full of lice and fleas and sores and everything else. Of course, we didn't know, really, how bad, but we heard later that they were loaded with fleas carrying typhoid fever. And they were all over us. They hugged us, doing everything like that."

A prisoner named Max Garcia who spoke English wanted to guide Persinger and his men on a tour of the camp. They went with him, even though it was emotionally very difficult.

"It was hard to put up with—very hard. Just that alone, but walking amongst the dead bodies and seeing them piled around the crematorium, and then into the crematorium. Things like that was what make you feel much worse than looking at those poor people that didn't have no garments or [were] starving to death."

And then they walked into one of the barracks. "Absolutely terrible. People lying on the barracks that would probably be more than half dead, because their eyes never made contact with you at all. Those folks were in very bad shape. Some alive, too, in there. If you were not sick and crying by now, you would be before you exited."

That evening, they went back down the mountain to the hotel in Ebensee that the American unit had taken over. Their message to the commanders was simple: the people had to be fed, and they were the only ones able to do it. "The following morning," Persinger says, "we started collecting vegetables, including potatoes, cabbage, and anything that we could use to make a soup from the surrounding countryside." They gathered food from stores in the area and bread from bakeries. In one case Sergeant Pomante used the big gun on a tank to

Robert Fasnacht with one of the mementos brought to the 80th Infantry Division reunion at Carlisle, Pennsylvania, in 2008.

persuade a village baker that his regular customers would have to wait; that day's output would go to the prisoners in the concentration camp.

By evening, they had a large amount of soup and bread to be served but knew the prisoners would be uncontrollable. They planned carefully and used the machine guns on two tanks to fire live ammo over the starving inmates' heads when they began to overrun the food lines. Persinger says many gulped the soup so fast that they ended up screaming in agony; some became very ill, and some died on the spot.

Within a day or two, Army hospital and quartermaster units moved in to care for roughly 18,000 inmates in the camp. Persinger's platoon stayed for another week before receiving orders to move on, aware that what faced them was a thirty-day furlough followed by a landing in Japan under General Patton.

While Bob Persinger went to Ebensee under orders, Bob Fasnacht actually made the visit as more or less a tourist. The Canton, Ohio, soldier was nineteen years old when he made the trip across Germany and into Austria with the 80th Division. He'd actually gone overseas with the 70th Division, but with the Battle of the Bulge chewing up infantrymen, he says, "fifteen of the least desirable men out of each company were transferred to the 80th Division, and naturally, I was one of them. They loaded us on trucks in the middle of the afternoon, and we never stopped until we arrived in Luxembourg the next morning about ten o'clock. A noncom said, 'You guys follow me.' And we followed him maybe half a mile over the front edge of a mountain, and he said, 'Dig in here.' And I said, 'What's that racket I hear over on the other side of the valley?' He says, 'Those are Tiger tanks.' I said, 'What are they doing?' He said, 'We don't know what they're doing.' Well, naturally, I dug awfully fast. That was my introduction to combat in the Third Army."

After the Bulge, Fasnacht froze his toes during the crossing of the Sauer River when he jumped into water nose deep to hold the boat against the shore while the rest of the guys got to cover on the beach. Unable to change his shoes or socks for five days, he ended up hospitalized for three weeks; then he returned to his outfit. Fighting all through Germany, he knew nothing about concentration camps, nothing about the Holocaust. But then, just days before the cease-fire, the 80th turned south in Austria, and Fasnacht, who'd become the headquarters photographer after looting a factory in Nuremberg of darkroom supplies and liberating an assortment of cameras throughout Germany, heard that one of its units had liberated Ebensee.

Ebensee had a very active resistance movement, and its members knew the Allies were approaching. According to reports, they collectively resisted an SS plan to force the prisoners into the tunnels, which would then be blown up. The camp commander and many of his staff fled before the arrival of the liberators. In that interim, there was a violent prisoners' revolt during which many kapos were murdered.

In fact, the brutally battered body of one of those collaborators was almost the first thing that Bob Fasnacht saw after he hitchhiked to Ebensee. "You couldn't tell if he was male or female, they had worked him over. And the inmates had propped his arm up into a Nazi salute." During the 80th's march through Germany, he'd seen small slave-labor encampments, but nothing like Ebensee. "Factories, big, big buildings, would have guys in striped uniforms working in there. They were slave laborers, but they weren't all being worked to death or anything.

"At Ebensee, I thought it was a mine. These people were working about twelve or fourteen hours a day, chopping rocks and that sort of thing, in this monstrous cave. And I didn't like being in there, so I got out as soon as I could. I remember going into this sort of a mine where they were working, and seeing these men that were just, just skin and bones, and they were still alive. And of course, you're young, you tended to not want to touch them or talk to them or anything else. The German I spoke then was pretty minuscule, and most of them were not Germans. So there was almost no communication between me and them.

"It's funny, even then you didn't realize the enormity of this. That humans could do this to humans. On such a big scale that—I've often wondered if Hitler knew, the scale of this sort of thing. Now, the pictures I've taken, I've showed those to people. They don't believe it. The enormity of that horror and the length of time it went on. And nobody did anything about it. And you can't tell me that American intelligence wasn't knowing what's going on there. I almost have a feeling that the Western world's attitude was 'Well, they're killing Jews—who cares?' Maybe I'm cynical."

A few years ago, Bob Fasnacht was invited to a synagogue in Cleveland to talk about the liberation. "This man who was maybe ten years younger than me was ushering me to my seat down in front in this auditorium, and he said, 'Where were you?' I said, 'Well, at Ebensee.' And he said, 'Can I hug you?' And I said, 'Why?' And he said, 'I was there when you came.'" He pauses. "You see, I get a little worked up over that; every time I try to tell that, I feel the same way. What a coincidence, but it's difficult to understand the enormity of those camps."

CHAPTER 15

GUSEN-MAUTHAUSEN

HOW SADISTIC CAN YOU BE?

MAY 5, 1945

NEAR GUSEN-MAUTHAUSEN, AUSTRIA

16 miles southeast of Linz

In the spring of 1943, Colvin Caughey—he doesn't like being called reverend now; pastor is okay—got taken in by an Army recruiter who said, "If you volunteer to go in the Army, take your basic training, then you can transfer to the Air Corps or the cadets." That's how the eighteen-year-old originally from Minnesota agreed to be voluntarily inducted and how, after getting into the Army ASTP program for troops who were college material and smarter than the average bear, he ended up in the armored infantry, riding a half-track in the 11th Armored Division.

Caughey's outfit, B Company of the 21st Armored Infantry Battalion, landed at Cherbourg on December 16, 1944, which just happened to coincide with the start of the Battle of the Bulge. They were

Corporal Colvin Caughey of the 21st Armored Infantry Battalion in 1945 and Pastor Caughey of Auburn, Washington, in 2008.

rushed up to northern France in two days, held in reserve, and on the 29th they moved to Bastogne. After several days of tank battles and artillery barrages, the memory of those hours was burned into his brain. More than six decades later, he can still see it and hear it.

"We were a green bunch; the unit had never experienced combat before. First, we had a barrage of artillery against the German positions; it was for fifteen minutes with everything they could fire. And you've never heard such a rumble and roar—I mean, it was just unbelievable. Not only the guns firing behind us, you know, over our heads, all these shells sizzling through the air, and then the horrible rumble, just like a huge roll of thunder, continuously, over where they were landing. There's nothing like it. You just think, how can anyone survive that kind of barrage, you know? And then in war—the way it's supposed to work, you give them a big artillery barrage, and then as quickly as possible you rush in the infantry before they can recover. You got to get there quick to get the effect of that barrage."

Caughey's job was to carry a 38-pound machine gun and, with the two others on this team, provide cover for the riflemen. Sometimes it worked, and sometimes it didn't. His outfit had come under mortar fire, and rather than take cover in a bomb crater, they opted to just hit the ground, counting on incoming blasts to go skyward. "We were still walking, moving forward, when I saw this one thirty yards away. A good big burst. And you know, it's not like in the movies where you have a big red flash. It's kind of a black-gray puff, and all these little lines go flying out from there. And I saw this one headed right for me. People wouldn't believe this, I saw it comin'. I didn't know where I'd get hit, but I knew it was comin' right at me. And then all of a sudden, I was hit. I got hit in the face, and I can remember it very clearly. It felt like I'd been hit by someone with their fist, as hard as they could hit me. It hit me right in the jaw, and the world began to spin. I thought I was spinning, but I realized what was happening. I passed out and fell on the ground there."

Caughey was hauled back to the nearest command post, where a couple of runners and the first sergeant had no clue how to help him. Now he thinks it's funny, but back then, when the top sergeant told a buck private to "get out a little handbook and look under 'Face wounds,' " it wasn't exactly a thigh-slapper. Eventually, he was evacuated to Neufchâteau, Belgium, where, at the stroke of midnight on New Year's Eve, a doctor gave him a local anesthetic and pulled a chunk of shrapnel out of his jaw. Next stop: England, where it took a while to get to an oral surgeon who could remove the teeth that had been broken off, leaving jagged roots sticking out of his gums.

His mantra after that experience was "I need to get to the 11th Armored." And eventually he did, after riding planes, trains, and trucks, being strafed by the Luftwaffe, and ultimately finding his way back to his unit, where the only guy left from his original squad on the half-track was the driver.

By the time he got back to his outfit, they knew the end of the war was near—it was just a matter of chasing down the German dead enders, processing POWS in ever-increasing numbers, and not doing anything stupid that could get him another Purple Heart. Concentration camp liberation was not on their minds. Caughey says he'd read some articles about the camps, but didn't take them very seriously. They weren't a big issue for his unit.

Almost at the very end of April—he figures it was a week before they got to Mauthausen on May 5—they came upon a column of civilian prisoners on the road. "We didn't know it, but they were concentration camp prisoners that were being marched from a camp one place to a camp another place. First, we noticed as we drove along the road, we'd see these dead bodies, you know? People in those pajamas—striped suits? And every so often, there'd be another body. We'd say, 'What's that all about?' We finally caught up to the column, which was being guarded by a bunch of German soldiers or SS men— I don't know who they were. There were probably a dozen of them."

He says there were several hundred prisoners in the column. "They were men and women, and they were in terrible condition, they were just starving. They were all begging for food, which we gave what we had in our half-track, you know, extra food we had. And they were just killing each other, almost, over a bite of food. They were just wild."

And the Germans who were guarding them? "Well, that's another story," Caughey says. "Those were caught—they abandoned the prisoners and headed across a field toward the woods. And our column moved up fast enough that they didn't make it to the woods. Some of them might have, I don't know. But there were quite a few of them still; I mean eight or ten out on that field that didn't make it to the woods. That was a turkey shoot. They tried to surrender, they held up their hands. It was kind of sad, I hate to tell this, you know. They wanted to surrender and threw their guns down and everything, but the guys weren't taking prisoners that day. And they shot them all down."

The former prisoners of those Germans stood by the side of the road, waving at the GIs, saying thank you in a variety of languages. Then the troops moved on without stopping to question the people on the road. "The war was on—we didn't stop, we kept moving. But the guys were so furious that the next couple villages mostly burned down. They were just so mad, they just hated the Germans at that point. And I think later, those poor people that lived there, they didn't know what that was about. They didn't know why the Americans were so furious or what had happened. All they knew is they caught hell. And same way with those poor guys that were driving those prisoners. They were probably forced to do that," he says, with a charity rarely exhibited by ex-GIs who had seen the camps.

Twenty-year-old American kids who've killed the enemy and seen their buddies die aren't big on introspection. They're just trying to process what they've seen. Caughey said it broke down into two simple phrases: "You just can't believe it. How could people do that? And that," he says, "was just a taste of what was to come."

John Fague, now a retired veterinarian in Shippensburg, Pennsylvania, was also in B Company of the 21st Armored Infantry, also twenty years old at the time they found the column of prisoners on the road. "They had all these inmates on the road, they were in their pajama pants is what I called them, striped pants. And it just seems like there was hundreds of them on the road. Some of them would get down on their knees and thank us, but, of course, we couldn't do anything for them because we weren't equipped for that. And I always remember my dear captain, he was chasing one of the guards down through the field and swinging his carbine—why he didn't shoot him, I don't know."

When some concentration camp inmates saw the German-born American soldier Werner Ellmann, they were literally frightened to death: he spoke German, wore a uniform, and had a gun.

Werner Ellmann was born in Germany in 1924, but at the age of five, along with his mother and younger brother, he emigrated to the Chicago area, where he still lives. Ellmann was drafted and had to convince the Army that he could do more good for them in Europe, because of his language skills, than he could in the Pacific.

He fought at Bastogne with the 101st Airborne Division when it was surrounded, the Nazis demanded surrender, and the division's acting commanding general, Anthony McAuliffe, famously responded with one word: "Nuts!"

Ellmann suffered frostbite in that horrendous winter but was never wounded. His closest call came one night. They'd been warned about Germans using English-speaking troops disguised in U.S. uniforms to misdirect traffic or get in close enough to kill. It was a psychological tactic that played hell with the American troops. Soldiers in the line were constantly being challenged with questions like "How many touchdowns did Babe Ruth score?" That sort of thing didn't make Ell-mann very comfortable. "You know, all these kinds of questions—my thought was always that, Christ, they would know that as well as I do because they grew up there. And then they went back." If you've seen the movie *Stalag 17,* you understand.

Ellmann remembers his encounter with the fake Americans quite well. "One night, the captain and I had to go through the lines to get to the British, and we'd usually leave around one or two in the morn-ing, and the windshield for the jeep is down. And on the road are these two American soldiers. And I didn't stop, but that captain said, 'Stop, let's see what's going on.' Okay, well, right off the bat I thought some-thing was wrong, because these guys had pretty new uniforms. And you didn't have that at the Bulge. And they're already in the jeep, and they're sitting in the back and the captain and I are sitting in the front. And I kind of took his hand and squeezed it, giving him a signal. I slammed on the brakes, and these guys tumbled right over our heads. And it turned out that they were Germans. I mean, it was horrible."

Ellmann had his own encounter with concentration camp inmates on the road. He was part of a long convoy moving quickly toward a ren-dezvous with the Russians when suddenly "We don't know what the hell's going on. The first thing I saw, skeletons walking in certain kinds of uniforms. I go up to three or four of them, and I say, 'What goes on?,' and it's in German. *'Was ist los hier?'* And they died in front of me, in fright.

"Yeah, God, they were so close to dead anyway. All of a sudden, the guy collapses. In the meantime, my driver's feeding somebody, and he dies on him. He just falls down, and he's gone. We're in such amazement and such confusion; we don't know how to make anything out of this.

"It's so hard to describe because the condition of these people— they are obviously civilians and not soldiers. They don't have guns; we do. And they look at us, and they think we're Germans. I speak Ger-man, I'm in uniform, and I got a gun. And they're just scared shitless."

The obvious question: there were no American flags around? "No, that's movies," says Ellmann. "We're just a bunch of hard-fighting guys on our way to a river to hook up with the Russians. We're pretty sure the war's almost over."

Albert Adams was in the Headquarters Company of the 21st Armored Infantry Battalion, and he had a similar experience while on the road that eventually led to Mauthausen. The twenty-two-year-old who'd honed his shooting skills as a kid hunting deer in Washington State still remembers seeing prisoners coming out of the camps, "and we gave them all the food we could possibly give them, and we killed them. 'Death warmed over,' we called them."

Adams's half-track was slowly moving down the road when he came upon a scene that's stuck in his mind for more than sixty years. Prisoners had knocked a man off a bicycle, and they were beating him to death with the bike. He learned that the man had been one of the guards in the camp.

When they got to the camp itself, which he believes was Mauthausen, Adams was confronted by a completely unexpected sight: women behind a gate asking to be let out. "I found out later they were comfort ladies for the German soldiers. And they were young and well fed and well dressed. They had the barracks right inside the first gate."

While he was standing there trying to figure out exactly what he was looking at, a male prisoner came up to him. "He spoke very good English. I still don't know who he was or what he was, and he said, 'Can I borrow your carbine for a little while?' And I said, 'Well, what the hell, why not?' I figure he had a good use for it. So [he goes away and] I could hear some shots, and he came back and gave me the gun back. He said, 'Well, now there's several of them that you won't have to take to court.' And I said, 'Several what?' And he said, 'Kapos.' And I said, 'What's a kapo?' He told me they were prisoners in charge of barracks, like the one that got killed [with the bicycle]."

That business out of the way, the prisoner took Adams on a tour of the camp. The first thing he saw was buses used to transport prisoners from Gusen to Mauthausen, killing them in the process. "All of these buses had an enclosed thing for the driver, airtight, and the exhaust gases went back into the bus, and they killed the majority of the people getting from Gusen to Mauthausen." Each bus held forty or fifty people.

"And then the next thing he showed me was the gas shower. It was a shower room that held several hundred people, and the showerheads didn't put out water, they put out gas. So they would eliminate that group of people that way."

Adams says there were thousands of bodies strewn about the camp, which, of course, stank. "The ovens where they cremated them were still smoking hot when I went in. They'd probably used them the day before. There were bones in them, not bodies."

His guided tour continued with a stop at the rock quarry, where he was told how the Germans would kill prisoners by forcing them to carry huge rocks up the 180 steps from the bottom to the top all day long. If the work didn't kill them, the SS guards would shove them off the cliff and watch them fall to their death on the rocks below. The prisoner, whose name and nationality he never learned, took him to a building where medical experiments had been conducted and corpses dissected. Adams says that the psychological impact of what he was seeing was blunted because he and his buddies had seen terrible things during the war, including the Americans' brutal response to the Malmédy massacre, which had included an "absolutely no prisoners, none" unofficial order. Nevertheless, while Adams has told the woman he married in 1946 about some incidents during the war, including what he did to get a Silver Star, Bronze Star, and Purple Heart, he's never told her or their five children and thirteen grandchildren about the concentration camps.

As the first troops from the 11th Armored were entering Mauthausen, Stanley Friedenberg of the 65th Counter Intelligence Corps Detachment was coming into Linz. Since leaving the Ohrdruf concentration camp, he and his small team had been following the Danube all the way into Austria, not knowing if they were entering the country as liberators or conquerors. "So," he says, "the people threw flowers at us, and we kept submachine guns on our laps." The first thing they heard in Linz was that the 11th Armored had discovered a huge concentration camp across the river and just twelve miles to the southeast.

Hurrying to the camp, he saw a sight he's never forgotten. "The thing I remember is the inmates, wearing the striped pajamas, none of them weighing more than a hundred pounds. Haggard, unshaven, disease-ridden, clinging to the barbed wire with their hands, saying nothing. But the fact that they said nothing said a lot."

As he describes the scene while seated on the patio of his winter home in Placida, Florida, the retired lawyer doesn't even realize that his hands have formed themselves into claws, as though he, himself, were hanging from the Mauthausen barbed-wire fence. When I point this out, he says, "When we visited Yad Vashem [the Holocaust Memorial] in Israel, they had a series of photo murals there, and the last photo mural was maybe four by eight feet, the exact same thing, of the men of Mauthausen clinging to the wires. I came around a corner and came face-to-face with it, and I'm not an emotional man, but I sat down and just cried."

At the Mauthausen gate on May 5, because he arrived in an unmarked jeep wearing a uniform that concealed his rank and had the authority that counterintelligence agents carry, he was able to order the GIs who wanted to open the gate to keep it closed. He recalls telling them it would be bad for the prisoners. "They'd wander over the countryside, the Germans will harass them, they'll die of starvation and disease. Just keep them here and get on your radio and call back for medics, food, and so forth." Then he entered the camp.

"They had these long barracks with five-tier-high beds, little narrow aisles between them, and the Sonderkommandos, who were the Jewish people used as help by the Nazis and given a little extra food, used to go through there every morning and clean out the dead bodies. And the place smelled; there were still many, many people laying in the bed too sick to get out, just moaning.

"It was so emotionally involving, I just want to go in and see what I can do. I couldn't do a damned thing except hope for some professional help to come there. And we walked through it, and I can't say how long it was before medics and food wagons came, but it was possibly the end of that day, and they started setting up medical tents there. We set up a separate detachment for Mauthausen. We had three or four men there just to cover it, and try to get who were the guards, the atrocities we could document. Our mission had somewhat changed by now. Now we're involved in war crimes and tracking down war criminals as well as counterintelligence."

George Sherman was a member of the 41st Cavalry Squadron of the 11th Armored Division. The nineteen-year-old from Brooklyn had enlisted in the Army Air Corps just two months before his high school graduation, but he had turned out to be color-blind and thus unqualified for flight training. It wasn't a problem in an armored outfit, however. It was the Thunderbolts who were sent to the town of Malmédy, where elements of the German 1st SS Panzer Division had massacred at least seventy-one American POWs. Their job was to winch the frozen American bodies out of the field where they'd been murdered and up to a road where they could be put in body bags and loaded onto trucks.

The day Sherman arrived at Mauthausen started with a simple assignment: look for the Russians coming toward them from eastern Austria. They were patrolling on roads a few miles east of Linz in M24 light tanks when they began smelling an awful odor. Moments later, they came to a big wooden entryway and heard a lot of yelling on the other side. One of the tanks drove through the gate, and then the entire platoon of tanks rolled inside. Sherman says, "We were greeted with the sights, the piles of bodies, these people walking around like God knows what. We dismounted, and the scout sergeant radioed back to the squadron headquarters. He couldn't explain what the heck it was. And about half an hour or forty-five minutes later, a full tank battalion came up from the 41st, rumbling down with about twenty-odd big Sherman tanks."

Those tanks remained on the road outside the camp, but nearly all the men came inside. "We didn't know what the hell to think. We had heard through *Stars and Stripes* about a couple of the other camps that were [liberated] early on, the main one [Auschwitz] being found by the Russians. So we surmised what it was. We were dumbfounded. The people—the prisoners coming up to us and not knowing what to say. But it's just—you have no words. You're looking at this, and it's kind of hard to believe."

What Sherman and his buddies wondered was, where were the German guards? "That was the thing we were looking for. And there were only a handful, who were, at that point, dead. The prisoners beat them to death, and we were later told that the majority of them had taken off very early in the morning and the night before because they knew we were literally just four or five miles away in Linz. They took off in our direction; they didn't want to go where the Russians were, of course. So they went west, but we didn't see them." After approximately two hours in the camp, the American officers ordered their troops out and told them to continue with their mission.

T/4 John Stephens was in the village of Mauthausen the day D Troop of the 41st Cavalry liberated the camp. He was just watching what he describes as "little worn men wearing gray-striped pajamas who were still able to walk" come into town. He says, "A German lady came to me to complain that one of the men had stolen her bicycle. I just looked at her and shrugged. After the way the prisoners had been treated, they deserved to steal anything they could get their hands on.

"While walking around, I had passed a bakery in which customers were being served. So when two of the little men pleaded [with me] for food, I took them to the bakery. The door was now locked. I suppose the proprietors must have seen us coming. Determined to break down the door if necessary, I kept pounding until the baker and his wife leaned out of the upstairs window and told me they were closed. *'Machen Sie auf oder ich werde schiessen!'* [Open up or I'll shoot!] brought them downstairs on a run. They didn't know that the chances were considerably less than zero that I would shoot an unarmed civilian. So they came downstairs immediately and were exceedingly polite. *'Diese Männer müssen Brot haben'* [These men must have bread], I said. The men chose what they wanted and hurried away. I have often wondered what happened to them. There they were, emaciated and weak, surrounded by a sea of enemies and a long, long way from home. Did they ever manage to reach home? If they did, was anything there?"

Pastor Colvin Caughey's memories of Mauthausen are tied closely to recalling the rumors that the end of the war was near. "We're in this town, and we started taking prisoners by the hundreds and thousands. You couldn't believe it—Germans were marching in columns, whole units were coming in. There were much more of them than there were of us, but they were coming as prisoners. We couldn't even guard them; we'd just say, 'Go over in that field, there.' They were trying to get away from the Russians, that's the whole thing—they were eager to surrender to us."

It was in the midst of coping with the onrushing surrendering Germans that Caughey's unit got orders to move to Mauthausen. "They knew about the camp, our leaders did, and they told us, 'Now, we're going to this camp and don't give them any of your food.' We thought that was kind of a strange order, but we had no idea what we were getting into.

"As we went down the road we could see, up on top of this hill, this big gray rock, stone building. Like a penitentiary. And that was our first glimpse of Mauthausen. And then, as we got closer, we saw all the barbed-wire fence. And we came to a wire gate and went through there into Mauthausen. And down below us was another huge fenced area with all these barracks and so on, and everywhere we went there were these prisoners all begging for food. They were desperate. You could see how starved they were. And we ignored the orders we'd gotten—we just gave them everything we had."

Caughey and his men had driven their half-track quite a way into the camp, but they were unable to dismount because they were immediately surrounded by inmates. Though the camp had actually been liberated a day or two before his unit arrived, he'd been sent with his men to help occupy the place, which meant he had to get out and walk around. Inmates told him the fenced area they'd driven into was called the hospital unit, but the name was just another perversion. "What it really was," he recalls, "was a big encampment for those who were too sick to work or crippled or whatever. It was just a place for them to wait until they died. And that's where the bodies were stacked up in big piles. Another thing we noticed when we got there was the stench. This very strong odor—I couldn't figure out what this was, you know? And it smelled like something might be burning, the whole area smelled like that. And I couldn't figure what the hell it was all about until several days later I caught on. That was the stench of the crematorium that was still there, days after they'd shut it down. Burning flesh, that's what the smell was. Burning human flesh. You just shake your head and say how awful it was, just awestruck at how horrible it is. You don't know how human beings could do such a thing. You're just—disgusted. Some guys threw up. I didn't."

Colvin Caughey hadn't been a religious person before the war, but he acknowledges getting religion in combat. As he puts it, "I had a real Christian experience that first day of battle, before I was hit." By the time he got to Mauthausen, he had committed his life to the ministry, and the horrors of the concentration camp only strengthened his belief. "All you can see is the dire need for something; human nature needs God. I mean, they couldn't be Christian people doing that. And of course, most of the people in there—not all of them but a vast majority of them—were Jewish people. And you just felt such compassion for those people. You didn't even know the half of what they'd suffered."

Caughey's unit stayed at Mauthausen for about six weeks. It was springtime, sunny and bright, and they could see the Danube River from up in the camp—although the beautiful blue Danube was dirty brown. They were quartered in a development of fairly new homes built for the SS officers within sight of the prison and stayed to help the medical and quartermaster units brought in to feed and treat the thousands of inmates suffering from malnutrition and disease. He saw the quarry and the death camp barracks. "They were so crammed in there, they just had these big bunks with a little straw if they were lucky, maybe a couple feet between bunks, clear to the ceiling, about four different decks. The bunks were three or four foot wide. And they'd have to sleep four people on each bunk, clear up to the ceiling, and just a very narrow aisle down the middle of the barracks. Just crammed in and dark. I talked to one of the guys there—I remember he wanted something to read, and that was so strange. The only thing I had was my New Testament. I said, 'Here, that's all I got.' He was probably Jewish, and I laugh about it, but it's all I could give him to read."

The inner prison at Mauthausen, the big stone building, was being used by the Americans to keep special German prisoners locked up in cells. Caughey's squad was assigned to help deal with roughly twenty of those prisoners. That's when he saw that inmates inside the camp had wreaked their revenge on some of the guards who hadn't managed to escape. "In that inner prison, I saw big Germans butchered, really, laying down in the inner camp near the gas chamber. The floor was covered with an inch of blood, and several of the German guards, or whoever they were, had been murdered or killed by the inmates. They were fat and healthy, and they had clothing.

"I was charged with work detail. I had one of these prisoners to do the work, and I was to guard him while he did the job. And he tried to talk to me. He was a big, strong, good-looking guy. Probably SS. And he said in German, 'What are they going to do to us—or me?' I forgot which. And I said, *'Ich weiss nicht.'* I don't know. And he said, 'Why? What have I done?' He said this in German, of course. I said, *'Der Lager ist schrecklich,'* the camp is terrible. He said, 'I was a guard on the gate. I didn't do any of that. All I was, was a guard at the gate.' "

In order to efficiently process the inmates and help them recover, the Americans got the upper camp cleaned up and kept them there. They also set up a hospital tent camp in an open field outside the Mauthausen wire. Eventually, they brought the German prisoners down into the fetid lower camp and forced them to clean out the huge latrines. Caughey says, "We had one guy on our squad who could speak German pretty good. And those prisoners were going to use the hose, stand outside and kinda hose it down from the outside. He just ordered them to get in there, and you-know-what was flying everywhere. Boy, oh boy, in a couple of hours, they had that place cleaned up."

The fact that his outfit remained at the camp for quite some time gave Caughey and his buddies a real sense of satisfaction. "We're just glad we got there when we did. You felt some gladness that we liberated that darn place, and we felt pretty good about things improving. Gradually, that camp is getting cleaned up, and those people who were there were starting to recover. So there was some good feelings about being there and doing what you were doing."

For Werner Ellmann, the fact that he was German-born and could communicate with both local Germans and prisoners inside the camp was not necessarily a positive thing. While his buddies were in shock, some of them throwing up and crying, Ellmann was asking questions. The answers were arguably more disturbing than the atrocities he could see. Take, for example, the stone quarry, where he found and questioned several German civilians who worked in the camp. "They remembered when two hundred American flyers had been captured because they had to parachute from their disabled planes. They took

[them] to Mauthausen, and they started them one morning to go down and get those rocks, didn't stop them until they were dead. Either they collapsed, they were shot, bayoneted, or whatever, but all two hundred of them were liquidated that way. That's what they did with the prisoners. How sadistic can you be? And how can you walk away with any kind of good feelings about the people who did it, much less than that's my ancestry?"

Ellmann can still see the camp in his mind's eye, and the dying inmates. "We had seen killing. For Christ's sake, that was nothing new to us, but this was too hard to handle.

"I want to help people, but I didn't know how. When you're looking at a person in that state, you either think to yourself, 'If I touch him, he'll fall apart.' Or maybe it was even—I don't know—disgust. I don't think that was in my mind. I think it was more subconscious. But I do feel that I had a compulsion to go through that place without running out of there. Some guys did."

After going inside the walls and wire of Mauthausen, Ellmann lost it. "I went crazy. I did. You know, when I went out into that field and I saw these farmers out there and I stopped them and said, 'What goes on in that camp?,' and they said they didn't know. I carried a Thompson submachine gun, .45-caliber. I was just about ready to blast those people. Those people were in jeopardy, because that hatred was instilled in me at that point. And I had to kill people; why the hell couldn't I kill them? My jeep driver backed my gun down.

"And then I went back in, and I said to the commanding officer, 'I think every one of those people in that village should be made to come into this place, see what exists here, and then be made to clean it up. Bury those people with a proper ceremony and a proper grave, and make every one of them see what's going on here.' And they did that."

Like Ellmann, Shelby Keeton, a veteran of the 11th Armored Division from Monticello, Kentucky, has been unable to put the war out of his mind. He was born in 1918 and was married and had three children before he volunteered to leave the farm and join the Army in 1944. He'd been married more than fifty years before he told his wife about being at Gusen and Mauthausen with the armored infantry. Her reaction was shock, but he believes she understood why he hadn't told her all those years. Telling her at last, he said, was necessary. "I had to talk to somebody, to get the pressure off of me, I guess. You don't forget something like that. You can't forget something like that. It leaves scars on you. Your memory is scarred."

Keeton says that unless you've been through it, it's impossible to imagine the burden. Not only was he at Mauthausen, he was also at one of the nearby Gusen subcamps shortly after it was liberated. "One of those commanders at Gusen, the inmates lynched him and hung him. And he had a little twelve-year-old boy, and they brought this boy up and showed him his dad hanging there dead, and the boy spit on him. In disdain. He was just disgusted with his father and spit on him. They called him Junior. He had a .22 rifle, and he would use the inmates, prisoners' heads, for target practice. We heard he killed over two hundred inmates, shot 'em."

Keeton graphically describes other encounters between the newly freed inmates and German guards they'd captured, adding that the Americans didn't intervene—"they couldn't." What the Americans did do is force the local German civilians to come to the camp to bury the dead in trenches dug by bulldozers. Just as at other camps, the locals protested that they hadn't known. "Oh, bull feathers," says Keeton. "They lied. They could smell 'em for two miles. I know it. But we didn't swallow that line, you know? We made 'em put 'em down there." The GIs made them do it at the point of a gun or a bayonet, whatever it took to make sure that the victims got a proper burial.

Duane Mahlen, a buddy of Keeton, was part of Headquarters Company in Combat Command B. By the time he got to Mauthausen, he'd seen what he described as "the most shocking thing ever" at Flossenbürg, not quite two hundred miles to the north, a camp where thousands had been killed and "the survivors looked like they were dead." But what he remembers most from Mauthausen is the piles of dead. "I always picture this like a stack of cordwood."

Orville Larson, from San Diego, was also a friend of Keeton. He's now ninety-one years old and still has visions of "dead people all over, piles of them" but says it didn't affect him the way it did the younger soldiers. He was twenty-seven at the time and took great satisfaction in forcing the Austrian civilians to bury the dead.

LeRoy Petersohn was a medic with the 11th Armored Division when he saved a three-week-old baby's life at Mauthausen.

Duane Mahlen says, "I was there when they dug one of the massive holes to bury them. The mayor had lots of locals over there to look at it, and it was their first, allegedly, look—but we'll never really know how much they did know. Everybody was mad at the Germans and Austrians for allowing it. But we were all deeply stunned, obviously, and surprised.

LeRoy "Pete" Petersohn, a close friend of Mahlen, is one of the few surviving liberators of Mauthausen who has a positive story to tell—one that started at the end of the war and continued into the next century. Born in 1922 and now living in Montgomery, Illinois, he was a T/5 medic in the 11th Armored Division who had his first taste of combat when Patton's army charged across France to help rescue the beleaguered 101st Airborne Division. Pete has two Bronze Stars, the Combat Medic Badge, a Purple Heart, and shrapnel inside him from the Battle of the Bulge.

Around 11 A.M. on May 5, his unit got a radio message ordering it to proceed to a position where it would meet an element of the 41st Cavalry Reconnaissance Squadron (Mechanized) and drive to Mauthausen. The trip from the Gusen camps was about a dozen miles, but when they were still about five miles out, men in the six-vehicle convoy—scout cars, a light tank, and jeeps—began smelling a foul odor.

When they arrived at the camp, Petersohn was approached by an inmate who spoke perfect English and offered to take him on a tour of the camp. Since the doctor he was traveling with, Combat Command B surgeon Major Harold Stacey, had gone into the office formerly occupied by the SS guards, the young medic accepted the offer. He was shown the crematorium furnaces, which were still burning, piles of bloody victims who had been recently killed by blows to the head, and what he describes as "the most devastating sight at that moment was piles of bodies, piled against the walls. And the piles were full of rats eating on the dead bodies, which was a horrible sight to see.

"The camp," he recalls, "was enclosed on three sides with quarry stone. And the fourth side, they had a high-wattage barbed-wire fence, and during the course of this fellow taking me through the camp, I was standing with him talking, and there were two women that appeared that just threw themselves against the barbed-wire fence. And of course, that being charged, they immediately were killed. And then the fellow told me that they probably were gals that were prostitutes for the German soldiers. And he said that many of the inmates knew them and what they did, and he said they probably didn't want to be taken alive."

Petersohn didn't think to ask the inmate serving as his guide where he was from, but the man did tell him that he'd been a college professor and that's what had led to his being arrested. "I taught kids, and I was an anti-Nazi. It didn't take them long before they caught up with me."

Despite having been warned by Dr. Stacey to stay away from the inmates as much as possible because they were diseased, Petersohn, who was wearing a helmet with the Red Cross symbol of a medic on three sides, was unable to resist calls for help. "The very first barracks I went in, a fellow came up to me, and he had a slash on his arm. I couldn't get a word out of him as to what happened, but there was a fellow laying in the top bunk, and he had his arm hanging out. I went over and felt his arm, and he had a slight pulse, very faint. But then I walked over and checked another fellow, and he had a good, strong pulse. He was younger. I went back to the fellow with the arm hanging out, and he was gone.

"The inmates just swarmed around me, and in one case, there was a fellow had gone down, he fell or just fell over, and come to find out he had been an SSer, and somebody had taken a piece of glass and had hit his heart. There were several of them that had changed clothes and were trying to mingle in among the inmates, hoping to convince us. But the inmates recognized them and killed them.

"I had seen a lot before we ever got to that camp, but I was more affected by seeing the people that were starved and just skin and bone. And all the things that they did to those people affected me far more than having to be out in the field, patching some of our men up."

But then there's the one incredibly positive experience Pete Petersohn had at Mauthausen. He had gone into one of the women's barracks and discovered a mother with a little baby girl that was "a mass of infection." She was covered with furuncles—pus-filled boils that, if not treated, could result in a staph infection spreading to her spinal cord, brain, and internal organs, ultimately killing her. The infant, a girl named Hana, was just twenty-four days old and had been born in a slave-labor camp called Freiberg, one of the Flossenbürg subcamps.

Her mother, Priska Loewenbein, had been shipped to Freiberg from Auschwitz to work in a converted textile factory that was manufacturing warplanes. The day after Hana's birth, she and her mother were loaded onto cattle cars with two thousand other women to begin what turned into a seventeen-day stop-and-start journey to find a camp with the facilities to kill them.

Years later, Hana's mother told her daughter about the kindness of strangers that had probably saved her life during that journey. The train had headed south from Freiberg into Czechoslovakia and at one stop, people in the station at Horni Bříza, near Pilsen, heard the baby crying. Though the prisoners were receiving little or nothing to eat, the

German guards were also hungry and running out of provisions. Hana's mother told her that the townspeople bargained with the guards. "If they were allowed to help the mother and child, they will provide for the guards. And that happened, the guards allowed that." They even provided clothing and diapers for her. Until then, she'd had nothing but a little shirt and hat (which are now part of the collection at the Holocaust Memorial Museum in Washington).

The distance between Freiberg and Mauthausen was only about 240 miles as the crow flies, but the train ride lasted an excruciating seventeen days as the Germans moved every which way to avoid the advancing Russian and American armies. The irony is that the delay in getting to Mauthausen probably saved their lives, because just before they arrived one evening, the Nazis killed a final batch of prisoners in the gas chamber—and then ran out of poison gas.

When they were unloaded from the train, the camp guards took everything Hana's mother had been given for the baby. And then she was told that no children were allowed in the camp. Hana says her mother told her, "When the guards tried to remove me from her hands, she started to fight with them, at which point a woman who was Polish, a guard, came to her and said she didn't see a child for six years and wanted to play—so she saved my life by saying she wanted to play with me, which apparently she did, and allowed my mother to watch it from outside through the window."

After examining baby Hana, Dr. Stacey determined that her body was riddled with skin infections, and since the hospital at Mauthausen was a filthy mess, they would have to take the baby to the hospital at Gusen. Pete recalls the doctor explaining it to Hana's mother in German, although Hana says her mother was fluent in English and would have understood. Nevertheless, there were a lot of tears when her mother handed the baby to the doctor and watched the two Americans drive away with her in a jeep.

As soon as they got to Gusen, Petersohn went to the nearby 81st Medical Battalion to get some vials of penicillin that they had under refrigeration. By the time he returned, the doc was working on the child. "He was already lancing these blisters, and then my job was to take swabs and penicillin and clean them out. There were some that were in bad enough shape that we had to stitch."

The antibiotic did the trick, and they returned the child to her mother at Mauthausen, where Dr. Stacey offered to help Hana's mother come to the United States because he thought additional medical treatment was necessary, treatment she was unlikely to get in postwar Europe. But she wanted to go back to Bratislava, Czechoslovakia, and look for her husband. The two of them had originally been taken to Auschwitz in September 1944, when Mrs. Loewenbein was two months pregnant.

Near the end of May, Hana and her mother boarded a boat going down the Danube for the 160-mile voyage to Bratislava, and Pete Petersohn was left to wonder for nearly sixty years what had happened to them.

———

Combat troops weren't the only Americans to enter the concentration camps. At Gusen and Mauthausen, female nurses of the 131st Evacuation Hospital helped save lives as well.

Phyllis LaMont Law from Leroy, Pennsylvania, was twenty years old and just out of nurse training when she volunteered for the Army because she wanted experience and excitement. As a second lieutenant, she was attached to the 131st at Fort Jackson, South Carolina, and around Christmas 1944, the unit boarded the *Queen Elizabeth* in New York harbor to sail across the Atlantic at thirty knots, zigzagging the entire way. She remembers all forty nurses being told to keep their clothes on for the voyage in case there was a submarine attack and they had to abandon ship.

The unit went from England to France and then rode railcars and trucks to Bierbach, Germany, where they set up to care for the wounded. From there, all their travel was by covered truck. "We never saw the countryside at all," Law says. "We were inside covered trucks because of snipers, they told us."

The 131st was set up near Nuremberg as a fully functioning hospital servicing combat units throughout the area. It had a total of 277 personnel, including 32 doctors, dentists, and medical service officers,

The caption Army nurse Phyllis LaMont (right) typed in 1945 appears to say all that needed to be said about the concentration camp known as Gusen.

the 40 nurses, and 205 enlisted men—lab and X-ray technicians, sterilization specialists, medics, clerks, drivers, and cooks. They performed all their services in tents that could be broken down, loaded onto trucks, transported, and set up again in a matter of a couple of days. As early as April 12, unit records indicate that they had hired freed Russian and Polish slave laborers to help with meals, but even by late April, the 131st hadn't been sent to any of the liberated concentration camps.

On May 9, a day after the war in Europe officially ended, the 131st arrived at Mauthausen, tasked to "take care of malnourished and typhus infected DPs."

Initially, in an act of what today would be considered male chauvinism, the female nurses were separated from their unit and sent elsewhere. Phyllis Law says, "We were left in a field for a few days until the boys went into the concentration camp. Our colonel wouldn't let us go into the camps." When the prohibition was lifted, the nurses were trucked into Gusen One but first they were all dosed with DDT from hand-pumped flit guns as a precaution against typhus, which is carried by fleas and lice. Law remembers the morning well. "They dosed us down and let us in, and we had to make up a lot of supplies first. And what we saw were all these horrible, horrible people in bunks that were five and ten across, and every one of them emaciated, and no clothes or few clothes, dirty clothes and whatnot. And they all had diarrhea and all kinds of sickness, so what we had to do was just pass pills at first. And some of the boys had set up intravenous and blood [transfusions]. Some of them were dead before they were completed.

"You feel bad. That's about all you can do; it's kind of a shock, you know, when you're young. The situation is kind of hopeless. You just hope you can save a few. You know how it happened because they talk about it all the time while you're there. And to see all the piles and piles of people that are outside, stacks of them, bones, and that's about all. Watch them being thrown into a big hole in the ground."

By May 11, a 1,500-bed hospital had been established near the main camp and a 600-bed female hospital was started near the town of Mauthausen. By May 12, a total of 1,804 patients were being treated at Mauthausen, Gusen One, Gusen Two, and the Quarry Camp. Existing buildings were converted to hospitals, and at the Mauthausen camp, more than 600 patients were cared for in the former SS barracks. By May 15, the 131st Evacuation Hospital was caring for 3,496 patients in buildings and tents, in beds and litters, and it had begun dispatching displaced persons back to their home countries, with an initial shipment of 950 Poles from Gusen One.

Phyllis Law, who was at Gusen from early May through July 1945, says they weren't allowed to write home about what they were doing, because everything was censored. And when she got home, she says, "nobody wants to hear about it, anyway." She didn't try talking about it, either. "My folks just weren't interested, you know. All they were interested in was me, I got home. And they were farmers and went about their work and didn't have radios or anything like that to keep up with anything. That was my experience. My sister was a nurse, but she was also busy in a hospital. People don't think about it. They think about the war, sure, but they were more concerned with the war than what we'd been through."

CHAPTER 16

YOU ARE STILL INDIVIDUALLY AND COLLECTIVELY RESPONSIBLE

MAY 7, 1945

FALKENAU AN DER EGER (NOW SOKOLOV), CZECHOSLOVAKIA

50 miles north-northeast of Flossenbürg, Germany

107 miles northeast of Nuremberg, Germany

At 2:41 A.M. local time, the German high command surrendered all land, sea, and air forces unconditionally to the Allied forces. The surrender act was signed at Reims, France. The order went out to American units that on receipt of this news in the field, "all offensive operations are immediately halted, and organization of defensive positions is to begin."

The day before, elements of the 9th Armored Division attached to the 1st Infantry Division had attacked into Czechoslovakia along the Cheb-Falkenau road. This area was the Sudetenland, inhabited mostly by ethnic Germans. On the morning after the signing of the surrender, they reached what was then called Falkenau an der Eger.

Owen Tripp, now of Bremerton, Washington, was a member of C Company of the 27th Armored Infantry Battalion. He'd been sent overseas just a few months earlier, had joined the 9th Armored Division as a replacement, and had fought with it at the Remagen bridge. He'd been aware of the concentration camps before going to Europe, but he'd never expected to see one.

On the morning of May 7, Tripp's outfit came across three 40 and 8 boxcars sitting on a rail siding outside the main entrance to what they learned was the Flossenbürg subcamp of Falkeneau. "This sticks with me because they each were about a third full of bodies. Nude bodies. Some I suspect were not completely dead but very close to it. I don't think they'd been there any great length of time, as there was no odor or anything of that nature. It was a revolting scene."

After spending perhaps a half hour going through the boxcars, he got orders to enter the camp, which was empty. "We did go in and clear the barracks, which I hated with a passion because every time I did— I went into a camp and went through the barracks—I got loaded with fleas, much as I tried to avoid it."

The only people his squad of five men saw were local civilians. He recalls that the concentration camp consisted of about a dozen one-story buildings surrounded by barbed wire with a few guard towers.

MAY 7, 1945
LUDWIGSLUST, GERMANY
   4 miles south of Wöbbelin
   73 miles east of Hamburg

On May 2, after reaching an agreement with the Russian army units nearby, the 8th Infantry and 82nd Airborne Divisions liberated the Nazi concentration camp at Wöbbelin. The camp had been opened just three months earlier, in March, as a subcamp of Neuengamme. It was a dumping ground for prisoners evacuated from other camps by the SS, who were attempting to follow Himmler's order that none should fall into Allied hands.

The living conditions of the approximately 5,000 inmates were abominable, with starvation and disease rampant and cannibalism reported. The camp had no utilities, no showers, primitive latrines; the barracks were unfinished. At least a thousand men had died and been buried in mass graves in nearby woods. Two hundred bodies were scattered about when the Americans arrived.

One of the 82nd Airborne soldiers at the scene had a unique and personal connection to the Holocaust. In 1938, at the age of fourteen, Staff Sergeant Manfred Steinfeld had fled Germany for the Chicago area, leaving his mother, sister, and younger brother, who were unable to get exit visas.

In 1944, while he was a student at the University of Illinois, he was drafted, and because he spoke fluent German he was assigned to military intelligence headquarters in London, where he was an order-of-battle specialist, an expert on the German army. When two additional airborne divisions were created, the skills he possessed were needed in combat outfits. He volunteered, went to jump school in England, and joined the 82nd Airborne Division, an assignment that ultimately took him to the concentration camp at Wöbbelin. Though he knew that his mother and sister had not been able to get out of Germany before the war, he didn't know their fate. His brother escaped to fight with the partisans and ultimately emigrated to Palestine and fought with the Israeli underground against the British, who killed him. Steinfeld's mother and sister, having been swept up by the Nazis, survived until just three weeks before the liberation of Wöbbelin. Steinfeld didn't learn until months later that they had been killed by the SS at the Stutthof, Poland, concentration camp rather than being freed to fall into the hands of the advancing Russians.

Steinfeld recalls his first visit to the Wöbbelin camp. "Conditions were terrible. When we got there, none of the barracks had windows; none of them had been completed. We found most of the inmates were very close to dying."

Five days after liberation, burial services were held for two hundred of the victims in the Ludwigslust town square. The decision to take

*American soldiers of the 82nd Airborne Division observe a moment
of silence at a mass funeral held on May 7, 1945, on the palace
grounds of the archduke of Mecklenburg in Ludwigslust, Germany,
where they forced the townspeople to bury two hundred of the
prisoners who had died in the nearby Wöbbelin concentration camp.
At the time of the burial, it was estimated that one in four of the
unidentified victims was Jewish, and as a result, the Star of David
was inscribed on 25 percent of the crosses that had been prepared to
mark the graves.*

the park in front of Castle Ludwigslust as a burial ground was made by
the commanding general of the 82nd Airborne, General James M.
Gavin, who'd taken over the castle as his headquarters. Steinfeld was
in charge of coordinating some of the activities with the local mayor's
office. He recalls, "It was a very solemn ceremony. And, of course, the
Germans felt what we were making them do—to walk by the deceased
bodies—was an insult to the Germanic character, so to speak. Everybody claimed, 'We didn't know.' It was their standard excuse. No one
spoke out loud, but since I spoke German and listened to some of the
conversations, I could gather that they resented the fact we made
them walk by."

The after-action report of the 82nd Airborne notes that "German
civilians of every social strata and occupation in Ludwigslust removed
the bodies from the concentration camp and prepared them for burial,
dug the graves, and filled the graves after the services." At the head of
each grave was a cross. Steinfeld, now retired as founder of a success-

ful furniture manufacturing company and still an important philanthropist in the Chicago Jewish community, says that it was estimated that at least 25 percent of the dead were Jews and that though the sight was jarring, a Star of David was painted on every fourth cross.

A eulogy by Major George B. Wood, an 82nd Airborne chaplain, also served as a rebuke to the Germans in attendance:

> We are assembled here today before God and in the sight of man to give a proper and decent burial to the victims of atrocities committed by armed forces in the name of and by the order of the German Government. These 200 bodies were found by the American army in a concentration camp four miles North of the city of Ludwigslust.
>
> The crimes here committed in the name of the German people and by their acquiescence were minor compared to those to be found in concentration camps elsewhere in Germany. Here there were no gas chambers, no crematoria; these men of Holland, Russia, Poland, Czechoslovakia, and France were simply allowed to starve to death. Within four miles of your comfortable homes 4,000 men were forced to live like animals, deprived even of the food you would give to your dogs. In three weeks 1,000 of these men were starved to death; 800 of them were buried in pits in the nearby woods. These 200 who lie before us in these graves were found piled four and five feet high in one building and lying with the sick and dying in other buildings.
>
> The world has long been horrified at the crimes of the German nation; these crimes were never clearly brought to light until the armies of the United Nations overran Germany. This is not war as conducted by international rules of warfare. This is murder such as is not even known among savages.
>
> Though you claim no knowledge of those acts you are still individually and collectively responsible for these atrocities, for they were committed by a government elected to office by yourselves in 1933 and continued in office by your indifference to organized brutality. It should be the firm resolve of the German people that never again should any leader or party bring them to such moral degradation as is exhibited here.

It is the custom of the Unites States Army through its Chaplain's Corps to insure a proper and decent burial to any deceased person whether he be civilian or soldier, friend or foe, according to religious preference. The Supreme Commander of the Allied Forces has ordered that all atrocity victims be buried in a public place, and that the cemetery be given the same personal care that is given to all military cemeteries. Crosses will be placed at the heads of the graves of Christians and Stars of David at the heads of the graves of Jews; a stone monument will be set up in memory of those deceased. Protestant, Catholic and Jewish prayers will be said by Chaplains Wood, Hannah and Wall of the 82nd Airborne Division for these victims as we lay them to rest and commit them into the hands of our Heavenly Father in the hope that the world will not again face such barbarity.*

MAY 8, 1945
SCHWÄBISCH HALL, GERMANY
107 miles southeast of Frankfurt am Main
140 miles northwest of Munich

David Nichols Pardoe spent no more than fifteen or twenty minutes with the 255th Regiment of the 63rd Infantry Division at Landsberg, but it was enough. He saw the walking skeletons tottering around in striped uniforms. He observed that they walked as though they were lost. "Suddenly they had their freedom, and they didn't know what to do. Where were they going to go? Where was their family? What happened, and how do we get there? We have no one—no anything."

He knew the job of the Americans was to get rid of this kind of thing. And he acknowledges a sense of accomplishment when he says, "I guess one of the big success stories of the twentieth century, which has very few success stories, [was] to liberate people."

*The Army Signal Corps' silent film of the interment and services can be seen online in the Steven Spielberg Film and Video Archive on the Web site of the U.S. Holocaust Memorial Museum.

Former Army nurse May Macdonald Horton on her seventy-fifth birthday in 1988.

Pardoe refuses to glorify his participation. If anything, he minimizes his personal war. "I just want to tell you one thing. I had one of the luckiest wars. Everywhere our company was sent, it seemed that the battle was just over. And somebody else had done the dirty work, and we got sent in for relief. And this may not be at all what happened, but it seemed that way to me."

It's correct to infer from his humility that the honor of being called "liberator" should accrue, as was stated in this book's introduction, to all the Americans—and the Allied forces as well—who fought and died to free Europe.

On VE Day, David Pardoe's unit was in a town called Schwäbisch Hall, and they were celebrating in a community center with French soldiers from General Jacques Leclerc's French 2nd Armored Division. "There were all these French guys who all seemed to know how to sing, and one guy after another would get up. One guy would give an imitation of Hitler, another would sing '[Lili] Marlene,' and it was just a beautiful time. One of the happiest memories of World War II was that afternoon with the French soldiers."

The 120th Evacuation Hospital's nursing supervisor, Lieutenant May Macdonald, wrote home at war's end, "This is VE day in Germany, but so far the only change is in our head-gear. We wear the helmet liner now instead of the whole business. All we live for right now is our day of release and the fact that Roosevelt is dead or VE is proclaimed doesn't cut too much ice with us as long as we can't see our way out of the Army."

At the time she wrote this, Macdonald's nurses were occupying a German family's home, sleeping on real beds, using indoor plumbing, eating on china in a modern café with radio and piano that served as their mess. "The lights are shaded, soft music plays, and we sit in comfortable chairs or divans thinking of cafes like this one where we've spent many a pleasant evening in days gone by."

Macdonald wrote that the attitude of the troops to the Germans was standoffish but admitted that it was difficult to be an enemy of little children begging for candy. "We know that it's very important not to be taken in by flattering words or kind attitudes of German civilians. You find yourself saying, 'Someone must be guilty of the atrocities we've seen.' And then you look around trying to find the criminals. Can you blame the old peasant in the field helping a pair of oxen plow the soil while his wife and children pitch manure? Or the woman who scrubs the hospital floor and helps feed the patients? Obviously they're not war criminals. I can't help wondering where the boys are who were behind this whole thing. We saw a few SS men who were caught at Buchenwald and some of our soldiers got a lot of steam off by letting them have it, but these, after all were only the dogs of the masters. I haven't seen the masters brought to justice yet. It's too early for the War Crimes Branch to start wholesale trials, but unless and until they do, I for one won't be satisfied even though I've seen German cities razed to the ground. A city is made of bricks and labor. It's not the equivalent of three to ten years in a concentration camp."

She went on to bemoan that the Germans felt the American forces should be taking care of them, transporting them home, and "be the Big White Father from across the seas." That attitude made her angry, made her want to say, "Dammit all, don't you——"—here she left out the epithets that truly conveyed what she thought of them—"know you started this bloody mess and you're the cause of all this loss of life, home and cities?

"They just don't seem to understand that we're supposed to be their enemies and not their big brothers. Perhaps it's just a pose and the soft nature of the American is again being utilized by a practical people. But actually we don't give a damn what they think or how they feel. All we want to do is to get the hell out of Germany, Europe, and every other theater and go home."

CHAPTER 17

AFTER THE WAR, AND
LONG AFTER THE WAR

Many of the nearly 150 veterans interviewed for this book have stories of postwar experiences that need to be heard if we are to have a complete understanding of their time in the service and how it impacted their lives. Some are unique, while others could be told by tens of thousands of war veterans. Here is a sampling.

Jerome Klein
New York, New York
and
Sidney Glucksman, né Stashek Gleiksman
New Haven, Connecticut
DACHAU

Freedom was not necessarily pretty for the former prisoners of Dachau. Shortly after liberation, Stashek Gleiksman and others took

Holocaust survivor Sidney Glucksman (left) and 14th Armored Division veteran Jerome Klein at the wedding of Sidney's granddaughter in 2009.

revenge on civilians living in the town of Dachau, close to the concentration camp. "We went into some of the buildings, just asking, 'Did you know what went on right next door at the camp?' They claimed they didn't know there was a camp. They didn't smell it? It stunk, the whole city stunk, but they didn't know that there was a camp. That's how they lied. And that's what made us so mad, because everybody said the same thing. We thought, maybe those people killed my parents, my family, somebody from my family. They were all mostly Gestapo people."

A few weeks after liberation, Stashek began riding a bicycle once or twice a week from Dachau to Munich, an eleven-mile trip, to meet with some former prisoners. Then he and his friends moved to Munich. "We saw a house; we would throw out the German family. We all had guns, you know, the American soldiers gave us guns. And we were not afraid to kill a German. We were full of hate. We went into a house and said to leave everything and to get out of the house. We're taking over the house. Nobody would stop us. We could do everything we wanted, maybe, for three, four weeks. Even kill in the street, Germans. We went around looking for a few that we thought would be somewhere in Munich, and we found a couple."

It was in Munich that Stashek reconnected with Jerry Klein, who had befriended him inside Dachau, and it was the special camera the soldier had been given by the German army doctor he'd captured that brought the two of them together. The camera was called a Robot. It was designed to be quick-loading and to take a series of rapid exposures without the photographer having to use a lever to advance the film. Klein was looking for a way to modify the spring that powered the autoadvance; he didn't need to take thirty quick exposures. Stashek discovered that the inventor of the camera was living in Munich, and he made arrangements for the camera to be modified, which led to frequent visits between the former concentration camp prisoner and the American GI.

Eventually Klein was shipped back to the United States, but he'd taken film to a Munich film processor before he left and was unable to pick it up. He gave Stashek his New York address and asked him to pick up the film when it was ready and send it to him. That led to a series of letters back and forth.

It took some time, but one day the young Dachau survivor received a letter from Jerry's mother asking him if he would like to come to America. "I wasn't able to read it, English. I had it translated, and then I said to myself, 'How can I go to America?' " He had no relatives in the United States, but he also knew he had no relatives alive in his hometown near Auschwitz in Poland. He wrote back, saying he wanted to come but didn't know how. And then he heard again from Jerry's mother. She'd made arrangements through the Hebrew Immigrant Aid Society (HIAS). It would provide the papers and bring him to America.

In about three months, Stashek Gleiksman sailed from Bremerhaven to New York, got an Ellis Island name change to Sidney Glucksman, and moved into the Klein family's apartment in Crown Heights. Jerry was thrilled. "I never had any brothers or sisters, so for that period, it was like having a younger brother around."

After about six months, Sidney moved to New Haven, where a community of concentration camp survivors had gathered. Jerry went back to City College, got a degree in business administration, and ultimately became a commercial photographer, owning a photo agency that represented other photographers. He married, but it lasted only seven years, and they never had children.

Sidney had met a girl in a displaced persons camp in Munich. She eventually came to the United States, and they were married. He put his skills as a master tailor to work and fifty years later still operates a well-regarded custom tailoring shop in New Haven. He and his wife have two daughters and several grandchildren, and Jerry Klein, one of the soldiers who freed him at Dachau, is, for all practical purposes, a member of the Glucksman family.

And is the Nazi era behind them? Not quite. Before Dachau, Klein had been a religious Jew. Every morning, whether in the trenches or in a half-track, he'd put on his tallis, the Jewish prayer shawl, and tefillin, and prayed. "All the fellows in the half-track kept quiet while I said my prayers. I'm sure they were convinced that God was protecting them along with me. And then, when I saw Dachau, I just lost faith. I have been a nonbeliever ever since."

His loss of faith happened very quickly. "I realized that there could be no essence of any kind that, having the ability to control human behavior, would allow such a thing to happen, so I had to believe that there was no such an essence."

It's a conclusion that requires the free-will counterargument, that God gave mankind free will and therefore God can't interfere with whatever man does. "Then God did a lousy job," responds Klein without hesitation, "and I can't believe that this almighty creature would have, if it existed, done such a lousy job."

Sidney Glucksman, on the other hand, is a believer. Even more, he believes God has given him a mission to make certain that people don't forget the Holocaust. "I'm still working. I have my own shop, but when they call me [to speak], I say, 'Anytime.' I drop everything, and I make a date, and I go. Because I always say that I'm alive because God wanted me to be alive so I should be able to tell the story about it."

One of those calls got him involved with the production in New Haven of *The Gray Zone*, a dramatic play by Tim Blake Nelson that takes place in Auschwitz-Birkenau in 1944. Sidney became, in essence, a technical adviser. At the conclusion of one performance in front of an audience of hundreds of people, a woman stood up to ask him a question. "She says, do I feel guilty to be alive? So you know what my answer was? I asked, 'What nationality are you?' She told me, 'German.' So I said to her, 'Well, God wanted me to be alive so I should be able to tell the true story of what happened, what you people did to us. That's why I am alive. And that's why I'm doing what I'm doing. And now you can go to hell,' and I walked out." To hearty applause, he added.

Morton Brooks, né Brimberg
Boynton Beach, Florida
BERGA

The soldiers who liberated the concentration camps came home to the United States intent on getting on with their lives. They had the GI Bill, and most of them had the thanks of a grateful nation. There were exceptions . . .

Morton Brimberg, who managed to survive as a prisoner of war in the slave labor camp at Berga, was physically rehabilitated, discharged from the Army at the end of 1945, and enrolled in college at Buffalo a month later. He completed his undergraduate program in a little over two years. Then Brimberg the veteran, Brimberg the ex-POW, Brimberg the Jew ran smack into the lack of that gratitude of a grateful nation everyone hears about during those Veterans Day speeches.

"I wrote letters asking for applications to graduate schools, and I wasn't getting a response just asking for the application, and someone said to me, 'Maybe it's because of your name.' I had written letters [signed Brimberg, and then] I sent out postcards to the same schools under Brent, Brandt, and Brooks, and I got immediate responses to the postcards. So I said to my wife, 'Maybe it is the name, and how do you feel about changing it?' She says, 'Fine,' so I put in for a name change."

So Morton Brimberg, who was sent to die in a Nazi slave-labor camp because he was a Jew, came home and had to deny his Jewishness. He was accepted to graduate school and became a PhD clinical psychologist and assistant director of a department at the University of

U.S. Army veteran and Berga survivor
Morton Brooks, PhD.

Buffalo Medical School, where he was responsible for integrating the behavioral sciences with the medical. The discipline that had helped him survive Berga helped him survive overt discrimination in postwar America. "I learned about camouflage, and I felt, if this is helpful, the hell with it. It's dealing with the situation, just doing something to cope and deal with the situation."

Brooks dealt with dreams and nightmares from the beginning and, when interviewed for this book, said he still has post-traumatic stress disorder and still goes to an ex-POW group at a VA hospital. He's been able to deal with the hate, to deal with the dreams of pinning the Berga commandant up against a wall and carving him up with a knife. But he had difficulty with the final years of the Bush presidency. "It scares me with Bush that in terms of how close his behavior has been to Hitler in terms of legally making rules and regulations in violation of constitutional law. And that the Congress didn't stand up more to him with some of the things that he's done. When they pass a law that says he shall go to court and prove the need to examine someone's communications and just disregard it, to me this is Hitler behavior, and it's scary."

Norman Fellman
Bedminster, New Jersey
BERGA

Unlike Mort Brooks, Norman Fellman kept his Berga experiences bottled up, in part because before the Army would discharge him, it made him sign an official, classified document agreeing that he wouldn't disclose anything that had happened to him while he was a prisoner of war. The ostensible purpose of the document was to keep other enemy countries from knowing what activities American POWs might have undertaken that were inimical to their captors.

Nevertheless, Fellman told his parents what he'd been through, and he did tell Ruth, his future wife, about his experiences. "When I realized that we were serious and I wanted to ask her to marry me, I thought she had a right to know that she was getting damaged goods. And so we talked for hours, and I answered her questions." But for the first fifty years after the war, he says, "nobody even knew I was in the service. I never spoke of it."

He didn't tell his older daughter until she was eighteen or nineteen. His younger twin daughters didn't know about Berga until they were grown up and married. The first time they heard the story was when he gave a talk at their temple.

Keeping the secret had consequences. "I knew I was sitting on a ton of anger and I was repressing it, and when I was younger, I was able to repress it pretty good, but it has been spilling out. It still spills out. It's the chief reason that we have marital differences that we have now, and we're married fifty-eight years. And they tell me at the VA that it's PTSD spilling out, so the anger has been coming out in bits and pieces." Except that he didn't begin going to the VA POW rap sessions until 1986.

The sessions were a start at changing his life. "The first time I walked into that room, it was like somebody took a ton off my shoulders, and I had never realized. Not having to guard myself, not having people disbelieve. I've had doctors who don't believe some of the things that happened—and said so."

One of them was a VA doctor, who some years back said to Fellman

U.S. Army veteran and Berga survivor Norman Fellman and his wife, Ruth, outside their home in Bedminster, New Jersey.

that he was making it all up, that it had never happened. "I would've gone over the counter for him, but luckily, I didn't. No, it's been a long road. [And I'm] still walking it. I find that each time I tell the story, there's a little less anger."

He's able to talk about his experiences now, and he can calmly put them into context and perspective. "We were just one little element. We had 350 military. The rest in Berga were all civilians, and there was torture going on and everything else. Everything else that went on in a concentration camp was happening there. It was a work camp, but they worked you to death, and I'm serious. The purpose of a POW camp, and they had slave labor in those POW camps, but the idea was to feed you enough to get the most amount of work out of you for the least amount of food and keep you alive. In a concentration camp, the idea was to work you until you couldn't work anymore, and when you couldn't work anymore, they killed you or you died on the job. The end result was your demise."

He didn't grasp the magnitude of the Holocaust until long after the war. "I don't think I did while I was there, because it was a microcosm that I was in; it was all I knew. But when you begin to see the number of camps—Dachau and on and on and on, only then could you begin to get the magnitude. We were a pimple; we were a blister. What happened in our camp was a very tiny part of what was going on, but whatever happened in any camp happened there."

And then there's the matter of survival. "Your mind has a lot to do with whether you manage to live or not. You can endure more than you can conceive of if you refuse to believe that it's going to kill you. If you don't give up."

Ultimately, there's the question about God. "Do you still believe?"

"Yes."

"Why?"

"Why not? I'm here, you know."

"It's the quintessential Jewish response."

"Exactly. *Voo den?* [What else?]"

Bernhard "Ben" Storch
Nyack, New York
SACHSENHAUSEN, SOBIBOR, MAJDANEK, and CHELMNO

It didn't take long for Ben Storch and his new bride, Ruth, to realize that not only was there no life to rebuild after the war in their native Poland, the odds were high that as returning Jews, they'd both be killed by anti-Semitic Poles who didn't want the Jews coming back and reclaiming their property. So they set off on an odyssey that took them through several displaced persons camps before arriving in Munich, where they registered to immigrate to either the United States or Palestine.

In March 1947, they were notified that they'd been granted a visa to go to the United States. They sailed for New York from Bremen on April 10 and arrived on April 22. They were met by his uncle, who lived in Brooklyn. Ben Storch spoke no English, but he was a master tailor and was able to get a job working in a factory in Long Island City. At the end of 1952, he became an American citizen.

"I did not speak about the Holocaust stories for twenty-eight years," he says. "My head was not healthy. I had headaches, dreams. I'd smoke

Bernhard "Ben" Storch, wearing medals he earned serving with the
Polish army attached to the Russians in World War II.

overnight." He saw a psychiatrist and "got healed, mentally. Everything
cooled down. Then children came, and I stopped smoking. Mentally,
the children brought me back to life, really. When I came back after
the war, I never hated. Don't ask me how, I did. I just want to have
peace." His equanimity is all the more remarkable when one considers
that his mother died in the extermination camp at Belzec, Poland,
along with 400,000 other Jews, and his three brothers were murdered
in Auschwitz. But he bears no malice toward the German people. He
says, "I want to have those kids, when they grow up in Germany, they
should have peace. [But] they should be told everything."

In 1985, he became active in the Jewish War Veterans of the
United States of America, ultimately becoming New York state commander. He also received his World War II medals from the Polish government, which he proudly wears every Memorial Day.

Storch makes a point of speaking to school groups about the Holocaust, not to describe the gore but to speak of the consequences of
hate. And when he was interviewed in 2008, he said that talking to the
kids continues to help him heal. "When I speak, I speak always for myself and for my friends which were with me, and all the other soldiers.
And when we say a prayer to this day, when I go to a synagogue, which

I do, I always say a prayer for the dead, regardless who they were, Jewish or not Jewish. The rabbi once asked me, 'How come you're praying?' I said, 'Listen, I can say prayer 365 days, there are so many people which are laying there, which don't have one person to say a prayer for them.'"

Vincent Koch, né Kucharsky
Dobbs Ferry, New York
LANDSBERG

The horrors of the Kaufering camps and the war have remained with Vincent Koch. At age eighty-three, even as he acknowledges that his experiences made him "become hard, very, very hard," he says the memories they engender are still with him and still hurt. "My kids used to tell me that I used to get up screaming in the middle of the night—even to this day. Not as much now as it was years ago—call it nightmares or whatever."

A few years before his eightieth birthday, his daughter-in-law suggested that since his granddaughter was studying the Holocaust in school, she should ask Grandpa about it. "So right there, she started to ask me questions. And that was the first time that I remember really getting into a discussion about it. I didn't want to talk about it, that was for sure. It brought back too many memories that I didn't want to revive, because when I talk about it even now, it brings back some of those vivid memories and they're all very real, that's the remarkable part of it—that even at this stage of my life, they're still very, very real memories."

One of the recollections that hurt Vincent Koch the most is the realization that many of the people he found in the Kaufering camp were beyond his help. "It was a terrible thing, for the simple reason that I could not communicate with them. I was so anxious to be able to do whatever I could for them, you understand? I would have done anything for them, I felt so bad, so sorry for what they went through. And there wasn't a thing in the world that I could do. I mean, they weren't even there, to be frank with you. I think their mind was somewhere else. They were out of it, almost, that's how emaciated and strictly

Vincent Koch

bones, and their facial expressions, cheekbones—it was just a horrible, horrible thing."

Koch, who was an observant Jew when he went into the service, still gets big laughs describing an experience he had at a training camp in the deep South. He had brought his tefillin with him to camp and made it a practice to get up at 5 A.M., an hour before the rest of the troops, in order to put on the tefillin and pray.

After several nights of this, a soldier named Clint who slept in the bunk next to his took Koch aside and asked in a deep southern voice, "Are you okay? Is your health all right?"

Koch responded, "Why do you ask?"

And Clint said, "Because the guys here are trying to figure out why you take your blood pressure every morning."

Koch laughs and says, "I don't think he ever saw a Jew before."

And Koch remained a believing Jew, despite what he'd seen at Landsberg. "I hear plenty of comments today, too, where you get into social situations and people are questioning God. I never question. That's God's will. Maybe it's a good thing that kind of brought you through in times when it might have been pretty difficult to get through them."

Stanley Friedenberg

Stanley Friedenberg
Old Westbury, New York
OHRDRUF and MAUTHAUSEN

Stanley Friedenberg, who had been raised as an Orthodox Jew but was never a religious believer even though he attended temple with his father, found that his wartime experiences lessened his belief in God. "With all the rationalization that God was looking at this and God was doing that, my answer was 'Where was he?' Six million of us so-called chosen people were being killed, abused, perished, degraded, and he had a master plan behind it? You speak to Orthodox people today about this, and they have all kinds of rationalizations for it. Doesn't work, doesn't wash. I'm told by Methodists and Baptists that I'm gonna burn in the fires of Hell and my parents are burning in the fires of Hell. Well, what can I do?"

Friedenberg is much more concerned with wondering whether it could happen again. "It's happening in other countries, and to a great extent, religion seems to be the cause of it." He points to the religious Germans, the good Lutherans and the Catholics. "And this [Holocaust] was entirely separate from their religion. They could not see this as being barred by their religion. It just didn't make any difference. It never seemed to occur to them that this was not just morally wrong but against their religion and everything else. A strange situation."

And he sees parallels today. "We seem to be selective in our outrages. We can be outraged by something in one country; the same thing happens in another country, and we turn a blind eye to it. I can't explain that."

Dallas Peyton
Tucson, Arizona
DACHAU

Dallas Peyton is another World War II veteran who didn't tell anyone about what he'd seen in the war—not his wife, nor his children. It wasn't until 2002, when one of his grandsons who was teaching high school history in Tucson asked him to be a guest lecturer and talk about the war, that he opened up. "I started talking to these kids and didn't do bad until I got to Dachau, and then from there on, I was crying more than I was talking."

His fear was that the kids were thinking, "You old fool, up there crying," but when he saw the looks on their faces, he knew it wasn't so. The word spread after that first class, and before the day was out, students from all over the school asked to hear him speak. Even with that positive experience, it took time for him to accept the fact that he had a story to tell. The encouragement of Jewish survivors helped.

Now he speaks often about his personal experience with the Holocaust, and he's reached the point where he can do it without breaking down. He ends most of his talks to school kids with the famous words of a onetime inmate at Sachsenhausen and Dachau, Reverend Martin Niemöller, who himself was answering a student who asked, "How could it happen?":

> First they came for the Communists, but I was not a Communist, so I did not speak out. Then they came for the Socialists and the Trade Unionists, but I was neither, so I did not speak out. Then they came for the Jews, but I was not a Jew, so I did not speak out. And when they came for me, there was no one left to speak out for me.

Leonard Lubin
St. Petersburg, Florida
WELS II

Leonard Lubin is able to describe his witnessing of the opening of the Wels II camp in precise detail, yet he is openly hostile to being called a liberator in its most common context. He knows there is a relative handful of Americans who were at the camps that the Germans had fled, and he acknowledges being one of them. But liberator? "It all sounds so exalted, so glamorous. But we didn't do anything to liberate anybody. It's a bunch of bull. Just a soldier, putting one foot in front of another like I was told to do, happened to be walking down that road like I was told to do, and walked into this thing. No Germans there to fight, so I didn't do anything heroic. I hate the term 'liberator.' It's a false thing.

"Most of us were draftees, and even if we weren't, we were just ordinary people like lots of people today, nothing special. People hear you're a liberator, their eyes glass over and they speak in hushed terms."

But he'll accept "eyewitness," even as he acknowledges that from 1945 to 2006 he never discussed his personal contact with the Holocaust with anyone. But unlike many of the other veterans, he can explain why, in emotional detail. "I'll answer you about that, what it's all about. You come back here, 'Oh, great, happy to have you home. Tell us, what was it like?' So you tell 'em. 'Concentration camp?' 'Yeah.' 'Well, what was it like?' 'Well, all these dead people.' 'Well, tell me about it.' 'Whaddya want me to tell you? They were dead people, stacked up, dead.' And then if you look like you're getting emotional or anything, they say, 'Hey, forget it! It's over now, you're back home, whoopee! Let's have a picnic. Let's have a party. Let's buy a car, get some clothes, get a beer.'

"So here you are and you've got this dichotomy—here, a great society, cars, happy people, well-fed, happy people. Over there, destroyed society, gone to rubble, the men gone, the women you could have all you wanted for a pack of cigarettes. And cigarettes were free to us, so the women were free. And a destroyed society. One of the most ad-

Leonard Lubin

vanced cultures in the world. You look through *Who's Who* of the 1800s on through until the advent of Hitler, every other name of achievement, the Germans. They had Social Security long before we did; it was gone. People's savings were gone. The currency was worthless, a totally destroyed society. Spiritually gone and confused.

"Over here, the other end of the dichotomy, everything was fantastic, terrific, get on with it, good. Forget it, like you could turn the spigot off and forget it. So you didn't. And there was, for Jewish soldiers like myself, not that I was an observant person, nothing like that, very American, assimilated like so many American Jews are, not just Jews—Catholics, Irishmen—all of us were assimilated as Americans. But nonetheless, have to say it's true—a certain embarrassment here—over there you're talking to these people, you asked me what they smelled like. They stunk. They were whining and pleading and crying and begging and assuming postures of begging and adoration, kissing your feet or trying to. Humiliating, the whole thing. And you're thinking to yourself, there but for the grace of somebody, why them and not I?

"But you talk to a German, they're well fed, no matter what you've heard to the contrary. They've got cigarettes to smoke, they're healthy, they can talk to you on an intellectual level, they can tell a joke. Over here you've got these whining, filthy people, abhorrent. Your instinct is just to get away from them. And I think—I can't speak for others—but I believe most Jewish soldiers who saw that, were involved in that way, had to be embarrassed and humiliated and torn. I know I was.

"Embarrassed because you want your people to be strong and healthy and well. And these were not strong and healthy and well at all; you could almost have contempt for them. You know, why did you allow the bastards to do this to you? Why didn't you resist? Why didn't you fight? Why didn't you take a bullet? It's hard to explain."

And Leonard Lubin comes back to the original question: why didn't he talk? And he acknowledges finally figuring out, after participating in a program at the Florida Holocaust Museum in St. Petersburg, that it wasn't just a Jewish thing. A non-Jew said he'd never talked. "People didn't talk. I always thought it was because of the Jewish context that I just described, but it was something else as well. Part of it was, really, nobody wanted to hear it. They'd say to you, 'Tell me about it,' [but then it was] 'Let's get on with it, have a good time, forget it. It's over, forget it, we won. Hooray.' And something about that tells you people don't want to hear about it. I have talked to survivors, not liberators, survivors of concentration camps with numbers on their arms, and they'll tell you the same thing. People didn't want to hear it."

When the war ended, Lubin's squad occupied a house in a little mountain village in the Alps that was owned by an old farmer and his wife. He went out to the field by day, and she was a housewife. "There over the mantle of the fireplace were pictures of four Germans, black-and-white pictures of four German soldiers. They were sons, every single one of them, killed on the Russian front. These were the loveliest people in the world. I didn't like Germans. I was prepared to kill 'em. Here was a mother, she lost all four of her sons, had no idea what the hell it was all about. And she somehow chose to believe that I reminded her of her youngest son, so she wanted to feed me and clean my clothes and press my clothes, and these were people—here were my corpuscles fighting with each other: hate, love, love, hate. A mother, a parent. It's just too much. I had enough conflict for a number of lifetimes, my mind and my spirit and my emotions.

"I was speaking to a graduating class at a Christian religious school, twelve-, fourteen-year-olds, and one little girl raised her hand. She says, 'Mr. Lubin, do you hate Germans? I'm German.' And I said, 'My God, child, no, of course not. They're people. Of course not.' And so all of this stuff in your head [is] the content of my nightmares. The minute I hear the word 'Holocaust,' what flashes through my mind is that engraving in my brain of that guy cutting himself to pieces trying to get some nourishment out of that tin can. That to me is the Holocaust. The content of my nightmares."

LeRoy "Pete" Petersohn
Montgomery, Illinois
and
Hana Berger Moran
Orinda, California
MAUTHAUSEN

It took fifty-eight years for Pete Petersohn to learn the fate of Hana, the three-week-old baby he'd rescued from the filthy woman's barracks at Mauthausen in the final days of the war. In 2003, he learned that the baby had grown up and become Hana Berger Moran, PhD, a U.S. citizen living in the San Francisco Bay Area with her husband. Here's how it happened.

On a trip to the United States from her home in Czechoslovakia in 1981, Hana's mother had begun encouraging her to find the soldiers who saved her. But Hana is a self-acknowledged procrastinator as well as being a very private person who admits she "didn't have the gumption to start looking for them." Nevertheless, she tried, but her initial attempts through the National Archives and the Simon Wiesenthal Center came to naught.

In 2003, around the time her son, Thomas, was married, she found

Hana Berger Moran and LeRoy Petersohn, reunited at the 60th-anniversary celebration of the liberation of the Mauthausen concentration camp in Austria.

the 11th Armored Division Association Web site and wrote a letter asking for help in locating the men who'd saved her life. The responses came quickly from veterans who'd been at Mauthausen, and soon she heard in writing from Petersohn, who said, "I always wondered what happened to that baby."

It took a lot of e-mail between them before Pete decided to call her. "I just happened to catch her at home, and boy, she let out a scream, 'Pete! Pete!' She wanted to know how I'd been, and the last thing she said to me was that she loved me and thank you for keeping her alive, and that I promise her to keep in contact with her."

Through regular e-mails and occasional phone calls, he learned that Hana had fled Czechoslovakia when the Soviets had invaded in 1968 and gone to Israel, where she had family members. She'd received her doctorate at the Weizmann Institute of Science and in 1977 had come to the United States on a fellowship at the University of Chicago as an organic and natural products chemist with expertise in governmental and scientific affairs. The baby Petersohn helped save now speaks five languages and has been responsible for more than thirty investigational new-drug filings with the U.S. Food and Drug Administration and nine drugs approved by regulatory authorities in both the United States and Europe.

Since Petersohn was in the Chicago area and Hana lived near San Francisco, they never had the opportunity to meet in person until she was invited to attend ceremonies being held by the Austrian government to commemorate the 60th anniversary of the liberation of Mauthausen. Hana had visited the former death camp when she was twenty years old with her mother, and she describes it as having been a difficult trip. She was not looking forward to repeating the experience, but when told that Pete was going to be there, she agreed to attend.

In May 2005, Petersohn and his two sons were flown, all expenses paid, to Frankfurt and then on to Linz, where they were taken to a hotel at Mauthausen the evening before the official events began. Hana was already in the restaurant with other invited guests. She can replay the moment in her mind, second by second. "Suddenly I heard these people coming through, and I knew it was him. So I kind of waited until he settled down, and he was very tired, and I kind of crept in next to him, and I just sat next to him. I didn't say a word. I didn't talk. He described the trip, and suddenly I noticed that everybody went quiet. His sons were quiet, and Pete was still talking. I'm not saying anything, I'm just looking at him, thinking, 'Wow!' And then I put my hand on his knee and he turned around and he said, 'Hana.' And of course it was very emotional. And here as I'm talking about it I have goose bumps."

Pete Petersohn remembers the moment a bit differently. "She came in the door, and she hugged me so tight I thought she was going to kill me."

In Hana's mind, she'd always held the image of a young soldier. She never thought of him as being an adult in his early eighties. "When I met him," she says, "it just kind of made sense. It just felt very safe. It felt very comfortable to meet him. I was just totally choked up.

"As hokey as this may sound, I have two birthdays. I was born on April 12, and then, thanks to LeRoy Petersohn and the 11th Armored, I was born again on May 5."

Bernard Schutz
Skokie, Illinois
LANDSBERG

When Bernie Schutz came back to Chicago, he went with two other bachelors to a social at Temple Sholom, the prestigious Reform Jewish Congregation facing Lincoln Park on the city's North Side. There he met Elizabeth Knoop—Betty—a Jewish Dutch girl who had survived the war only because she'd been helped by a church that was part of the underground. It had smuggled her out of the Amsterdam ghetto, and with her fair complexion and blond hair she was able to work as a housekeeper in the home of a gentile family. Her parents also survived the war, hidden by the underground in a clothes closet for two years.

Bernie learned that the only way Betty could stay in America legally was if she married a citizen. He qualified. And that's what happened. It's also how he ended up in the art business, with her relatives in Holland buying European art and shipping it to his gallery in Illinois to be sold.

Before the Army, Bernie describes himself as being "very Jewish but not practicing religion." Before he saw Landsberg, he believed in God—he says he'd often say, "God help me." After Landsberg, he had a big question. "I still have a feeling that there is something, but I have no knowledge of what it is, and after what I saw—" He doesn't complete the thought. He recalls a conversation about the Holocaust with an Orthodox Jewish man whose answer was "He knows best."

Schutz says, "You know, I envy people who have blind faith. I think that's wonderful, no matter what you say or what happens, they believe. I question. I want to believe, but it's very difficult."

Don Timmer
Mansfield, Ohio
OHRDRUF

Don Timmer came home and didn't talk about the two days he'd spent in and around the concentration camp at Ohrdruf. His family knew, but no one else. He finally broke his silence and went public after

Don Timmer

hearing about a board of education meeting in Loudonville, Ohio. A high school teacher was reviewing her itinerary for the senior class trip to Washington. Proposed stops included the Lincoln and Jefferson memorials, the Smithsonian, and the United States Holocaust Memorial Museum.

He says that one of the school board members "flew into a rage and said that the Holocaust was grossly exaggerated and that the students shouldn't be forced to go to the museum and listen to 'a fabrication.' He said he'd 'had enough of those damn Jews.'

"When I heard what the guy said, it made me go back to my memory of those days in April 1945," he said, anger rising in his voice. Since then, he's spoken often about the Holocaust.

Ernest James
Santa Rosa, California
NORDHAUSEN

By his own estimation, Ernest James has talked about the Holocaust to more than 15,000 high school students, primarily telling them they have a responsibility to remember how it came about and why, and what they can do about it. Most of the time, he says, this is new to them. But a couple of times—these are the ones that really stick in his memory—he has run smack into deniers.

There was "the little town in the gold country here in California, a lot of redneck types, and the school was hearing from the kids that they didn't believe it happened. And so I went up and talked to them about it—these kids had been told by their parents that it didn't happen. And after it was over, I was surprised, girls would come up and throw their arms around me and thank me, and guys would come up and shake my hand and almost to a person would say, 'We didn't realize that that happened that way.' What they were really saying is that 'Our parents told us different.'

"Then I had another one where the school in Elk Grove, California, where the teacher warned me that there was a girl that didn't believe it happened. Her parents, her grandparents had moved over here from Germany because they wanted to get away from Hitler. But they were Hitler supporters. And the grandparents convinced the [girl's] parents that all of this did not happen, that it was a big lie."

When it was announced at the school that James was going to speak, the granddaughter objected and her parents refused to give permission for her to attend. Somehow, however, she was at his presentation. "Afterwards, I talked a little to her, and she was absolutely convinced that I was wrong, it didn't happen. No matter what my arguments were. And then she wrote a thesis where she put down all of her arguments, and they were, right down the line, the arguments you hear from the nasty types. And there was nothing I could do to convince her. She absolutely refused to believe it. Here's two generations that had refused to believe it and were passing it along to a third."

James says that kind of reaction is unusual, certainly the exception. But he believes that it does point out the need for continuing education on the subject and raises concerns about finding credible people to engage and enlighten schoolchildren once the World War II generation of eyewitnesses is gone.

Melvin Waters

Melvin Waters
Dallas, Texas
BERGEN-BELSEN

Melvin Waters says he came home from the war, where he drove an ambulance for the American Field Services, and completely forgot about his experiences, including those at Bergen-Belsen. "I never had a nightmare, I never even thought about it. And then, about thirty years after the war, I went to a movie with my wife one Sunday afternoon, and it was *Sophie's Choice.* Do you remember that? And when we went out and got in the car and I started the car up, and then I just completely broke down. And I guess what got me was the scene where she had to make a choice between her two children, do you remember that one? And I had thought that the surroundings remind me—and I told Jo—I said, 'I think that that was Belsen, the way it looked.' Probably all of them looked alike in some form or fashion. But of course, the daughter immediately went to the gas chamber, and there wasn't one in Belsen.

"But my feeling was really and truly a feeling of not feeling like I was compassionate, as much as I should've been. In other words, I just treated it like a day at the office instead of what it really was." Waters acknowledges that acting that way in the midst of the horror was his way of getting through it—but it's easy to infer that, despite this, he's still filled with guilt. He made a trip to visit the AFS archives in New York, and he says he completely broke down. "Seeing the whole thing again, seeing the atmosphere, seeing the pictures of everybody. I was to the point that I really felt like I couldn't talk about it in public. I never did try to talk about it." Interviewed for this book, he says his bad feelings have somewhat abated but he still has feelings of guilt. "I still feel like that I was not compassionate enough, that I didn't do enough when I was there."

Werner Ellmann
McHenry, Illinois
MAUTHAUSEN

The pain in Werner Ellmann's voice is palpable as he acknowledges how his shared German ancestry with the Nazis and their supporters has messed with his head for years. He says that he spent an entire year drunk after returning home to Chicago from the war. Eventually he got into therapy, which helped. Ellmann chose to attend what was then Roosevelt College because he says it was the only college in the United States at the time that had no quotas for Jews or blacks. And it also had an active core of young people getting involved in the nascent civil rights movement, so he was surrounded by turmoil while dealing with his own internal demons. "I was ashamed of being a German and of my relatives. I didn't like myself. I always remembered that I took life, and to this day, I still can't live with that."

Things didn't really change for him until 1972, twenty-seven years after the war. "I really went to work at destroying my hate. I got involved because of Roosevelt [University]. I set up a volunteer program. I got so engrossed in volunteer work as a penance for what I'd done. I'm not for gun control; I'm for completely destroying all of the guns. We don't need them. And I think I'm constantly trying to pay my penance. I was raised a strict Catholic, you know, Hail Marys and all

Werner Ellmann

that when you sinned, vow to never sin again, but you do. And I lost that religion. I lost all religion. I became an atheist. Today, I'm a deist. I'm in church 24/7. And I'm always acting in that context."

Ellmann remembers a religious epiphany just before his outfit was committed to battle in the Bulge. "We were told we could all go to a service of our denomination. I went to the Catholic Mass, and the priest did nothing but berate the other side and that they should pay for this crime and we should all be preserved and not be hurt, not to die. And I kept sitting there thinking, 'What the hell's going on here? My two [German] brothers over there, they're probably hearing the same thing, except now I'm the bad guy. What's going on?' I think that was the first time that I really began to question, and that doesn't happen overnight. That's a process."

At college, even while battling his drinking problem, he became heavily involved in fighting for the rights of others, at the same time dealing with the shame of being a German who had relatives on the other side during the war.

He also felt a burning need to go back to Germany and visit with family members who had been there during the war. "You know, in 1972 I said to [my wife,] Liz, 'I've got so much hatred in me, I have to get it loose, and I think the way to do it is to go back to Germany.' And we did. And I went to visit my brother, and I said, 'I want to be in a room with just you and me.' We stayed for six hours in that room, and I blasted him all over the map."

It was his oldest brother, Herbert, the oldest of four, about six years older than Werner, whom he confronted. "I told him how I felt about the Germans and what they did. And every time he said to me, 'Werner, I wasn't a Nazi,' I felt like blasting his face with my fist. When we walked out of that room, we had settled some stuff, and I began my healing."

In 2008, Werner Ellmann was still working on healing from the things he'd seen and done during World War II. He still wakes up at night screaming, still dreams of someone in a uniform coming at him. And he says he doesn't believe he'll ever be cured of that.

Morris Sunshine
North Belmore, New York
NORDHAUSEN

Morris Sunshine has the heart of a jazz musician. Unfortunately, his arteries are clogged with hate, and he hasn't been able to find a way to fix it. The smell of Nordhausen never goes away. He readily acknowledges the anger, saying, "My hate for the German language and the German people is terrible. It's something that I've never forgiven them for."

Even six decades later. He understands when he hears stories of veterans who didn't seem to be affected by the war, by seeing the camps, but after they retire begin having nightmares and exhibiting the symptoms of what the docs call delayed-onset post-traumatic stress disorder. "Yeah, I can understand that," he says. "I can understand it completely. If you've got this stuff stored up in yourself, it's gotta go someplace. I mean—the shock of seeing this kind of outrage, civilian outrage. It's unforgivable, absolutely unforgivable in my book.

Morris Sunshine

I'm very bad—everybody's taken me to task for this, including my wife, my kids. But if I heard German spoken by young people, anybody, my first reaction is this hate. I can feel it in the back of my head, you know, my hair standing up. Now, these people might be Jews, they might be Austrian Jews, and I have that. But my first emotion is the hate I have for the language and everything else."

He's been in therapy groups; no help. "They always come up to the same thing: you gotta forgive, and these children are really not responsible for what their parents didn't do or did do. They're showing me that's really the right way, but that's got nothing to do with my emotions. I still smell that, you see. In my head I understand that I'm crazy when it comes to this. But it's there, you know, and I can't forgive anybody for this kind of bestiality."

When you talk with Morris, it becomes apparent that his anger is directed more at the civilians who lived near the camps and denied knowledge of them than at the Nazi officials themselves. "It was always the same response—that they didn't know. *'Ich bin nicht ein Nazi.'* I am not a Nazi. And 'I had to be part of the Hitler *Jugend,'* all that kind of stuff. *'Ich bin kein Nazi.'* Might not be correct German, but, you know, it's close enough for jazz."

Jazz is probably what kept his hate from eating him alive. Sunshine went to music school when he got back home to New York, studying arranging with Eddie Sauter, who used to write for Benny Goodman, Artie Shaw, Ray McKinley, and Red Norvo. Eventually he began to teach music, and he began selling and repairing instruments. He married a girl he'd known in high school—they recently celebrated their sixty-second anniversary—and they had three kids.

And he told them about Nordhausen. He told everyone about Nordhausen. "Everybody I know knows that I opened up a concentration camp. That was like a banner that I used to walk around with. I always used to tell them, 'Never mind what you see in pictures. The smell of death is the strongest odor in the world.' And a massive smell, massive bodies, that odor sticks with you forever."

So he can't get rid of the smell—or the hate. But jazz has saved him. "Music is my love," Morris says, "and that's been passed down to the next generation. They play music, and we play together. I can sit down with the granddaughter, my daughter, my son, and we play. We swing. No greater force in the world."

Manfred Steinfeld
Chicago, Illinois
WÖBBELIN

There's no one size fits all with veterans on the matter of Germany or German people. Consider Manny Steinfeld. He was born in Germany; his mother and one brother were murdered by the Nazis just three weeks before he participated in the liberation of one of the camps. Yet he's gone back to Germany and become a benefactor of the current residents of the little town he left as a young teenager.

Actually, Steinfeld has been back to Germany many times. The first was in the late 1950s, when he went to the furniture show in Cologne. "I drove through the town I was born in; I didn't even stop. I didn't want anything to do with them." That's how he felt even while acknowledging that there had been very little anti-Semitism in the town where he had lived until the age of fourteen.

In the year 2000, he was contacted by a young man from the town, about seventy miles north of Frankfurt, who told him he'd been working on dedicating a memorial to the three Jewish families from the town who had been killed by the Nazis—families whose roots went back two hundred years. The man wanted Steinfeld to speak at the dedication. He went and brought eleven people with him. After the dinner, which the town paid for, he said, "Now that you have done this, what can I do for the town?"

The town fathers said they needed a youth center, and after lengthy correspondence, Manny Steinfeld agreed to pay for it, provided it was named for his younger brother, who had been killed in Palestine. In 2007, the town held a memorial service and dedicated the new building, with a plaque that told the story of his brother's short life in Germany.

On that same trip in 2000, Steinfeld paid a visit to the town of Ludwigslust, where he'd watched the funeral service for two hundred of the Wöbbelin victims at the end of the war. "I looked for the cemetery where we buried the two hundred bodies. No sign of the cemetery. Everything was gone." He contacted an official of the Wöbbelin museum, who told him that all the wooden crosses they'd erected had been removed during the winter of 1948 and burned when no coal or other fuel was available. The town had been in what was then East Germany, and the government had seen to it that only a stone monument remained, dedicating the site to two hundred victims of National Socialism.

In addition to his personal experiences in postwar Germany, Steinfeld says he's pleased that many towns with a population greater than 50,000 once again have Jews living in them, and he sees that as the Germans trying to make amends in some reasonable fashion. He also seems to take comfort in the fact that the new Berlin Holocaust Memorial and Jewish Museum is the most visited museum in the country today. "Are [these] all Germans and all young Germans who want to, maybe, clean their conscience?" he asks and then answers, "I don't know."

Despite his own history and his family's tragic past, Manny Steinfeld seems willing to keep an open mind about today's Germans. Nevertheless, he betrays a sense of caution by telling this story: "When Hitler passed the law that the middle name of any Jew is Israel or

Sarah, they went back to all the birth records and added the middle names to all of them. Can you believe that? Dead or alive. And then, in 1947, when it was rescinded, they went back to make the changes again. But that's the German mentality."

Harry Feinberg
Elmwood Park, New Jersey
OHRDRUF

The two dozen men gathered in a New Jersey hotel dining room in spring 2008 had brought wives, children, even grandchildren with them. The occasion was not a happy one. Harry Feinberg, who'd been president of their chapter of the 4th Armored Division Association since 1985, had to tell the membership that the time had come to disband—maybe one or two more meetings after that, no more. They used to meet four times a year, men only. Then they'd cut it to twice a year and let the wives in. Harry says they came from all over the area: Long Island, the Bronx, Brooklyn, south Jersey, upstate New York, Connecticut. But no more. "We're losing them, we're losing them too fast. I get these phone calls, I hate to get on the phone. Every time, [my wife will] say, 'Harry, it's for you,' and one of the children or a wife would tell me, 'Sorry to tell you this, but Bernie just passed away,' or Charlie. I just got one the other day, a son called. They're like brothers to me. What we went through, the bond from what we went through, we would do anything for each other. Believe it or not. You go to any of these meetings, and you'll see guys hugging each other, a kiss on the cheek, you know. And we're all straight men. But that's the way it is. I never saw anything like it in my life."

If reunions give the veterans a chance to remember the good times in the war—a concept nonveterans may find difficult to understand— they also have a chance to talk about the stuff that still screws with their heads. And the wives have a chance to talk among themselves about their husbands—the physical ailments and the mental.

Harry acknowledges that his wife, Edie, still has to help him keep it together. The memories of the concentration camps are still there, still vivid. And when the couple moved from the house they'd lived in for decades, the flashbacks got worse. The VA finally sent him to see a psychiatrist—this is more than sixty years after the war. "I go there every three months, every six months, whenever he gives me an appointment. And he wants to hear stories, and I keep telling him these stories, and he questions me. And I said, 'Doc, do you want me to pull punches?'

"And I start bawling myself, tears come out of my eyes, which I try to hold back. 'No, no, I want to hear you. Don't hold anything back,' he says. I never went to a psychiatrist in my life, but he wants to hear these stories. 'Do you dream about it?' I said, 'Yes, you know, at times my wife has to nudge me because I'll start moaning and jumping all over the bed, not vertically, but start tumbling around, and she'll say, 'Harry, what's the matter? Is it the war?' I'll say, 'Yeah, Edie, I was just dreaming about the war.' "

Feinberg says the dreams increased after he retired, and they got bad enough that he wanted to be medicated. "I asked Dr. Falcone, 'Isn't there a magic bullet? Give me a pill.' He says, 'Mr. Feinberg, you cannot forget it. You will never forget it.'

"I said, 'Why am I coming here? I want to forget about this; I want a pill that's going to soften everything. I don't want to think about this anymore.' So he says, 'There's no such pill, and you will never forget about it.' "

Ultimately, the psychiatrist put Harry on a medication that is supposed to help him relax. But he's still dealing with back problems that began during the war. "My back started acting up. You get up on the tank; to get down, you jump down. Every time I jumped, I would complain to my first sergeant. All he wanted to know is 'Any bones broken?' No. 'Any blood?' No. 'Get outta here.' And he wouldn't let me see a doctor. If I went over his head, I would be dead now. He would give me some detail."

Harry had his first back surgery in 1953; since then, he's had two more, but he's coping. And he's being very careful.

In 1999, he and some other 4th Armored veterans were invited to return to Gotha, Germany, where they were surprised to discover that the American soldiers were looked upon as saviors. Harry says the German officials insisted that the Americans had liberated them. "I said,

'How in the hell did we liberate you? We were fighting the German army.' And he said, 'No, no, you weren't fighting the German people; you were fighting the Nazis. All Germans are not Nazis.' And I opened my mouth, and I said, 'I can't believe this. I was there. Imagine that, all these things were kept from us. We thought we were fighting Germans. We were fighting Nazis. Can you believe that?'"

Morris Eisenstein
Delray Beach, Florida
DACHAU

By the time he participated in the capture of Munich, Morris Eisenstein couldn't count the number of German civilians who had pleaded with the American soldiers, *"Nicht Nazi."* "That was the favorite expression of all the Germans, *'Bitte, bitte, nicht Nazi.'*" One German, in particular, sticks in his mind. "He had been an exchange professor at the University of Chicago, in English or German literature. I said to him, 'How could you possibly have done some of this? You people who gave the world all the great minds in music and culture and art.' He says, 'What can I say? We were obeying orders.' Typical German."

Russel R. Weiskircher, PhD
Cleveland, Georgia
DACHAU

Russ Weiskircher knew that the Holocaust would be part of his life forever within minutes of his arrival outside Dachau. He puts it less elegantly. "Right after I tossed my cookies in the first boxcar, you know right then and there that you aren't going to live this one down. And when we got away from there, I didn't tell the world. I didn't even put a mention of it—not a word of it—in my letters home. I couldn't express it. I wanted to see what was going on, but I couldn't describe it, and I didn't really find myself able to discuss it until I got back to the States and I ran into the deniers, telling me that it was a Churchill/Roosevelt/Stalin myth, that there were no concentration camps, and my pictures were lies and I was brainwashed."

Russel Weiskircher

He was invited to speak at a German Evangelical United Brethren Church in McKeesport, Pennsylvania. And the pastor, who he says was a Nazi, told his congregation that everything Weiskircher had to say was a lie. "This was an ordained minister of God. A U.S. citizen. I got up and made him look like two cents, and I've been spieling ever since."

He'd been afflicted with nightmares immediately after the war, always about the crematory and the bodies stacked up. They came back when he was eighty-two years old, when his old commanding officer, Felix Sparks, died. They'd maintained a telephone relationship, and suddenly it ended.

He says that Dachau was the building block for the rest of his life. "I decided that bad things happened when good people shut up and don't do anything, so I started out on a crusade of one to let the world know you gotta get off the dime and do something." He drifts into the practiced cadence of the southern preacher he became, saying, "You ought to wake up, you gotta get up, you gotta stand up, you gotta speak up, and you don't dare shut up. That's been my creed for years and years and years."

Russ Weiskircher came home from the war with his belief in God strengthened. He believes he survived and that he's doing what he's doing because God wants it that way. He says, "The mission now is to do as much as I can to get people involved to study what happened, to overcome bias and prejudice to see that it doesn't happen again. To get people in a position where they speak up when it's wrong and when they're not afraid to do it. If we had opened our borders when the Jewish immigrants needed a place to go, we could've lessened the impact of the Holocaust by close to five percent. FDR didn't do one damn thing."

And he's not sure that if it were put to a vote today, Americans would save 200,000 people from certain death in Darfur. "It would be tough. I know how I would vote, but it would be tough to sell it. There'd be people who'd genuinely want to save them and people who didn't give a damn."

Which prompts the question, what do you think we learned from the Holocaust?

"What I think we learned is, you can't sit still and wait it out. You can't let the bastards get away with it. That's as simple as I know how to put it. You gotta speak up for your neighbor before they come for him and end up coming for you. The last man to go is me," he says, paraphrasing Reverend Niemöller.

Yet he's realistic. He believes the future depends on the impact his generation makes in spreading the word, and he, personally, is doing everything he can. The legacy of which he's proudest can be found in his work with the Georgia Commission on the Holocaust, which has established an institute that teaches public-school teachers how to use the Holocaust to overcome prejudice and bias.

"Teachers come to learn how to teach, and they get paid. If the school year is going, we pay a substitute to stand in for them. And they get their room and board, and promotional credits. We teach them how to handle diversity, how to create diversity, accept diversity in the classroom, and we teach them how to fight prejudice. We cover a lot of ground when we teach teachers."

Russel Weiskircher heard the call at Anzio, and it set him on a religious path for life. But it was at Dachau where he learned that bad

David Nichols Pardoe

things happened when good people shut up and do nothing. And that's what started him on "a crusade of one to let the world know you gotta get off the dime and do something."

David Pardoe, né Nichols
Huntington, Massachusetts
LANDSBERG

The story told by David Pardoe of the VE Day party with the French troops in Germany was an example of how men and women who've been through the worst that war has to offer can find good memories to talk about when they get together. He's pondered that effect and takes it a step further. "You know, I've thought about why it is that all the veterans' organizations support the government and support the wars that the government undertakes. None of them, the veterans' organizations like ours, ever oppose that kind of thing. And one of the essential reasons is that veterans' organizations are made up of, first of all, the survivors. And they—the memory system, our minds—tend to bury the unpleasant, the ugly, the things that are best forgotten, and to remember the good times, the happy times, the comradeship, the loyalty. And that's why so many veterans still support war. Because they survived, and the memory plays this terrible trick. It suppresses the ugly and the real brutality. It's true. But this is true in our personal lives, too, you know. It's much easier to remember the happy times than the hard times."

Frederick "Fritz" Krenkler
Lake Havasu City, Arizona
DACHAU

Driving to the reunion of the few remaining guys who served together in the 42nd Infantry Division, the Rainbow, Fritz Krenkler was listening to talk radio when someone called in to agree with the president of Iran saying the Holocaust never happened. At that moment, Krenkler's blood pressure probably went off the charts. "I'm still mad about it. I would like to go over there and grab him by the balls and pull his tongue out. That SOB that called in telling [talk-show host] Mike Savage it never happened. . . . I don't know where these people get this idea."

Fritz is another World War II veteran who has exhibited classic symptoms of post-traumatic stress disorder, but he lived with it without getting help. Truth is, there was no help for it that was readily available at the postwar VA when it began chewing up the lives of guys like Krenkler, who was at Dachau with the 42nd. "I'm afraid I was a different person when I came back than when I went over. I had an anger in me that I didn't understand. As a matter of fact, I didn't understand that anger until ten years ago, when I got a little psychiatric help. That anger expressed itself in many ways. I got pretty nasty, probably never realized why."

What got Fritz to a therapist was a severe blowup, the kind of anger that goes from A to Z in a second. And it nearly tore his family apart. "I never realized what was happening to me. I could have enjoyable weeks on end and have one, two, three days where my wife would want to just plain get rid of me. And I'd bury myself in work."

Frederick "Fritz" Krenkler

Though his wife stayed with him, Fritz Krenkler's explosions de-stroyed his relationship with two of his three children. "Two of them to this day won't have anything to do with me. Makes me very sad be-cause it's a big hurt. And my oldest girl has cancer, and that makes me sad. I carried a package—but we all carried a package. I was not alone, that's the big thing. I was even not as bad as some of them."

Half a century after the war, he finally found a private therapist who could help him—mostly, he says, by letting him rant and rave. The therapist told him to let it out. "And this was the thing that was bottled up much, much too long."

What he hasn't done is talk to his buddies, the guys he survived the war with, and tell them how therapy helped. As we sat in a corner at the Mobile, Alabama, hotel where the men of the Rainbow were hav-ing their reunion, Fritz said, "This has been very private—as a matter of fact, you're one of the first strangers I've mentioned it to."

I said. "You did it because I pushed."

And he responded, "Whether you did or not, it's because I wanted to answer."

Or maybe because it took only sixty-three years for a stranger to ask.

It wasn't called post-traumatic stress disorder in 1945, and, like the GIs who later returned from battlefields in Korea, Vietnam, the Persian Gulf, Afghanistan, and Iraq, the soldiers who came home from World War II, for the most part, just wanted to get on with their lives. Without official acknowledgment that combat messes with your head in a way that leaves invisible unhealed wounds, they were unlikely to seek help. And even sixty-five years later, they're still having the occasional nightmare and flashback to their war years. But, as Harry Feinberg was forced to acknowledge, the ones who still survive have fewer buddies to call, to talk it through with. They know a soldier's truth about war that those who've never been there will never know: a war doesn't end just because some general signed a piece of paper. In some respects, for some, wars never end.

The postwar stories you've just read from the soldiers who fought in World War II are not meant to be perceived as museum library contributions—little pieces of oral history that have no present-day application. What these men have gone through, and are still going through, should be recognized by everyone, ordinary citizens and especially our elected officials, as part of the price that's paid for going to war. The man or woman we send to war is not the same man or woman we get back. War is not that simple, that easy. If it didn't change those who experience it, we should be very worried about the kind of young people our civilization is producing. What we must do as a nation to help our veterans readjust is learn to write the check to beef up postwar health services at the same moment as we dispatch the first planeload or shipload of soldiers, sailors, marines, airmen, or coastguardmen.

Aside from letting your representatives in Congress and the president know how you feel about providing better-than-barely-adequate support for veterans, what's the message for you, the nonveteran reading this book? It's simple: if you know any veterans who have been lucky enough to come back from his or her war—whether World War II, one we are currently fighting, or any in between—do a good deed:

A memorial in the garden of the Hebrew Educational Alliance, a Denver Conservative synagogue, dedicated to the men of the 157th Infantry Regiment and to "all who liberated prisoners from Nazi concentration camps."

ask them to tell you about their wartime experiences. If they hesitate, tell them you can handle what they have to say. And then pay close attention, really listen, no matter how difficult or emotional it becomes.

If they turn you down once, ask again another day. Our veterans need to know that we support them, that we care. One of the best ways for an individual to do that is to explain that you want to know about their service to our country, that it's important that we all know. It's a demonstrably useful way to honor their service. No veteran should have to wait fifty years to be able to tell someone about it. You won't regret that you asked.

And don't put it off, especially with veterans of World War II. As Jim Bird, who was at Dachau with the 45th Infantry Division, warns, "Most of us are on the 'slippery slope' of life, and the leaves are falling every day."

———

U.S. Army Signal Corps newsreel footage of the liberation of many concentration camps has been made available online at the Steven

Spielberg Film and Video Archive of the United States Holocaust Memorial Museum. Many of the scenes described in this book can be seen in this newsreel collection.

At the same site, you can access thousands of Holocaust-related photos from the National Archives as well as from private donors that the USHMM has digitized and made available in a searchable online catalog. Go to www.ushmm.org/research/collections/search/.

If you find the USHMM collections useful, you might want to consider making a contribution and/or becoming a member. Your financial support will help the USHMM continue this worthwhile work. You might also consider supporting Holocaust museums and educational centers situated elsewhere in the United States or the world.

ACKNOWLEDGMENTS

I want to offer the largest possible measure of gratitude to the veterans who agreed to talk with me about the World War II experiences that brought them face-to-face with the Holocaust. Because they were willing to relive the unbelievable, future generations who, sadly, will not have the opportunity to hear from them directly will still have an opportunity to study the words of these courageous men and women who are America's witnesses to the Holocaust.

Tracking down veterans who were at the camps would have been much more difficult without the assistance of a key group of veterans (and a few nonveterans), some of whom have done their own research and writing about the liberators. Special thanks go to David L. Israel, the author of *The Day the Thunderbird Cried,* Dan P. Dougherty, Curtis Whiteway, Melvin H. Rappaport, Robert Enkelmann, Dee Eberhart, Forrest Lothrop, Russel Weiskircher, Jim Bird, George Slaybaugh, Jan Elvin, Donna Bernhardt, Mark Miller, Glen E. Lytle, and Robert Humphrey.

Lieutenant Colonel (Ret.) Hugh Foster generously provided me a place to stay while I attended the reunion of the 80th Infantry Division at Carlisle Barracks, Pennsylvania, shared his expertise on the liberation of Dachau and on World War II military history, weapons, and tactics, personally guided me in researching World War II records at the National Archives in College Park, Maryland, and carefully reviewed the manuscript.

I wish to express my gratitude to Walter H. Chapman for generously granting me permission to publish his wartime drawings of Salzwedel, and to his wife, Jean, for her logistical assistance. Thanks, also, to Dee R. Eberhart for permission to use his poem "KZ Dachau," and to Warren E. Priest for permission to use his poem "My First Encounter."

Of invaluable assistance in finding documents, photographs, liberators, survivors, and/or essential facts and details were: Geoffrey Megargee, PhD, applied research scholar at the United States Holocaust Memorial Museum in Washington, D.C.; Frank R. Shirer, chief, Historical Resources Branch, U.S. Army Center of Military History at Fort McNair, D.C.; Lillian Gerstner of the Illinois Holocaust Museum and Education Center, in Skokie; Dan Raymond, University of Illinois Library archive assistant in Urbana; Judy Janec, archivist at the Holocaust Center of Northern California, in San Francisco; Eleanora Golobic of American Field Service; Donna and Carl Phinney, Jr.; Gloria Deutsch of *The Jerusalem Post*; Baker Mitchell; and Theresa Lynn Ast, PhD, associate professor of history at Reinhardt College, whose encouragement and doctoral dissertation, "Confronting the Holocaust: American Soldiers Who Liberated the Concentration Camps," provided a starting point for my research.

As she's done for my previous books, Kathy Kirkland typed the interview transcripts, did an exceptional job of online research following leads generated by those interviews, and did her best to ensure that essential material was not overlooked.

Thanks to my information tech guru, Manuel Leyeza, who also served as my principal translator of German documents, and to my mother, Essie Hirsh, who was my go-to expert for Yiddish translations.

A select group of friends and relatives provided support, advice, and encouragement during the research and writing process, read early drafts, offered constructive criticism, and helped in other meaningful ways. They are Jon Eisenberg, Ira Furman, Todd Katz, Richard Greenwald, Peter Herford, Mike Farrell, Saryl Radwin, Leslie Sewell, Jennifer and Joel Weisberger, Rose and Robert Aronson, Richard and Laura Aronson, Sam Sola, and Jay Wolfson.

My agent, Matthew Bialer of Sanford J. Greenburger, Associates, was especially supportive of this project from the beginning, and was instrumental in shaping the proposal that ultimately resulted in this book. Thanks also to his assistant, Lindsay Ribar.

My editor, Philip Rappaport, and Bantam Dell's publisher, Nita Taublib, expressed immediate enthusiasm for this project, and expended extraordinary effort to make it successful. I also want to thank the book's designers, Casey Hampton and Barbara Bachman; the cover designer, Robbin Schiff; and the publicity department at Bantam Dell, especially its director, Theresa Zoro, and publicists Katie Rudkin and Diana Franco. Thanks also go to my editor's assistant, Angela Polidoro; the copy editor, Lynn Anderson; the proofreaders, Maralee Youngs and Tita Gillespie; the cartographers, Mapping Specialists, Ltd.; and the production editor, Steve Messina.

Living with someone who has chosen to bury himself in the ugliness of the Holocaust for an intense, albeit limited, length of time, has its downside. And that is why I conclude these acknowledgments with particular thanks and love to the woman who, for more than forty years, has made me a better person, my wife, Karen.

LIST OF INTERVIEWEES

Maroon, Dorothy	Gusen 1–Mauthausen	131st Evac
Marx, Art	Gusen-Mauthausen	11th AD
Maurice, Roger	Slave camp	99th ID
Melman, Nathan	Ampfing	14th AD
Moran, Hana Berger	Mauthausen	Survivor
Motzko, Edmund	Gardelegen	102nd ID
Myers, Gerald Virgil	Buchenwald	80th ID
Nachman, Monroe "Monty"	Landsberg	103rd ID
Ogle, Wayne L.	Ahlem, Salzwedel	84th ID
Olson, John R.	Dora-Nordhausen	104th ID
Oltjenbruns, Elton	Gardelegen	102nd ID
O'Neil, Eugene	Buchenwald	80th ID
Panebianco, Al	Dachau	45th ID
Pardoe, David	Landsberg	63rd ID
Parker, Leonard	Dachau	45th ID
Pauzar, Karl	Ampfing	14th AD
Payne, Charles T.	Ohrdruf	89th ID
Pecchia, Domenick J.	Landsberg/Kaufering	63rd ID
Persinger, Robert	Ebensee	80th ID
Petersohn, LeRoy	Mauthausen	11th AD
Peterson, Ray W.	Landsberg	63rd ID
Peyton, Dallas	Dachau	20th AD
Pierro, Aurio J.	Dora	3rd AD
Priest, Warren E.	Buchenwald	120th Evac
Rappaport, Melvin	Buchenwald	6th AD
Ray, Robert	Nordhausen	3rd AD
Rheney, John, Jr.	Nordhausen	104th ID
Rice, Rip	Dora-Mittelbau	104th ID
Robinson, Forrest	Nordhausen	104th ID
Rogers, Chan	Dachau	45th ID
Rood, Coenraad	Ampfing	Survivor
Rose, James	Dachau	42nd ID
Ross, Irv	Dachau	45th ID
Salvio, Sal	Buchenwald	4th AD
Saunders, Harry	Mauthausen	11th AD
Schlocker, Irvin	Landsberg/Kaufering	63rd ID

Schmidt, Max	Buchenwald	80th ID
Schutz, Bernard	Landsberg	5th Army
Selwood, Clifford	Mühldorf	99th ID
Serian, Leo	Hersbruck/Flossenbürg	65th ID
Sherman, George	Mauthausen	11th AD
Silva, Milton R.	Buchenwald	120th Evac
Simonson, Ted	Dachau	42nd ID
Snodgrass, Harry	Buchenwald	1st Army HQ
Steinfeld, Manfred	Wöbbelin	82nd Abn
Stephens, John	Mauthausen	11th AD
Storch, Bernhard	Sachsenhausen, Poland	Polish army
Straba, Robert	Mühldorf	14th AD
Sunshine, Morris	Nordhausen	104th ID
Sutton, William	Dachau	45th ID
Terepka, Edward A.	Dachau	45th ID
Timmer, Donald H.	Ohrdruf	89th ID
Tripp, Owen	Falkenau/Flossenbürg	9th AD
Vanacore, Joe	Ohrdruf	4th AD
Verheye, Pierre C. T.	Buchenwald	Survivor
Vitalone, Gabriel	Ohrdruf	89th ID
Waltzer, Joel S.	Landsberg	63rd ID
Wannemacher, Paul	Flossenbürg	90th ID
Waters, Melvin	Bergen-Belsen	AFS
Weiskircher, Russel	Dachau	45th ID
Whiteway, Curtis	Mühldorf	99th ID

BIBLIOGRAPHY

Abzug, Robert H. *Inside the Vicious Heart*. New York: Oxford University Press, 1985.

Adkins, A. Z., Jr., and Andrew Z. Adkins III. *You Can't Get Much Closer Than This.* Havertown, Pa.: Casemate, 2005.

Ast, Theresa Lynn. "Confronting the Holocaust: American Soldiers Who Liberated the Concentration Camps." PhD dissertation, Emory University, 2000.

Berenbaum, Michael, ed. *Witness to the Holocaust*. New York: HarperCollins, 1997.

Bridgman, Jon. *The End of the Holocaust: The Liberation of the Camps*. Portland, Ore.: Areopagitica Press, 1990.

Clinger, Fred, Arthur Johnston, and Vincent Masel. *The History of the 71st Infantry Division*. Whitefish, Mont.: Kessinger Publishing (reprint).

Cohen, Israel I. *Destined to Survive*. Brooklyn, N.Y.: Mesorah Publications, 2001.

Cohen, Roger. *Soldiers and Slaves*. New York: Knopf, 2005.

Dann, Sam, ed. *Dachau, 29 April 1945*. Lubbock: Texas Tech University Press, 1998.

D'Este, Carlo. *Patton: A Genius for War*. New York: Harper Perennial, 1996.

Draper, Lieutenant Theodore; maps and drawings by Sergeant Walter H. Chapman. *The 84th Infantry Division in the Battle of Germany*. New York: Viking Press, 1946.

Elson, Aaron. *Tanks for the Memories*. Hackensack, N.J.: Chi Chi Press, 2001.

Feig, Konnilyn G. *Hitler's Death Camps.* New York: Holmes & Meier Publishers, 1981.

Friedlander, Saul. *Nazi Germany and the Jews, 1933–1939: The Years of Persecution.* New York: HarperCollins, 1997.

———. *Nazi Germany and the Jews, 1939–1945: The Years of Extermination.* New York: HarperCollins, 2007.

Gilbert, Martin. *The Routledge Atlas of the Holocaust,* 3rd ed. London: Routledge, 2002.

Griess, Thomas E., series ed. *Atlas of the Second World War: Europe and the Mediterranean* (The West Point Military History Series). Wayne, N.J.: Avery Publishing Group (undated).

Gring, Diana. "The Death Marches and the Massacre of Gardelegen: Nazi Crimes at the Final Stage of World War II" (translation of pamphlet published in German). Gardelegen, Germany: Stadtmuseum Gardelegen, 1993.

Gun, Nerin E. *The Day of the Americans.* New York: Fleet Publishing, 1966.

Hackett, David A., trans. *The Buchenwald Report.* Boulder: Westview Press, 1995.

Hart, B. H. Liddell. *History of the Second World War.* New York: Putnam, 1971.

Israel, David L. *The Day the Thunderbird Cried.* Medford, Ore.: Emek Press, 2005.

Jones, James. *WWII: A Chronicle of Soldiering.* New York: Ballantine Books, 1975.

Keegan, John. *The Second World War.* New York: Penguin Books, 1990.

Laqueur, Walter, ed. *The Holocaust Encyclopedia.* New Haven: Yale University Press, 2001.

Levitt, Sergeant Saul. "Ohrdruf Camp." *Yank, the Army Weekly,* May 18, 1945, p. 4.

MacDonald, Charles B. *The Last Offensive of World War II.* New York: Barnes & Noble Books, 1995.

Maguire, Peter. *Law and War: An American Story.* New York: Columbia University Press, 2001.

Perry, Michael W., ed. *Dachau Liberated: The Official Report by the U.S. Seventh Army.* Seattle: Inkling Books, 2000.

Preil, Joseph J., ed. *Holocaust Testimonies: European Survivors and American Liberators in New Jersey.* New Brunswick, N.J.: Rutgers University Press, 2001.

Shirer, William L. *The Rise and Fall of the Third Reich.* New York: Simon and Schuster, 1960.

Supreme Headquarters Allied Expeditionary Force Evaluation and Dissemination Section G-2 (Counter Intelligence Sub-Division). *Basic Handbook, KL's (Konzentrationslager) Axis Concentration Camps and Detention Centers Reported as Such in Europe.* Undated. ISBN 0-85420-046-0.

Swift, Michael, and Michael Sharpe. *Historical Maps of World War II Europe.* London: PRC Publishing, 2001.

Toland, John. *The Last 100 Days.* New York: Random House, 1965.

U.S. Army. "The Seventy-first Came . . . to Gunskirchen Lager" (pamphlet). Augsburg, Germany: E. Keiser KG, 1945.

U.S. Army Center of Military History. *U.S. Army in World War II: Special Studies. Chronology: 1941–1945.* Washington, D.C.: U.S. Government Printing Office, 1960.

United States Holocaust Memorial Council. *The Liberation of the Nazi Concentration Camps 1945: Eyewitness Accounts of the Liberators.* Washington, D.C.: U.S. Government Printing Office, 1987.

Weber, Louis. *The Holocaust Chronicle.* Lincolnwood, Ill.: Publications International, 2001.

Whitlock, Flint. *Given Up for Dead.* Boulder, Colo.: Westview Press, 2005.

Young, Gordon R., ed. *The Army Almanac.* Harrisburg, Pa.: Stackpole Company, 1959.

Zelizer, Barbie. *Remembering to Forget: Holocaust Memory Through the Camera's Eye.* Chicago: University of Chicago Press, 1998.

INDEX

ILLUSTRATION CREDITS

Unless otherwise indicated below, World War II–era and recent photographs of interviewees were provided courtesy of the interviewees.

Drawings of Salzwedel on pages iv and viii courtesy of Walter H. Chapman.

Ohrdruf photograph on page 29 from the archive of the United States Holocaust Memorial Museum (USHMM), courtesy of National Archives and Records Administration, College Park, Maryland.

Buchenwald survivors photograph on page 52 by First Sergeant Percy Smith, courtesy of Gerald Virgil Myers.

Warren Priest 2007 photograph on page 78 courtesy of Ken Williams, *Concord Monitor.*

Salzwedel photograph on page 97 by Sergeant Maurice Miller, courtesy of his son, Mark Miller.

Photograph of Eisenhower at Ohrdruf on page 100 from the USHMM, courtesy of Harold Royall.

Gardelegen photograph on page 128 from the USHMM, courtesy of Vern Ecklund.

Gardelegen photograph on page 133 from the USHMM, courtesy of the photographer, John Irving Malachowski.

Dachau photograph on page 197 from *Allemagne, avril–mai 1945: Photographies d'Eric Schwab,* USHMM, courtesy of Michael Caskey.

Ampfing photograph on page 228 courtesy of Nathan Melman.

Ludwigslust photograph on page 279 from the USHMM, courtesy of Dr. Alfred B. Sundquist.

Moran/Petersohn photograph on page 303 courtesy of Brian Petersohn.

Memorial photograph on page 324 courtesy of 157th Regiment, 45th Infantry Division veteran John R. Hallowell.

Recent photos of the following interviewees were provided by the author: Irzyk, Feinberg, Myers, Rappaport, Nachman, Schutz, Eberhart, Eisenstein, Chaney, Fasnacht, Brooks, Fellman, Storch, Friedenberg, Lubin, Ellmann, and Krenkler.

ABOUT THE AUTHOR

Following a thirty-five-year career as a journalist and producer in radio, public television, and commercial TV, during which he won the George Foster Peabody Award, the DuPont-Columbia Citation, several Emmy Awards, a Writers Guild Award, several PBS and CPB Awards, as well as many other awards for documentaries and specials that his wife says she's tired of dusting, MICHAEL HIRSH opted to write his way out of television. *The Liberators* is his fifth nonfiction book. He was embedded with U.S. Air Force pararescue and combat search-and-rescue units in Afghanistan, Pakistan, and Uzbekistan to write *None Braver: U.S. Air Force Pararescuemen in the War on Terrorism*. In 1966, Hirsh was a combat correspondent with the Army's 25th Infantry Division at Cu Chi, Vietnam, where he was awarded the Combat Infantryman Badge. He and his wife, Karen, live in Punta Gorda, Florida. He can be contacted at liberatorsbook@gmail.com.

ABOUT THE TYPE

This book was set in Fairfield, the first typeface from the hand of the distinguished American artist and engraver Rudolph Ruzicka (1883–1978). Ruzicka was born in Bohemia and came to America in 1894. He set up his own shop, devoted to wood engraving and printing, in New York in 1913 after a varied career working as a wood engraver, in photoengraving and bank note printing plants, and as an art director and freelance artist. He designed and illustrated many books, and was the creator of a considerable list of individual prints—wood engravings, line engravings on copper, and aquatints.